Dio non
ha creato che
l'acqua…
l'uomo ha fatto
il vino.

God created the water…
man made the wine.

Mr Rav,
    Have a great Fathers day.
    Your the best.
            love,
                Mark.

ALSO BY MARIO BATALI

Mario Batali Simple Italian Food

Mario Batali Holiday Food

MARIO BATALI

the **Babbo**

COOKBOOK

Photographs by CHRISTOPHER HIRSHEIMER

CLARKSON POTTER/PUBLISHERS, NEW YORK

TO SUSI,
Benno, and Leo
and the MANHATTAN SKYLINE

Published by Clarkson Potter/Publishers, New York, New York.
Member of the Crown Publishing Group.

Random House, Inc. New York, Toronto, London, Sydney, Auckland
www.randomhouse.com

Clarkson N. Potter is a trademark and Potter and colophon are registered trademarks of Random House, Inc.
Printed in Japan

Art Direction by Lisa Eaton and Douglas Riccardi.
Design by Memo Productions.

Library of Congress Cataloging-in-Publication Data
Batali, Mario.
The Babbo cookbook / Mario Batali; photographs by Christopher Hirsheimer.
1. Cookery, Italian. 2. Babbo Ristorante e Enoteca. I. Title.
TX723.B323   2002
641.5945–dc21   2001055469

ISBN 0-609-60775-8

10   9   8   7   6   5   4   3   2

ACKNOWLEDGMENTS

I would like to thank the following for their invaluable contributions to this book:

My partner, Joe Bastianich. Our collaboration really makes half of this his;

Chef Andy Nusser, whose energy, style, and tenacity are reflected on every page of this book and every day at Babbo;

Pastry chef Gina DePalma, whose unbelievable desserts and overall style help make Babbo what it is;

Present and past sous-chefs Elisa Sarno, Memo Trevino, John Eisenhart, Patty Collins, Frank Langello, Jared Lewin, Liz Chapman, and Chris Juliano, for strength and fire;

My present management team: Alfredo Ruiz, Jim Logan, Nancy Seltzer, David Lynch, John Maineri, Amanda Steurer, and Caroline Jackson, for simplifying my life and improving Babbo through their constant thought and hard work;

My other partners, Jason Denton, Mark Ladner, Dave Pasternack, Simon Dean, and Lidia Bastianich, for their vision and intensity;

Food artists Frank Langello, Kirsten Goldberg, and Steve Rooney, for help and plates;

Christopher Hirsheimer and Natasha Milne for beauty, style, and wisdom on the page;

Lisa Eaton, Douglas Riccardi, and the Memo team for design and wit;

Pam Krauss and her team at Clarkson Potter: Amy Boorstein, Marysarah Quinn, Leigh Ann Ambrosi, Liana Faughnan, Jane Treuhaft, and Joan Denman;

My assistant Laurie Woolever, for a lot of work on the recipes and text and for keeping me in the game;

Michael Stipe, for songs, inspiration, and humor;

Marcia Kiesel, for the right measurements and quantities;

And to Food Network, for continuing to give me a soapbox.

CONTENTS

INTRODUCTION

If I had to distill the essence of Babbo Ristorante and Enoteca it would probably come down to one concept: Italian hospitality . . . but with a decided American twist.

When you walk into Babbo one of the first things you feel is a sense of well-being coupled with a buzz of energy. The restaurant has a personality all its own that informs the hundreds of decisions that I and all the others who keep Babbo humming make every day. How we carve a rabbit in the dining room, how we serve a new aperitivo, what we think of a new linen company, how we address countless glitches on a weekly basis—at this point, three years down the road, our approach is almost intuitive.

Many people ask me what type of Italian food we serve at Babbo, and I have no pat answer. While there are certainly a few dishes on the menu that are faithful renditions of beloved regional dishes, like braised shortribs *(brasato al Barolo)*, most of them are nothing you would find in an Italian trattoria or home. Yet they feel and taste like dishes you might eat in Italy. Like Italian cooks, we use locally grown products with a near fanaticism to express the flavor of our dirt, our wind, our rain.

This, of course, gets us back to the basic premise I will always harp on, that your cooking can only be as good as the ingredients you buy. An active collaboration with the butcher, fishmonger, baker, gardener, or oil merchant is as critical as the proper execution of a recipe in making something truly delicious. What elevates a mere list of ingredients and techniques to something really great is the personalization of the ingredients.

Shop hard and shop smart. Italians walk into every store with the intention of taking home the very best stuff in the store. They think of this as their God-given right and responsibility—not just an option when they feel like splurging. This does not mean buying veal chops every time you hit the butcher shop. It means talking with the butcher, finding out what is really special this week, discussing the options, and taking home the prize. It is not every day that veal breast or lamb shoulder are available, but when it is, it should be going home with you. In the worst-case scenario, you grind it and make the world's most delicious meatballs or sausages; in the best case, you'll braise it slowly with some root vegetables and create an ethereal ragù.

I'm not claiming to be a pioneer here; this is the premise of the California cuisine epitomized by Alice Waters, Jeremiah Tower, and Judy Rodgers in the early eighties. And just as they did, we try to handcraft as many of our components, from salami to preserves, in our own kitchen. Recognizing that the element of the homemade in your jam, pickles, tomato sauce, wine, antipasto, or whatever is as important as the recipe is what will make your cooking as good as, if not better than, the cooking at Babbo.

One thing the savvy cook will quickly notice is the total absence in this book of the reduced stocks and demi-glaces often found in many restaurant cookbooks. This is not my way of dumbing down the technique to make it easier on the home cook; this is truly the way we cook at Babbo. I am not interested in making intense reductions that in my opinion overwhelm the pure flavors I want to present in a dish, nor am I that excited about the glutinous, viscous texture of these bone stocks—or the way they get sticky as they sit on a plate. These are not the lessons I learned during the time I spent in Italy. What I observed there was a looser, less reduced sauce on the plate that was closer to a pan juice, maybe "broken" with some rivulets of olive oil at the last minute and certainly not thickened with roux or any other liaison. Many of my contemporaries in other restaurants are observing the same thing and treating much of their food with similar lightness, particularly in the sauce and condiment departments.

What ends up on your table reflects a lot on you, the cook. I enjoy using offbeat ingredients like tripe or cardoons in many of our dishes because New York City's voracious eaters want the intellectual stimulation of trying something few of them will cook at home. These perhaps challenging ingredients are then tempered by a trattoria-style simplicity, creating hybrids that are neither highbrow nor blue-collar—just different and more personal. Such innovation is not, however, the raison d'être of the Babbo kitchen. Many of the dishes we serve at Babbo are really classical home-cooking standards gussied up with a single untraditional ingredient, and it is much more important to me to have a firm respect for the tradition of the Italian table than to create a tricky, cerebral new combination.

With any innovation the most important things to remember are flavor and impact. Food should really taste good and feel good to eat. We talk a lot about mouth feel in relation to everything from simple wines to the deep brown crust on our bread to the way the filling oozes from a beef cheek ravioli when you bite it. We never forget that dining is an all-sensory experience. To hit a real home run, sometimes taste, sight, and smell must be augmented with the thought-inducing stimuli of the unfamiliar or the reimagined. Add auditory and tactile sensation and you have a very provocative series of juicy elements vying to create the perfect dining moment.

Balance is another critical factor, whether it be the acid balance of a vinaigrette, the condiment-to-noodle balance of a plate of tortelloni, or the Louis Armstrong–to–REM balance on the stereo throughout the evening. The same holds true in menu composition. I try to strike a balance between traditional and contemporary dishes, between challenging ingredients and comfort food. In the end, it all comes down to personal choices and tastes.

Guests at Babbo sometimes have questions about how our menu "works": Is it okay to have a pasta as a *secondo*, or main course? Can one make a meal of antipasti? Does one order the cheese course instead of or in addition to a dessert? My answer is that any and all of the above are fine, either at Babbo or at home. For those who insist on being led by the hand we usually recommend our guests order an antipasto, split a pasta, then have a *secondo* followed by some cheese and then a dessert. And for very special occasions they might indulge in one of our tasting menus, one more traditional, with four small courses plus cheese, pre-dessert, and dessert, the other consisting of five consecutive pastas. We devote a great deal of time and thought to constructing these menus, orchestrating every moment of the meal and varying the tempo of flavors and textures over the course of an evening. By the same token, we are very happy to be thought of as a neighborhood place where regulars can drop in when they just feel like a bowl of pasta and a salad.

You should approach the recipes in this book the same way, asking yourself first and foremost: What do I feel like eating? If you are feeling very ambitious you may want to devise your own tasting menus. More probably you'll make one of the entrées or pastas (especially easy if you've made them ahead and frozen them), perhaps a *contorno* (a vegetable side dish), with a *dolci* (a sweet dish) or just some cookies and coffee to round things out.

The recipes that follow present the dishes precisely as they are served at the restaurant, so you, the cook, can prepare them with all the condiments, garnishes, and other accompaniments you would find on your plate at Babbo if you choose. I would be remiss not to acknowledge, however, all the help I have in the kitchen in getting these dishes on the table. For that reason I have included suggestions for simplifying some recipes that require hard-to-find ingredients, or numerous components. They may not be exactly the real deal, but I guarantee they will still be delicious and definitely will be a little easier on the cook.

Whichever way you go—whole hog or scaled back—you can and should make every meal an event. Many times it's all about getting a simple, casual meal on the table. Other times you may want to entertain on a more elaborate level, and really spend some time on it. In either case, the Italian ideal of total care and attention to every detail can, and should, be foremost.

It can be the most minute detail that brings you, as the host, and your guests a certain level of satisfaction and joy. Throughout this book my partner, Joe Bastianich, and I offer musings on different aspects of our service at Babbo. To some, these may seem a bit fussy or even a waste of time, but I include them because these are the details we think about every day, every week, every time we entertain, every time we eat a sandwich, and every time we eat at someone else's restaurant. They are where the fun comes in.

The experience of dining, as opposed to simply eating, has as much to do with your surroundings, the company, and numerous other factors that you may or may not even register on a conscious level as with the food on your plate. What makes eating out fun is seeing the different perspectives and flourishes of an individual restaurateur. It is as interesting in my opinion as understanding how a writer or painter approaches his craft. Of course, I may just be that crazy to think that everyone else regards dining as a pursuit as intriguing as going to the theater or a museum. When people say they love the ambience at Babbo, though, they are talking about something to which we've given a great deal of thought.

When you walk in the door the creamy colors and lighting create an almost theatrical effect that is enhanced by low votive candles; these cast an intimate mood at each table and softly illuminate the central table, where we finish certain dishes and prepare the wine service. Each table is set in a minimalist fashion, with only a water glass, bread plate, folded napkin, and essential silverware, but cabinets around the dining room hold five different kinds of wine glasses from Spiegelau, each meant to complement a specific style of wine. There is no art on the walls, but there is always music playing: It might be soft jazz, light pop, or even the music of the day (sometimes playing relatively loud). The uncarpeted floor is stained hardwood and the only floral decoration is a large, spare arrangement in the center of the room. The list could go on but my point is that every single detail represents a choice we have made in creating an environment that our guests will find conducive to a comfortable and yet personal experience.

You have the opportunity to do exactly the same thing at home. I am not suggesting that you must or should buy everything we have at Babbo in order to make a great dining experience; to the contrary. I am suggesting that you think about all of these details when you're planning a special meal, and do something about them in a way that pleases you. What it comes down to is a presentation of your individual brand of style. Because my partner and I both come from Italian-American families (with other stuff thrown in on my side), aligning ourselves with the Italian style was obvious and natural to us. Discover what feels natural to you. Recognize that you can set a tone with the kind of bread you serve, the kind of glasses you use, the kind of music (if any) you play, the type of napkin and the intricacy (or lack thereof) in its fold. Whether there are candles, printed menus, and flowers, or just a great picnic table with the right paper plates and a big bottle of prosecco, each component depends on you.

Throughout this book you'll find some notes on service, wine, and other aspects of hospitality that we think contribute to what makes Babbo unique. They were contributed by my partner, Joseph Bastianich, who has put his stamp on the front of the house as indelibly as mine is in the kitchen.

APERITIVI

The first thing that is offered to me when I go to a friend's house or a restaurant is a beverage. Nine times out of ten this means a glass of wine or a bottle of beer, and very occasionally I might get a mixed drink. None of these is a bad option; they quench my thirst and soothe the New York City angst in me. But by resorting to such a predictable array of choices—much the same as what I've been drinking since college—my host has missed an important opportunity to show a bit more thought and have a bit more fun.

In Italy the aperitivo moment is almost as deliberately pondered as the first course. A diner might be presented with a glass of prosecco flavored with a bit of fresh fruit juice or a more elaborate mix of sweet vermouth, gin, and fruit puree. It could even be as simple as Campari and soda with a splash and slice of something unexpected, but it is always carefully considered.

Almost as important as the taste of an aperitivo is its presentation: It needs to *look* delicious. This is not to say that you need a full battery of glassware, just a few variations on the theme. I suggest that you invest in a set of martini glasses, because everything looks sexy in a chilled martini glass. I also recommend champagne flutes for anything that goes with prosecco, and some medium tumblers, for the Campari or sweet vermouth drinks. If you had to choose just one type of glass, however, a reasonably large white-wine glass with a stem could actually stand in for all of these.

My point is that if I am going to spend a couple of hours creating a great dinner for my friends (or restaurant customers for that matter), a little extra time spent creating a special taste to introduce the evening is time well spent. It will also help make my guests feel special, which is, of course, the ultimate objective of entertaining guests.

OPPOSITE, LEFT TO RIGHT:
Blood Orange Bellini;
Anna 'Sta Notte; Amarina

BLOOD ORANGE BELLINI

SERVES I

½ ounce **BLOOD ORANGE JUICE**

3 ounces **PROSECCO**

Pour the juice into a champagne flute. Top with prosecco and serve immediately.

ANNA 'STA NOTTE

SERVES I

1 teaspoon **GRAPPA**

1 **SUGAR CUBE**

½ ounce **LIMONCELLO**

3½ ounces **PROSECCO**

Place the grappa in a large spoon and add the sugar cube. When it has absorbed the grappa, place the sugar cube in a champagne flute. Top with the limoncello and prosecco and serve immediately.

BLOOD ORANGE COSMOPOLITAN

SERVES I

2 ounces orange-flavored **VODKA**

¼ ounce **COINTREAU**

¼ ounce fresh **LIME JUICE**

½ ounce **BLOOD ORANGE JUICE**

ORANGE TWIST, for garnish

In an iced shaker, combine the vodka, Cointreau, and juices. Shake to combine and pour into a chilled martini glass. Garnish with the orange twist.

AMARINA

SERVES I

1 teaspoon Angostura **BITTERS**

1 **SUGAR CUBE**

½ ounce **LIMONCELLO**

3½ ounces **PROSECCO**

Place the bitters in a large spoon and add the sugar cube. When it has absorbed the bitters, place the sugar cube in a champagne flute. Top with the limoncello and prosecco and serve.

Blood Orange Cosmopolitan

BABBO NEGRONI

SERVES 1

¾ ounce Junipero **GIN**

¾ ounce Cinzano **SWEET VERMOUTH**

¾ ounce **CAMPARI**

3 drops orange **BITTERS**

ORANGE TWIST, for garnish

In an iced shaker, combine the gin, vermouth, and Campari. Shake well to combine and pour into a chilled glass, straight up or over ice. Add the bitters and garnish with the orange twist.

CIN CYN

SERVES 1

2 ounces Junipero **GIN**

½ ounce Cinzano **SWEET VERMOUTH**

½ ounce **CYNAR** (artichoke liqueur)

Orange **BITTERS**

ORANGE TWIST, for garnish

In a chilled shaker, combine the gin, vermouth, and Cynar. Shake until well combined and pour into a chilled martini glass, straight up or over ice. Add a few drops of orange bitters and garnish with the orange twist.

THISTLE

SERVES 1

1½ ounces orange-flavored **VODKA**

½ ounce **COINTREAU**

¼ ounce **CYNAR** (artichoke liqueur)

1 ounce fresh **ORANGE JUICE**

Dash or two of **BITTERS**

ORANGE TWIST, for garnish

In a chilled shaker, combine the vodka, Cointreau, Cynar, and orange juice. Shake until well combined and pour into a martini glass, straight up or over ice. Garnish with a dash of bitters and the orange twist and serve.

Babbo Negroni

CHAPTER ONE

Antipasti

Antipasto for many has become the way to sample a restaurant's style by indulging in a series of smaller courses, so their guests can indulge in a wider variety of tastes. One of my biggest complaints when I go out to eat is large portions. I simply tire of chewing the same thing for ten or fifteen mouthfuls and am much happier ordering three antipasto courses, and then maybe a pasta or two to follow. This keeps my meal more interesting and gives me a lot more flavors to try.

Antipasto has not always been a part of the Italian table. Throughout the nineteenth century, antipasto was thought of in many households as an affectation of the wealthy. The style and quantity of food served at traditional meals in that largely agrarian society were dictated primarily by availability and financial necessity. Protein was perceived as a luxury and therefore rarely served in abundance, except on religious or family holidays. The first course, or *primo,* was usually pasta- or grain-based and comprised the true bulk of the meal. A *secondo,* or second course, generally followed, and consisted of a small portion of meat or fish or perhaps some cured meat. A piece of cheese and some fruit were the extent of the dessert offerings.

Today an antipasto would generally be a part of any Italian restaurant meal, but in many regions the only antipasto offered is sliced meats, called *affetati.* This reflects the grand tradition of *salumi* (otherwise known as sausage-making) throughout all of Italy. The pig and Italian dining culture are as entwined as Romeo and Juliet, as Hansel and Gretel, as Laurel and Hardy; that is, they are bound together in a true chemistry. At Babbo, we are quite proud of our *salumi*, nearly all of which we make by hand in the style of Italian artisans. This chapter contains two recipes for creating your own cured meats. Follow them closely the first few times and then start to personalize, small step by small step. Eventually you will create your very own style, and that is where cooking becomes most joyous—and most Italian.

But not all our antipasti are meat-based. We love our local farmer's market and support our farmers enthusiastically. Seasonal vegetables that have not seen refrigeration since they were picked are the essence of the kind of Italian simplicity I have long advocated. And seafood, such as marinated anchovies or mixed seafood salad, needs little embellishment to shine like diamonds.

The antipasti that follow could easily make a fun meal served in a series of two, three, or four courses, one of which might be a simple frittata or even just some great prosciutto on grilled bread. Pair that with an elegant seafood salad or a selection of marinated raw and cured fish and you've got the idea. The main point is that you should not feel tied to a rigid progression of dishes when you cook or entertain at home. Do as I do and cook what *you* feel like eating; that way you will enjoy the process even more, and that pleasure and passion will be obvious on the plate.

BRUSCHETTA

Bruschetta is an excellent way to start a meal, either passed while everyone is still socializing or as the first course at the table. There are many restaurants in Italy that approach bruschetta as the main event. Their menus read like the offerings at a pizzeria, with a plethora of toppings. The following three are variations on a theme, but let your imagination run wild. The most important thing here is the quality of the bread, so find a great one. Mine comes from Sullivan Street Bakery in New York City, where Jim Lahey makes bread that matches perfectly with our food.

ROASTED BEET *and* PARMIGIANO
bruschetta

1. Preheat the oven to 400°F.

2. Wrap the beets in aluminum foil and roast in the oven for 30 to 45 minutes, or until they are easily pierced with a paring knife. Remove from the oven and, once cool enough to handle, peel the beets and cut into ¼-inch cubes. Set aside to cool completely.

3. Preheat the grill or broiler.

4. In a medium bowl, combine the beets, vinegar, oil, caraway seeds, chives, and salt and pepper.

5. Grill or toast the bread until crispy and golden brown. Top each slice with some of the beet mixture, then grate the cheese over each piece. Serve immediately.

SERVES 8

1 pound **BEETS**

1 tablespoon **BALSAMIC VINEGAR**

3 tablespoons extra-virgin **OLIVE OIL**

1 teaspoon **CARAWAY SEEDS**

1 teaspoon chopped fresh **CHIVES**

KOSHER SALT and freshly ground **BLACK PEPPER**, to taste

8 ¾-inch slices of crusty **PEASANT BREAD**

¼ pound **PARMIGIANO-REGGIANO**

TOMATO *and* SHEEP'S MILK CHEESE
BRUSCHETTA

SERVES 8

2 **TOMATOES**, cored, seeded, and
cut into ¼-inch cubes

10 fresh **BASIL** leaves, finely
shredded

Freshly ground **BLACK PEPPER**,
to taste

4 large **GARLIC** cloves, 1 halved,
the other 3 sliced paper thin

8 ¾-inch slices of crusty
PEASANT BREAD

2 tablespoons extra-virgin
OLIVE OIL

KOSHER SALT, to taste

¼ pound **CACIO DI ROMA** or
other semi-soft sheep's milk
cheese

1. Preheat the grill or broiler.

2. In a medium bowl, combine the tomatoes, basil, black pepper, and sliced garlic. Set aside.

3. Grill or toast the bread for 2 to 4 minutes, until golden brown. Rub one side of each slice of bread with one of the garlic halves, then brush with some of the olive oil. Season the tomato mixture with salt, and spoon some of the tomato mixture onto each of the eight slices of bread. With a vegetable peeler, shave cacio over each piece and serve immediately.

CECI BRUSCHETTA

1. Preheat the grill or broiler.

2. In a mixing bowl, gently stir together the beans, olive oil, olive paste, vinegar, red pepper flakes, rosemary, basil, and garlic. Season lightly with salt and pepper.

3. Grill or broil each slice of bread until lightly toasted, about 2 minutes.

4. Spoon the bean mixture onto each of the grilled bread slices and serve immediately.

SERVES 4

1 cup cooked CECI (garbanzo) BEANS

4 tablespoons extra-virgin OLIVE OIL

2 tablespoons BLACK OLIVE PASTE

2 tablespoons BALSAMIC VINEGAR

½ teaspoon hot RED PEPPER FLAKES

½ teaspoon chopped fresh ROSEMARY

2 tablespoons fresh BASIL leaves, finely shredded

1 GARLIC clove, thinly sliced

KOSHER SALT and freshly ground BLACK PEPPER

4 1-inch slices of Italian PEASANT BREAD

ACORN
SQUASH
sformato

An intense autumn squash flavor and incredibly light texture make this dish an interesting eat. The julienne of raw squash over the top of this baked custard adds another intriguing note and could easily be served as a salad on its own.

1. Preheat the oven to 325°F.

2. Cut the squash through the equator to create 3 pieces: a 1-inch-thick ring and 2 end pieces. Wrap each end piece in foil. Wrap the onions in another piece of foil. Bake the squash and onions for 1 hour, then unwrap and allow to cool.

3. Turn the oven up to 400°F. Lightly grease eight 4-ounce ramekins or custard cups with butter or oil.

4. Peel the cooled squash and cut the flesh into cubes. Pulse the cubes in the bowl of a food processor until pureed, or mash vigorously with a fork. Transfer the squash to a large bowl, add the egg yolk, eggs, Parmigiano-Reggiano, mascarpone, nutmeg, salt, and pepper, and stir gently to combine. Beat the egg whites to soft peaks, then gently fold them into the squash mixture.

5. Divide the batter equally among the prepared cups, and place them in a baking pan large enough to hold them all without tipping. Fill the pan halfway with warm water, cover the whole pan tightly with aluminum foil, and bake for 35 to 40 minutes, or until a toothpick inserted in the center of a custard comes out clean. Keep warm.

6. While the squash bakes, place the shiitakes in a small baking pan. Drizzle with 1 cup of the olive oil, sprinkle with the chopped sage and garlic, and gently toss the mushrooms to coat. Roast until the mushrooms are tender, 15 to 20 minutes. Remove and allow to cool. Strain the oil and reserve.

(continued on next page)

SERVES 8

1 **ACORN SQUASH** (2½ pounds)

4 **CIPOLLINE ONIONS**

1 **EGG YOLK**

3 **EGGS**

¼ cup freshly grated **PARMIGIANO-REGGIANO**

¼ cup **MASCARPONE** cheese

¼ teaspoon freshly grated **NUTMEG**

1 teaspoon **KOSHER SALT**

¼ teaspoon freshly ground **BLACK PEPPER**

2 **EGG WHITES**

½ pound **SHIITAKE** mushrooms, stems removed

3 cups plus 1 tablespoon extra-virgin **OLIVE OIL**

10 fresh **SAGE** leaves, finely chopped, plus 8 whole **SAGE** leaves

2 **GARLIC** cloves, finely chopped

2 tablespoons **SAGE OIL** (page 51)

⅓ cup **SHERRY VINEGAR**

PARMIGIANO-REGGIANO, for grating

7. While the shiitakes and custards are cooking, heat 2 cups of the olive oil to 300° F. in a small, heavy-bottomed saucepan. Deep-fry the sage leaves in the hot oil, four at a time, until they are dark green and crispy, about 25 seconds. Remove from the oil with a slotted spoon, drain on a plate lined with paper towels, and set aside.

8. Peel the reserved squash ring and cut the flesh into julienne strips. Place the squash in a small bowl, add the remaining tablespoon of olive oil and salt and pepper to taste, and toss well to coat.

9. To make the mushroom vinaigrette: Pour the vinegar into a small bowl. Gently whisk in 1 cup of the strained mushroom cooking oil and season with salt and pepper.

10. To assemble the dish, carefully unmold one custard onto each of eight warmed dinner plates, running a knife around the edge of the cup to loosen the custard if necessary. Carefully halve the onions through the equator and place one half on each plate. Surround the custards with some of the roasted mushroom mixture, garnish with the julienned squash, fried sage leaves, sage oil, and wild mushroom vinaigrette, and grate plenty of cheese over each plate before serving.

BABBO STYLE

Many restaurants identify themselves as owner-operated—*un ristorante padronale*—but at Babbo we take this concept to heart. For Mario and me, Babbo is much more than a business or even an eating establishment; it's a personal expression of our cumulative life experiences, commitments, and passions. Our commitment to offering *le cose giuste* in food, wine, and service is uncompromising. We don't just feed our diners, they become part of the Babbo experience, sharing in the rich culture of the Italian table. Eating in our restaurant is like spending a little time in our world. You may never want to live there, but it's a great place to visit.

—J.B.

sweet pea FLAN

with CARROT VINAIGRETTE

SERVES 6

KOSHER SALT

1 cup fresh **MINT** leaves, packed

¾ pound green **PEAS**, fresh or
frozen

3 large **EGGS**

¾ cup **HEAVY CREAM**

1 teaspoon fresh **LEMON JUICE**

Freshly ground **BLACK PEPPER**,
to taste

1¼ cups **CARROT JUICE**

1 teaspoon **HONEY**

1 tablespoon **CHAMPAGNE
VINEGAR**

½ cup extra-virgin **OLIVE OIL**

2 cups young **PEA VINES** (about
¾ pound)

¼ cup **PARSLEY OIL** (page 50)

PARMIGIANO-REGGIANO, for
shaving

This is the Babbo version of peas and carrots. Juice your own carrots
if possible, or stop by your local juice bar.

1. Bring about 3 quarts of water to a boil and add 1 tablespoon
salt. Set up an ice bath nearby. Blanch the mint leaves and the peas
in the boiling water for 1 minute, then drain and immerse them in
the ice bath. Drain again and puree them together in the bowl of a
food processor until smooth. Pass the mixture through a food mill
into a large bowl and combine with the eggs, cream, lemon juice,
salt, and pepper.

2. Preheat the oven to 350°F.

3. Coat six 4-ounce ramekins with cooking spray. Divide the pea
mixture evenly among the ramekins, filling them two-thirds full.
Place the ramekins in a baking dish and fill it with enough hot
water to come halfway up the sides of the ramekins. Cover the baking dish with aluminum foil and bake for 25 to 30 minutes, or until
the centers are just set. Remove from the oven, taking care not to
splash any water into the ramekins, and allow to cool.

4. Meanwhile, place 1 cup of the carrot juice in a small, heavy-
bottomed saucepan and bring to a boil over high heat. Reduce the
heat to medium and cook the juice until it is reduced to ¼ cup,
taking care not to let it scorch. Remove the juice from the heat and,
in a medium bowl, combine it with the honey and champagne
vinegar, whisking to blend. Slowly whisk in the olive oil, then stir
in the remaining ¼ cup of raw carrot juice. Season with salt and
pepper.

5. To assemble the dish, carefully run a knife around the inside
edge of each cooled ramekin and unmold one flan onto the center
of each of six chilled dinner plates. In a large, nonreactive bowl,
toss the pea vines with the carrot vinaigrette and season with salt
and pepper if necessary. Divide the pea vines among the six plates,
partially covering the flan. Drizzle with carrot vinaigrette and parsley oil, shave a few curls of Parmigiano-Reggiano over each plate,
using a vegetable peeler, and serve immediately.

GOAT CHEESE
truffles
THREE WAYS *with* PEPERONATA

The three coatings create a different mouth feel for each of the truffles in this dish, the most distinctive of which is rolled in *pimentón*, a Spanish paprika. Chef Andy Nusser brought a cache of this smoky treat back from a recent trip to Spain and the kitchen just loves it.

1. To make the *peperonata:* In a 12- to 14-inch sauté pan, heat the 2 tablespoons of olive oil over high heat until almost smoking. Add the red and yellow peppers and sauté over high heat for 4 minutes, or until browned at the edges and softened. Add the sherry vinegar, salt, and pepper, reduce the heat to medium, and continue to cook for 5 to 7 minutes, or until the peppers are tender. Adjust the seasonings and set aside to cool.

2. Place the goat cheese in a medium bowl and season with salt and pepper. Divide the cheese into 12 portions and gently roll each portion into a ball. Roll four balls in the *pimentón* to completely coat, then roll four in the fennel and four in the poppy seeds. Set aside.

3. Preheat the oven or broiler to 400°F.

4. Bring 4 quarts of water to a boil and set up an ice bath next to the stove. Drop the arugula in the boiling water, blanch for 10 seconds, then remove with a slotted spoon and immediately refresh in the ice bath. Remove from the ice bath, gently squeeze out the excess liquid with a paper towel or clean dish towel, and place the arugula in a medium bowl. Toss with the 3 tablespoons of olive oil, the lemon juice, salt, and pepper.

5. Toast the bread slices in the oven or broiler for 2 minutes, until slightly browned and crispy.

6. To assemble the dish, divide the arugula and *peperonata* among four dinner plates. Place one of each flavor of goat cheese truffle on each plate. Drizzle with the olive oil, lean three slices of toast up against each trio of truffles, and serve.

SERVES 4

Peperonata

2 tablespoons extra-virgin **OLIVE OIL**

1 **RED BELL PEPPER**, cored, seeded, and cut into thin strips

1 **YELLOW BELL PEPPER**, cored, seeded, and cut into thin strips

2 tablespoons **SHERRY VINEGAR**

KOSHER SALT and freshly ground **BLACK PEPPER**, to taste

2 cups fresh **GOAT CHEESE**, preferably firm Coach Farm

¼ cup ground *PIMENTÓN* (Spanish paprika)

¼ cup ground **FENNEL SEEDS** or **FENNEL POLLEN**

¼ cup **POPPY SEEDS**

1 pound **ARUGULA**

3 tablespoons extra-virgin **OLIVE OIL**

1 tablespoon fresh **LEMON JUICE**

12 ½-inch slices from a **BAGUETTE**

Best-quality extra-virgin **OLIVE OIL**, for drizzling

cool roasted SHIITAKES

with BARBECUED ONIONS *and* BASIL OIL

SERVES 4

½ cup plus 1 tablespoon extra-virgin **OLIVE OIL**

10 fresh **SAGE** leaves, finely chopped

1 sprig of fresh **ROSEMARY**, leaves finely chopped

4 **GARLIC** cloves, 2 finely chopped and 2 thinly sliced

1 pound **SHIITAKE** mushrooms, stems removed

KOSHER SALT and freshly ground **BLACK PEPPER**, to taste

1 tablespoon **ANCHOVY PASTE**

1 tablespoon **BALSAMIC VINEGAR**

2 large **RED ONIONS**, sliced crosswise into ½-inch slices

BASIL OIL (page 50)

Shiitake mushrooms are a prime example of the Babbo approach to ingredients. While never used in Italy, they have such a great flavor and texture that we can't get enough of them. This, combined with the fact that they are grown locally in nearby Kennett Square, Pennsylvania, makes them a perfect choice for any mushroom dish.

1. Preheat the oven to 350°F.

2. In a small bowl, combine ¼ cup of the olive oil, the sage, rosemary, and chopped garlic and whisk to blend. Place the mushrooms in a small roasting pan or casserole and pour the oil mixture over. Season the mushrooms with salt and pepper and roast, uncovered, for 20 minutes.

3. Drain the mushrooms (saving the strained oil for a mushroom vinaigrette like the one on page 30) and set aside in a medium bowl to cool. In a separate bowl, combine the sliced garlic, anchovy paste, balsamic vinegar, salt, and pepper. Gently whisk in 3 tablespoons of the olive oil and pour the mixture over the mushrooms.

4. Preheat the grill or broiler.

5. Brush the onion slices with the remaining 2 tablespoons of olive oil, season with salt and pepper, and grill on the hottest part of the grill until tender and grill-marked, about 4 minutes on each side. Remove the onions from the grill and divide them evenly among four warmed dinner plates. Remove the mushrooms from the marinade and mound them evenly atop the onions. Drizzle each plate with basil oil and serve immediately.

5
AUTUMN VEGETABLES

with GOAT RICOTTA **AND PUMPKINSEED OIL**

Vegetarian appetizers always sell well—almost as well as pure pork ones—and this easy dish really captures the flavor of October. I would double the recipe because for me this is breakfast, too.

1. Preheat the oven to 475°F.

2. Place the butternut cubes and chopped sage on a cookie sheet, drizzle with 1 tablespoon of the olive oil, and roast until light golden brown, 8 to 10 minutes. Set aside in a large salad bowl to cool.

3. Place the Jerusalem artichokes on the same cookie sheet and toss with 1 tablespoon of the olive oil. Roast in the oven for 6 to 7 minutes. Remove and set aside with the squash.

4. Place the parsnips on the cookie sheet and toss with the cumin and 1 more tablespoon of olive oil. Roast for 6 to 7 minutes, then set aside with the other vegetables.

5. Bring 6 cups of water to a boil and set up an ice bath near the stove. Plunge the leeks into the boiling water and cook until tender, 2 or 3 minutes. Remove the leeks from the boiling water and submerge them in the ice bath until cool. Remove the leeks from the ice bath, pat dry with paper towels, and set aside.

6. Add the leeks, celery root, and mizuna to the salad bowl. Add the remaining olive oil, the sherry vinegar, salt, and pepper and toss gently to coat well.

7. Divide the mixture evenly among four chilled dinner plates, mounding it like a haystack. Smear each baguette slice generously with fresh goat cheese and place on top of each "haystack." Drizzle the sage and pumpkinseed oils around each mound. Serve immediately.

SERVES 4

½ pound **BUTTERNUT SQUASH**, peeled and cut into ½-inch cubes

4 fresh **SAGE** leaves, finely chopped

½ cup extra-virgin **OLIVE OIL**

¼ cup **JERUSALEM ARTICHOKES**, scrubbed and sliced into ⅛-inch disks

2 **PARSNIPS**, scrubbed and sliced into ¼-inch disks

1 teaspoon ground **CUMIN**

1 **LEEK**, white part only, cut into 3-inch julienne

½ **CELERY ROOT**, peeled and cut into julienne

¼ pound **MIZUNA**, watercress, or frisée

2 tablespoons **SHERRY VINEGAR**

KOSHER SALT and freshly ground **BLACK PEPPER**, to taste

4 1-inch **BAGUETTE** slices, toasted for 2 minutes in a 400°F. oven

¼ pound fresh **GOAT CHEESE**

¼ cup **SAGE OIL** (page 51)

2 tablespoons **PUMPKINSEED OIL** (available at specialty stores)

SEA SCALLOPS *crudo*

with SHAVED FENNEL *and* OLIO NUOVO

SERVES 4

4 large, very fresh **SEA SCALLOPS** (preferably freshly shucked)

½ **FENNEL** bulb, cored and very thinly sliced, fronds reserved for garnish

Juice of 1 **LEMON**

¼ cup best-quality **OLIO NUOVO** (first-pressed extra-virgin olive oil), plus more for drizzling

KOSHER SALT and freshly ground **BLACK PEPPER**, to taste

2 tablespoons finely chopped flat-leaf **PARSLEY**

The *crudo,* or raw, concept for fish is something that I worked on with my partner Dave Pasternack at Esca. This dish is a variation on the first *crudo* dish we served at Esca, pared down a bit.

1. Slice the scallops horizontally as thin as possible and place in a large bowl with the fennel. Add the lemon juice, olive oil, salt, and pepper and toss well.

2. Remove the scallops and place 4 or 5 slices on each of four chilled dinner plates. (If you like, arrange the *crudo* in a large scallop shell, as shown.) Add the parsley to the fennel, toss again, and divide the salad evenly among the four plates. Top each salad with a clean, beautiful fennel frond, drizzle each plate with a little more olive oil, and serve immediately.

insalata DI MARE

The most important ingredient in this dish is freshness. If you ask the fishmonger for the four most pristine items in the case, he or she will probably contribute a great deal to the quality of your insalata.

1. In a pot large enough to hold both of the lobsters, bring 6 quarts of water to a boil. Set up an ice bath nearby. Add the lobsters to the boiling water and cook until they are bright red and the meat is cooked through, about 10 minutes. Remove the lobsters, reserving the cooking liquid, and set aside to cool. In the same boiling water, cook the shrimp until they are just cooked through, about 1 minute. Remove and refresh in the ice bath. Remove the lobster meat from the shells, and peel the shrimp. Place in a large bowl and set aside.

2. In a large skillet with a lid, combine the wine and shallots and bring to a boil. Add the clams and mussels and cover. Cook over high heat until all the bivalves have steamed open, about 5 minutes; discard any that have not opened after this time. Remove from the pan, reserving the cooking liquid, and set aside to cool. Remove the clams and mussels from their shells. Remove the filter sac from the razor clams and cut them into thin strips, on the bias.

3. Add all the bivalves to the bowl with the lobster and shrimp. Add the frisée, lemon zest, lemon juice, olive oil, a splash of the reserved cooking liquid, and salt and pepper. Toss well by hand to combine. Divide evenly among four chilled dinner plates and serve immediately.

SERVES 4

2 small **LOBSTERS**

1 pound medium **SHRIMP**

1 cup dry **WHITE WINE**

2 **SHALLOTS**, finely chopped

1 pound razor **CLAMS**, scrubbed

1 pound **MUSSELS**, scrubbed and debearded

1 head of **FRISÉE**, torn into pieces

Zest of 1 **LEMON**

2 tablespoons fresh **LEMON JUICE**

6 tablespoons extra-virgin **OLIVE OIL**

KOSHER SALT and freshly ground **BLACK PEPPER**, to taste

MARINATED
FRESH ANCHOVIES
with "GIARDINIERA" *and* LOBSTER OIL

SERVES 6

Juice of 6 **LEMONS**, plus zest of
    1 lemon

3 **GARLIC** cloves, thinly sliced

2 tablespoons fresh **THYME**
    leaves

¾ cup extra-virgin **OLIVE OIL**

KOSHER SALT and freshly ground
    BLACK PEPPER, to taste

18 fresh whole **ANCHOVIES**,
    filleted

2 medium **CARROTS**, peeled and
    cut into thin strips

½ **FENNEL** bulb, cut into strips

1 head of **CAULIFLOWER**, cut into
    florettes

2 **SHALLOTS**, peeled and thinly
    sliced

1 cup **CHAMPAGNE VINEGAR**

½ cup **SUGAR**

½ cup **KOSHER SALT**, plus more
    to taste

½ pound **HARICOTS VERTS** or
    green beans

10 flat-leaf **PARSLEY** leaves, finely
    shredded

BAGNA CAUDA VINAIGRETTE
    (page 241)

¼ cup **LOBSTER OIL** (page 51)

These are not the anchovies of corner pizzeria fame—this is what the seaside tastes like in Italy. If you don't want to deal with the fresh anchovies yourself, you can find excellent stand-ins from Italy and Spain in fancy delis, where they are called *alici marinati* or *boquerones*. But I urge you to give these a try; they're a revelation if all you've experienced are the sorry specimens that come in a can.

1. In a small, nonreactive mixing bowl, combine the lemon juice, garlic, and thyme. Using a whisk or fork, whisk in ½ cup of the olive oil until emulsified. Season with salt and pepper.

2. Place the anchovies in a nonreactive dish just large enough to hold them in a single layer. Pour the marinade over the fish, shaking them slightly to completely surround them with the liquid. Cover and refrigerate for 24 hours.

3. In a large, nonreactive bowl, combine the carrots, fennel, cauliflower, shallots, vinegar, sugar, and ½ cup salt. Mix well to combine, and add enough water to cover the vegetables completely, about 5 cups. Cover tightly and refrigerate for 24 hours.

4. Bring 4 quarts of water to a boil and add 2 tablespoons of salt. Fill a large bowl with ice cubes and cold water, and place it next to the stove. Cook the green beans in the boiling water until just barely tender, about 3 minutes. Drain the beans and plunge them into the ice water. When they have cooled, drain the beans again and spread them on paper towels to dry. Stir the blanched green beans into the marinated vegetable mixture.

5. To assemble the dish, lift the vegetable mixture out of the marinade with a slotted spoon. Pat off the excess marinade, then divide the vegetables evenly among six chilled dinner plates and sprinkle with the parsley. Remove the anchovies from their marinade, pat them dry, and arrange the fillets in a circular pattern atop the salad, six per serving. Drizzle each plate with bagna cauda vinaigrette and lobster oil, top with lemon zest, and serve immediately.

marinated *baccalà*

with BABY FENNEL

AND ACETO TRADIZIONALE

SERVES 4

1 pound *BACCALÀ* (2 thick pieces, center cut)

1 cup plus 5 tablespoons extra-virgin **OLIVE OIL**

⅓ cup **CHAMPAGNE VINEGAR**

½ **RED ONION**, thinly sliced

Zest of 1 **LEMON**

1 tablespoon hot **RED PEPPER FLAKES**

10 to 15 **BLACK PEPPERCORNS**

2 heads of baby **FENNEL**, bulbs and fronds separated, bulbs cut in half lengthwise

KOSHER SALT and freshly ground **BLACK PEPPER**

ACETO TRADIZIONALE (see sidebar), for drizzling

I stole this dish from one of my favorite places in the whole world, Ristorante Lancelloti in Soliera, near Modena. They serve the *baccalà*, or salted cod, with a salad of the most incredibly fragrant herbs and flowers from their garden, accented by angelica. I love the simplicity of the baby fennel. Note that the *baccalà* requires soaking in advance.

1. Place the *baccalà* in a bowl with water to cover and soak for 48 hours, changing the water daily. Drain and pat dry. In a small, non-reactive casserole, combine 1 cup of the olive oil, the vinegar, onion, lemon zest, red pepper flakes, peppercorns, and fennel fronds and stir well. Add the *baccalà* and shake the pan to coat the fish. Marinate in the refrigerator for 4 hours, turning once or twice to marinate the fish evenly.

2. Bring 3 quarts of water to a boil and add 1 tablespoon salt. Set up an ice bath nearby. Blanch the halved fennel bulbs in the boiling water for 30 to 45 seconds, then remove and immediately refresh in the ice bath. Once the fennel has cooled, drain and pat dry.

3. Preheat the grill or broiler. Brush the fennel bulbs with 2 tablespoons of the olive oil, and season with salt and pepper. Grill or boil the fennel bulbs, cut side down, until they are charred and cooked through, about 5 minutes. Cool slightly, then roughly chop the fennel and place the pieces in a large bowl. Set aside.

4. While the fennel cooks, remove the *baccalà* from the marinade, pat dry, and slice very thin, as for gravlax or carpaccio. Divide the slices evenly among four chilled dinner plates.

5. Strain the solids from the marinade mixture and whisk together the liquid ingredients to emulsify. Drizzle enough of the dressing over the fennel to coat lightly, 3 to 4 tablespoons, and season with salt and pepper. Divide the salad among the plates. Drizzle each plate with the remaining 3 tablespoons of olive oil and a few drops of *aceto tradizionale;* serve immediately.

Aceto Tradizionale

At Babbo, we reserve the "good stuff"—*aceto tradizionale di Modena* or *di Reggio*—for a very few dishes, both because of its prohibitive cost (about $40 per ounce) and because to splash it all over the menu would be like having your birthday or Christmas every day. This is the *real* balsamic vinegar, aged for a minimum of twelve years, with a flavor so complex and unique that, in Italy, a small vial of a family's own balsamic is included in a bride's dowry.

The oils can be refrigerated in a sealed container for up to 1 week unless noted otherwise.

Parsley Oil

Makes 2 cups

1 bunch of flat-leaf PARSLEY, chopped
2 cups extra-virgin OLIVE OIL, chilled for 2 hours
1 teaspoon KOSHER SALT

Place all of the ingredients in a blender and puree until nearly smooth and uniformly green. Strain through a fine sieve. The oil can be refrigerated for 24 hours.

Basil Oil

Makes 2 cups

1 cup packed BASIL leaves, chopped
2 cups extra-virgin OLIVE OIL, chilled for 2 hours
1 teaspoon KOSHER SALT

Place all of the ingredients in a blender and puree until nearly smooth and uniformly green. Strain through a fine sieve.

Chive Oil

Makes 2 cups

2 bunches of CHIVES
2 cups extra-virgin OLIVE OIL, chilled for 2 hours
1 teaspoon KOSHER SALT

Bring 6 cups of water to a boil. Blanch the chives for 30 seconds and shock in an ice bath until cooled. Drain and pat dry with paper towels. Place the chives, oil, and salt in a blender and puree until nearly smooth and uniformly green. Strain through a fine sieve.

Sage Oil

Makes 1 cup

2 bunches of fresh SAGE, leaves
  only
1 cup extra-virgin OLIVE OIL,
  chilled for 1 hour
KOSHER SALT, to taste

Place the sage leaves in the bowl
of a food processor and pulse to
form a coarse puree. With the
motor running, slowly drizzle in
the olive oil. When all of the oil
has been incorporated and the
mixture is a uniform green, pass
through a fine sieve; discard the
solids. Season with a bit of salt.

Lobster Oil

Makes 4 cups

6 LOBSTER carcasses
1 CARROT, peeled and chopped
½ medium ONION, chopped
1 CELERY stalk, chopped
2 teaspoons PAPRIKA
4 cups extra-virgin OLIVE OIL

Preheat the oven to 400° F.

Place the lobster carcasses on
a baking sheet and roast for 15
minutes. Transfer the carcasses to
a large saucepan and add the
remaining ingredients. Bring to a
boil, then reduce the heat and simmer for 25 minutes. Remove from
the heat and let the mixture cool;
strain the oil, discarding the solids.

Red Pepper Oil

Makes 2 cups

2 cups extra-virgin OLIVE OIL
8 JALAPEÑO PEPPERS, seeded and
  chopped into ⅛-inch dice
2 tablespoons hot RED PEPPER
  FLAKES

Place the oil, jalapeños, and red
pepper flakes in a medium
saucepan and place over medium
heat. Heat to 175°F., remove from
the heat, and allow to cool. Allow to
stand overnight and strain out the
solids.

STEAMED
GULF SHRIMP
and **MAHOGANY CLAMS**
in a GREEN CHILE–BASIL *BRODETTO*

The mahogany clams in this brothy dish have a particularly fat flavor and an almost meaty texture, which we find to be an excellent counterpoint to the sweet flavor and softer texture of steamed shrimp. If you cannot find them, Littlenecks or New Zealand cockles make a fine substitute.

1. In a 12- to 14-inch sauté pan, heat 3 tablespoons of the olive oil until almost smoking. Add the garlic and sauté over high heat until lightly browned, 1 to 2 minutes. Add the jalapeños, clams, shrimp, and white wine and cover. Lower the heat to medium and cook for 3 minutes. The clams should open and the shrimp should be cooked through. Discard any unopened clams.

2. Add the parsley, toss gently over low heat for 1 minute, and remove from the heat. Add the remaining 6 tablespoons of olive oil and stir through. Divide evenly among four warmed dinner bowls, sprinkle with the basil, and serve immediately.

SERVES 4

9 tablespoons extra-virgin **OLIVE OIL**

6 **GARLIC** cloves, thinly sliced

2 **JALAPEÑOS**, seeded and finely chopped

20 mahogany **CLAMS**, scrubbed

12 gulf **SHRIMP**, peeled and deveined

1 cup dry **WHITE WINE**

¼ cup finely chopped flat-leaf **PARSLEY**

10 fresh opal **BASIL** leaves, finely shredded

STEAMED COCKLES

in a HABANERO CHIVE BROTH

SERVES 4

¼ cup extra-virgin **OLIVE OIL**

½ **RED ONION**, finely chopped

4 **GARLIC** cloves, thinly sliced

1 **HABANERO CHILE**, finely
   chopped

1 bunch of **CHIVES**, cut into
   1-inch lengths

2 pounds New Zealand **COCKLES**,
   scrubbed

2 cups dry **WHITE WINE**

½ cup **BASIC TOMATO SAUCE**
   (page 220)

KOSHER SALT and freshly ground
   BLACK PEPPER, to taste

New Zealand cockles have a flavor reminiscent of the Adriatic clams I loved so much in Italy, only they travel better; any briny clam will do, however. Be careful with habaneros if you have not worked with them before; they are *pericolosi* (that's Italian for dangerous). Wear kitchen gloves while you chop and seed them.

1. In a large skillet with a lid, heat the olive oil over high heat until almost smoking. Add the onion and garlic and cook for 5 minutes, or until soft and lightly browned. Add the chile, half of the chives, the cockles, wine, and tomato sauce and bring to a boil. Cover and cook until all the cockles steam open, about 5 minutes. Discard any cockles that do not open.

2. Season the broth with salt and pepper. Divide the cockles and broth evenly among four warmed bowls, top with the remaining chives, and serve with the bread.

WARM MUSSEL SALAD

WITH GAETA OLIVES *and* ORANGES

I love warm seafood salads as appetizers or even as light main courses. Prince Edward Island mussels are especially good here.

1. In a 12- to 14-inch sauté pan, combine the onion, thyme, and wine and bring to a boil. Add the mussels, cover tightly, and steam over high heat until the mussels open, about 5 minutes. Uncover the pan, remove from heat, and set aside to cool. Remove the mussels from their shells, taking care to keep them intact. Cover and refrigerate.

2. In a small saucepan, bring ½ cup of the orange juice to a boil and cook until it reduces by half, adjusting the heat if necessary to avoid scorching. Remove from the heat, allow to cool, and whisk in the olive oil. Stir in the remaining 2 tablespoons of orange juice and season with salt and pepper.

3. In a 12- to 14-inch sauté pan, combine the mussels and just enough of the orange citronette to moisten the mussels. If necessary, drizzle with a little olive oil to keep the mussels from sticking, and toss over high heat for 2 minutes.

4. Place the frisée, radicchio, scallions, orange segments, olives, and sherry vinegar in a large bowl. Add the hot mussels and toss by hand to coat evenly, then season with salt and pepper.

5. Divide the salad evenly among four dinner plates, drizzle with the remaining orange citronette, top with orange zest, and serve immediately.

SERVES 4

1 **WHITE ONION**, chopped

4 sprigs of fresh **THYME**

1 cup **WHITE WINE**

2 pounds (about 50) **MUSSELS**, scrubbed and debearded

½ cup plus 2 tablespoons fresh **ORANGE JUICE**

¾ cup extra-virgin **OLIVE OIL**

KOSHER SALT and freshly ground **BLACK PEPPER**, to taste

1 cup (about ¼ pound) **FRISÉE**, cut into bite-size pieces

½ head of **RADICCHIO**, cut into 1-inch ribbons

2 **SCALLIONS**, sliced ⅛ inch thick

1 **ORANGE**, peeled and cut in segments

¼ pound **GAETA OLIVES**, pitted

2 tablespoons **SHERRY VINEGAR**

Zest of 1 **ORANGE**

Montauk LOBSTER SALAD
with MÂCHE, FLOWERING CHIVES,
AND SUNGOLD TOMATOES

SERVES 4

4 1-pound Montauk LOBSTERS
    or other small lobsters

1 bunch of flowering CHIVES,
    cut into 4-inch lengths

7½ tablespoons extra-virgin
    OLIVE OIL

1½ tablespoons SHERRY
    VINEGAR

KOSHER SALT and freshly ground
    BLACK PEPPER, to taste

1 pound tender young MÂCHE

Zest of 1 LEMON

1 tablespoon fresh LEMON JUICE

1 pint SUNGOLD TOMATOES,
    cut in half lengthwise

CHIVE OIL, for drizzling
    (page 50)

The lobsters that come from Montauk, Long Island, in the summer are called soft-shell at the seafood market and possess a sweetness and a flavor that make them inimitable, but any tender, fresh lobster will be delicious in this beautiful salad. Purslane, if you can come by it, is a cool substitute for the mâche.

1. Fill a pot large enough to hold all four lobsters three-quarters full of water and bring it to a boil. Add the lobsters and cook until just done, about 12 minutes. Drain the lobsters, let them cool slightly, then remove all the meat from the claws and tail. Set aside to cool completely.

2. In a large bowl, combine the lobster meat, chives, 4½ tablespoons of the oil, the sherry vinegar, salt, and pepper and toss well to combine and coat. In a separate bowl, combine the mâche, the remaining 3 tablespoons of oil, the lemon zest, lemon juice, salt, and pepper and toss well to combine and coat.

3. Divide the salad evenly among four chilled dinner plates and arrange in a mound in the center. Top the salads with the lobster mixture, divide the tomatoes evenly among the plates, drizzle with chive oil, and serve immediately.

COD *in saor*

The roots of this dish are in the Veneto, where it is traditionally made with sole. I use cod because of its abundance, but also because I like the texture of deep-fried cod when it is served at room temp, as it is here. *In saor* refers to the classic sweet-and-sour marinade with currants and pine nuts often served in the *bacari* (wine bars) of Venice.

SERVES 4

1. Heat 1 cup of the oil to 375°F. in a deep saucepan.

2. Season the cod pieces with salt and pepper. Dredge the fish in the seasoned flour and fry in the hot oil until golden brown, 4 to 6 minutes. Remove and drain on paper towels.

3. In a 12- to 14-inch sauté pan, heat ¼ cup of the oil over medium heat. Add the onion and cook until softened and just light brown, 10 to 12 minutes. Add the currants, sugar, pine nuts, and vinegar and bring to a boil. Cook for 5 to 6 minutes, or until the currants are soft, then remove from the heat and allow to cool.

4. When all the ingredients are cool, layer the cod pieces in an earthenware dish that just fits them, overlapping slightly. Top with the sweet-and-sour mixture and refrigerate for 24 hours. Remove the fish from the refrigerator 1 hour before serving and add the chives.

5. While the fish comes to room temperature, in a small bowl, combine the celery, lemon juice, the remaining 2 tablespoons of olive oil, and salt and pepper and toss well. When ready to serve, drizzle some of the marinade over each portion of fish, arrange some of the salad over each portion, and serve.

1¼ cups plus 2 tablespoons extra-virgin **OLIVE OIL**

2 pounds **COD**, filleted

KOSHER SALT and freshly ground **BLACK PEPPER**, to taste

½ cup **FLOUR** seasoned with 1 teaspoon each of kosher salt and freshly ground black pepper

1 red **ONION**, cut into ½-inch dice

½ cup **CURRANTS**

2 tablespoons **SUGAR**

¼ cup **PINE NUTS**

1½ cups **RED WINE VINEGAR**

3 tablespoons chopped **CHIVES**

1 **CELERY** stalk, sliced paper thin into 6-inch lengths (using a vegetable peeler)

Juice of ½ **LEMON**

MACKEREL
in scapece
with LEMON THYME *and* SWEET PEPPERS

An oily trash fish like mackerel is often a difficult sell, even in New York. This dish makes it easy to love because poaching the fish in a delicate yet acidic bath of onions and thyme cuts the oily quality.

1. Season the fish with salt and pepper.

2. In a wide, deep sauté pan, combine the vinegar, 2 tablespoons of the sugar, the lemon juice, lemon thyme, red pepper flakes, saffron, salt, and pepper and bring to a simmer. Add the fish chunks, adding a bit of water if needed to cover the fish, and simmer until the fish is just cooked through, about 5 minutes. Remove from the heat and allow the fish to cool in the liquid.

3. In a 12- to 14-inch sauté pan, heat 3 tablespoons of the olive oil over medium-high heat. Add the bell pepper, reduce the heat to low, and cook slowly to wilt the peppers. Once the peppers have begun to soften, sprinkle with the remaining tablespoon of sugar, the mustard seeds, and garlic. Cook until the garlic is softened, 3 to 4 minutes. Season with salt and pepper and set aside.

4. Remove the mackerel pieces from the scapece and arrange in stacks on four chilled plates. Spoon 1 tablespoon of the saffron liquid over each serving and then sprinkle with the red pepepr mixture. Serve immediately.

SERVES 4

1 pound **MACKEREL** fillet, cut diagonally into 2-inch diamonds

KOSHER SALT and freshly ground **BLACK PEPPER**, to taste

2 cups **RED WINE VINEGAR**

3 tablespoons **SUGAR**

2 tablespoons fresh **LEMON JUICE**

2 tablespoons **LEMON THYME LEAVES**

1 tablespoon hot **RED PEPPER FLAKES**

10 to 15 **SAFFRON THREADS**, crushed in a mortar and pestle

4 tablespoons extra-virgin **OLIVE OIL**

1 **RED BELL PEPPER**, cut into ¼-inch dice

1 teaspoon **MUSTARD SEEDS**

4 **GARLIC** cloves, thinly sliced

JELLYFISH SALAD

with GOLDEN TOMATOES,

OPAL BASIL, AND ARUGULA

SERVES 4

1 pound salted JELLYFISH

4 1-inch slices PEASANT BREAD,
   grilled or toasted

2 tablespoons best-quality
   extra-virgin OLIVE OIL,
   for drizzling

1 pint yellow and red PEAR
   TOMATOES, halved

10 opal BASIL leaves, finely
   shredded

1 bunch of ARUGULA

2 tablespoons SHERRY VINEGAR

¾ cup extra-virgin OLIVE OIL

KOSHER SALT and freshly ground
   BLACK PEPPER, to taste

I found this amazing salted jellyfish in a funky market in Chinatown and it turned out to be a perfect match for the bounty of tomatoes we have in the middle of September. If you just can't find it, an easy substitute would be calamari, thinly sliced and blanched in boiling water for just a minute.

1. Rinse the jellyfish under cold water. Remove and discard the tentacles, then cut the body into thin slices. Place the jellyfish slices in a large bowl.

2. Drizzle each bread slice with some of the olive oil.

3. Add the tomatoes, basil, and arugula to the bowl with the jellyfish. Add the vinegar, oil, and salt and pepper and toss well to coat evenly. Divide the salad among four chilled dinner plates and serve with a slice of bread.

OCTOPUS

with YUKON GOLDS

and SPICY TANGERINE CITRONETTE

SERVES 4

5 tablespoons extra-virgin **OLIVE OIL**

4 **GARLIC** cloves, thinly sliced

2 teaspoons hot **RED PEPPER FLAKES**

1 2-pound **OCTOPUS**, fresh or frozen

1 **WINE CORK**

KOSHER SALT

½ pound Yukon Gold **POTATOES**, cut into ½-inch dice

1 **RED ONION**, thinly sliced

1 cup fresh **TANGERINE JUICE**

2 tablespoons **CHAMPAGNE VINEGAR**

½ cup extra-virgin **OLIVE OIL**

KOSHER SALT and freshly ground **BLACK PEPPER**, to taste

½ **RED ONION**, finely chopped

1 tablespoon **RED WINE VINEGAR**

1 bunch of **CHIVES**, cut into 2-inch lengths

There's some magical chemical reaction when octopus is simmered with a cork; it becomes tender and yet retains the essential leathery mouth feel that I associate with eating it in Mediterranean countries. The tangerine citronette should be wet and broken, not thick and emulsified.

1. Preheat the oven to 300°F.

2. In a large Dutch oven, heat 2 tablespoons of the olive oil over high heat until almost smoking. Add the garlic and 1 teaspoon of the red pepper flakes and cook over high heat for 2 minutes. Add the octopus to the pan and cook on all sides over high heat until it has changed color and has released its liquid. Add the wine cork, cover the pan with aluminum foil, and bake for 1½ to 2 hours, or until the octopus is quite soft. Cool to room temperature.

3. Meanwhile, bring 3 quarts of water to a boil and add 1 table-spoon of salt. Fill a large bowl three-quarters full with ice and cold water and keep it close by. Cook the potatoes and sliced onion in the boiling water for 3 minutes, until somewhat tender but still firm. Drain the vegetables and plunge them into the ice bath. Drain again and spread on paper towels to dry.

4. In a small, heavy-bottomed saucepan, bring the tangerine juice and remaining teaspoon of red pepper flakes to a boil and cook until reduced by half, about 8 minutes. Allow to cool, then place in a small bowl with the champagne vinegar. Slowly whisk in the ½ cup of olive oil to barely emulsify and season with salt and pepper.

5. Carefully separate the octopus tentacles from the head. Cut the tentacles into 3-inch pieces; cut the head in half.

6. Place the potatoes, sliced onion, and chopped red onion in a large bowl and toss with the red wine vinegar, the remaining 3 tablespoons of olive oil, and salt and pepper. Divide the mixture evenly among four chilled dinner plates, mounding the potatoes on the center of each plate. Top with some of the octopus tentacles, drizzle with the tangerine citronette, garnish with the chives, and serve.

ASPARAGUS

The arrival of asparagus in the middle of April is an exciting moment in Babbo's kitchen. After a long winter of braised and slow-cooked foods with muted, rich flavors and colors, savoring the blast of spring so evident in the verdant, snappy first asparagus is divine. We love the idea of a *scorpacciata,* the Italian word describing a full attack of eating a particular ingredient in copius amounts and very often in its evanescent period of local perfection. The next three recipes capture a lot of what we love about the firm green kings, each with its own soft counterpoint.

ASPARAGUS *Milanese*
with PARMIGIANO *and a* DUCK EGG

1. Bring 3 quarts of water to a boil and add 1 tablespoon salt. Set up an ice bath nearby. Blanch the asparagus spears in the boiling water for 1 minute and 30 seconds, then remove and immediately refresh in the ice bath. Once cooled, remove from the ice bath with tongs and pat dry. Set aside.

2. In a 12- to 14-inch nonstick sauté pan, heat 3 tablespoons of the olive oil over high heat. Add the asparagus and toss in the oil over high heat for 1 minute, season with salt and pepper, then divide evenly among four warmed dinner plates.

3. Wipe out the sauté pan with a paper towel, add the remaining 3 tablespoons of oil, and heat over medium-high heat. Crack 2 of the eggs into the pan, taking care to keep the yolks intact. Cook the eggs sunny-side up until the whites are firm but the yolk is still runny. Season each egg with salt and pepper, then carefully slide 1 egg each onto 2 of the asparagus servings. Cook the remaining 2 eggs in the same way. Grate the cheese over each plate and serve immediately.

SERVES 4

KOSHER SALT

20 jumbo ASPARAGUS spears, tough ends snapped off

6 tablespoons extra-virgin OLIVE OIL

Freshly ground BLACK PEPPER

4 DUCK EGGS

PARMIGIANO-REGGIANO, for grating

ASPARAGUS VINAIGRETTE
WITH BLACK PEPPER PECORINO ZABAGLIONE

1. Bring about 6 quarts of water to a boil and add 2 tablespoons salt. Fill a large bowl about three-quarters full with ice cubes and cold water and keep it close by. Immerse the asparagus in the boiling water and blanch for 1 minute and 30 seconds. Remove the asparagus with tongs and immediately place it in the ice bath. Once the asparagus has cooled, remove it from the ice bath with tongs and allow it to dry on a plate lined with paper towels. Set it and the ice bath aside.

2. In a small bowl, combine the shallots, sherry vinegar, mustard, and salt and pepper to taste. Gently whisk in the olive oil until the mixture is emulsified. Set aside.

3. To prepare the zabaglione, in a stainless-steel or, preferably, copper bowl, whisk the egg yolks, 2/3 tablespoon of the pepper, and the Marsala until foamy. Place the bowl over simmering water and continue whisking until the mixture is thick and mounding, about 10 minutes. Set the bowl over the ice bath and whisk until chilled, 4 to 5 minutes.

4. Whip the cream until stiff peaks form. Carefully fold the whipped cream, 2 tablespoons of the Pecorino Romano, and 1 tablespoon of the pepper into the chilled zabaglione. Refrigerate until ready to serve.

5. To assemble the dish, place six spears of asparagus on each of four chilled dinner plates. Stir the parsley into the vinaigrette and drizzle it around and across the asparagus. Spoon a dollop of the zabaglione onto each plate, sprinkle with the remaining tablespoon of cheese, and serve immediately.

SERVES 4

KOSHER SALT

24 jumbo **ASPARAGUS** spears, trimmed and bases peeled

1 **SHALLOT**, minced

2 tablespoons **SHERRY VINEGAR**

1 teaspoon prepared **MUSTARD**

1 2/3 tablespoons freshly ground **BLACK PEPPER**, plus more to taste

6 tablespoons extra-virgin **OLIVE OIL**

5 **EGG YOLKS**

2/3 cup **MARSALA**

1/2 cup **HEAVY CREAM**

3 tablespoons freshly grated **PECORINO ROMANO**

10 flat-leaf **PARSLEY** leaves, finely shredded

snapper tartare

with GRILLED ASPARAGUS

SERVES 4

1 pound sushi-grade **SNAPPER** fillets

Juice and zest of 1 **GRAPEFRUIT**

Juice and zest of 1 **LEMON**

Juice and zest of 1 **ORANGE**

¼ cup plus 2 tablespoons extra-virgin **OLIVE OIL**

1 **GARLIC** clove, finely chopped

¼ cup green **JALAPEÑO PESTO** (page 220)

1 **SCALLION**, thinly sliced

1 teaspoon **SUGAR**

KOSHER SALT and freshly ground **BLACK PEPPER**, to taste

12 jumbo **ASPARAGUS** spears

1 **GRAPEFRUIT**, peeled and cut in segments

1 **LEMON**, peeled and cut in segments

1 **ORANGE**, peeled and cut in segments

ROASTED RED PEPPER JUS (see sidebar)

1 teaspoon hot **RED PEPPER FLAKES**

1. Cut the snapper very fine into ¼-inch cubes and place in a medium nonreactive metal bowl. Fill another bowl with ice, set the snapper bowl into the ice, cover, and refrigerate.

2. In a nonreactive metal bowl, combine the citrus juices and slowly and gently whisk in ¼ cup of the oil until emulsified. Add the garlic, pesto, scallions, and sugar. Season with salt and pepper and set aside.

3. Preheat the grill or broiler. Brush the asparagus with the remaining 2 tablespoons of olive oil and season with salt and pepper. Grill the asparagus on all sides until tender and cooked through, 8 to 10 minutes. Arrange three spears in a triangle on each of four plates.

4. Pour enough of the vinaigrette over the chilled snapper cubes just to coat, toss well, and season with salt and pepper. Divide the tartare evenly among the plates, and place some of the citrus segments on each plate. Drizzle with the red pepper jus, sprinkle the red pepper flakes around each portion, top with the zests, and serve immediately.

Roasted Red Pepper Jus

Makes 2 cups

8 **RED BELL PEPPERS**, roasted, cored,
   and seeded
½ cup cool **WATER**
2 tablespoons **SHERRY VINEGAR**
KOSHER SALT and freshly ground
   BLACK PEPPER, to taste

Place the peppers and water in a
blender and puree until very smooth,
then pass through a fine-mesh sieve,
pressing to extract as much juice as
possible. Add the vinegar and salt
and pepper.

DUCK EGGS

SUNNY-SIDE UP *with* *guanciale*
AND TRUFFLE VINAIGRETTE

SERVES 4

¼ pound *GUANCIALE,* pancetta, or
bacon, cut into large batons
(see sidebar)

1 head of **FRISÉE**, cut into
bite-size pieces

5 tablespoons extra-virgin
OLIVE OIL

1 tablespoon fresh **LEMON JUICE**

KOSHER SALT and freshly ground
BLACK PEPPER, to taste

4 tablespoons (½ stick) unsalted
BUTTER

4 **DUCK EGGS**

4 1-inch slices of crusty **PEASANT
BREAD**, grilled or toasted

¼ cup **TRUFFLE VINAIGRETTE**
(page 240)

We get our duck eggs from Quattro Farms in New York State and love
them for the viscous and decadent texture of their yolks. *Guanciale* is
the very distinctly flavored bacon made from the jowls and cheeks of
our hero, the pig. It has a depth of flavor and intense richness that is
simply not present in commercially made American bacon. It is quite
simple to make at home; we make fifty pounds a week at Babbo and
use it with abandon whenever possible.

1. In a 12- to 14-inch sauté pan, heat the *guanciale* over medium-
low heat until most of its fat is rendered. Remove the *guanciale* to
a plate lined with paper towels and discard the fat.

2. In a large bowl, combine the frisée, 3 tablespoons of the oil, the
lemon juice, and salt and pepper and toss well. Set aside.

3. In a nonstick pan, heat 1 tablespoon of the butter over high
heat until it foams and subsides. Crack one egg into the pan, taking care not to break the yolk, and cook without turning for 4 to 5
minutes, or until the white is cooked through and the yolk is
"sealed." Season with salt and pepper and remove from the pan.
Repeat with the remaining butter and eggs, working with two pans
if possible to speed up the process.

4. While the final egg cooks, drizzle each bread slice with some
of the remaining 2 tablespoons of olive oil. Halve each piece of
toast on the bias.

5. Divide the frisée salad evenly among four dinner plates and top
each with one egg. Sprinkle the *guanciale* batons over the salads,
drizzle each plate with some of the truffle vinaigrette, and serve
immediately with the toast.

Guanciale

Makes 2 pounds

½ cup **SUGAR**
½ cup **KOSHER SALT**
10 to 15 whole **BLACK PEPPERCORNS**
4 sprigs of fresh **THYME** leaves
2 pounds **HOG JOWLS**

In a medium bowl, combine the sugar, salt, peppercorns, and thyme. Coat the hog jowls with the mixture, rubbing gently. Place the jowls in a nonreactive casserole, cover, and refrigerate for 5 to 7 days.

Remove the jowls from the casserole and tie a piece of butcher's twine around the middle of each. Hang the jowls in a dry, cool place (it should not be warmer than 60°F.) for at least 3 weeks. They should be firm and dry, with a slight give. Slice and use like bacon or pancetta.

CENTER TABLES

The center table is the sun of Babbo's solar system. Each dining room has one, and they serve as focal points. They hold our cheeses, serving condiments, and seasonal fruit displays and provide a staging area for wine service, but they are also the spot where many dishes are finished. Whole roasted or grilled fish, a staple of the Babbo menu, are presented to diners in their entirety, then skillfully filleted on the center table by our floor staff. It is also where a rib-eye steak for two and *stinco di vitello* (veal shank) are deftly reduced to beautiful portions. By performing the finishing touches in full view of the entire dining room we highlight the simplicity and quality of our food while enhancing the theatrical quality of the meal.

—J.B.

CROSTINI toscani

with **FENNEL PICKLES** and **KALE**

These Tuscan toasts make a perfect light lunch with a salad and can be made with chicken or duck livers. The liver spread lasts a week in the fridge and can also be used as a condiment for pasta: Heat two tablespoons per person in a sauté pan with a healthy splash of pasta water and sauce some long strands of love.

1. To make the fennel pickles: In a large nonreactive saucepan, combine the vinegar, 2 cups water, the sea salt, peppercorns, garlic, fennel seeds, and sugar and bring to a boil. Add the fennel pieces and cook until just tender, about 5 minutes, then remove the pan from the heat and set aside to cool.

2. Preheat the grill or broiler.

3. In a 10- to 12-inch sauté pan, heat 4 tablespoons of the olive oil slowly over medium heat. Add the onion and cook slowly until soft but not brown, about 10 minutes. Add the livers, capers, anchovies, and red pepper flakes and cook until the livers are lightly browned, about 8 minutes. Add the wine and cook until only 3 to 4 tablespoons of liquid remain, about 15 minutes.

4. Transfer the liver mixture to a food processor and pulse on and off until blended but still lumpy—it should not be smooth like a purée. Season with salt and pepper and remove to a small mixing bowl.

5. Spread each bread piece with 1 heaping tablespoon of the liver mixture.

6. In a medium bowl, combine the kale, the remaining 3 tablespoons of olive oil, the lemon juice, and salt and pepper and toss well.

7. Divide the kale salad among six dinner plates. Drain the fennel pickles and divide evenly among the plates. Divide the toasts among the plates and serve immediately.

SERVES 6 TO 8

Fennel Pickles

3 cups **WHITE WINE VINEGAR**

2 tablespoons **SEA SALT**

15 **BLACK PEPPERCORNS**

2 **GARLIC** cloves, peeled

1 tablespoon **FENNEL SEEDS**

¼ cup **SUGAR**

½ **FENNEL** bulb, cored and cut into 2-inch strips

Chicken Livers Toscani

7 tablespoons extra-virgin **OLIVE OIL**

1 **RED ONION**, finely chopped

1 pound **CHICKEN LIVERS**

2 tablespoons **CAPERS**, rinsed and drained

2 salt-packed **ANCHOVY** fillets, rinsed, soaked in water, and patted dry

1 tablespoon hot **RED PEPPER FLAKES**

1 cup dry **RED WINE**

KOSHER SALT and freshly ground **BLACK PEPPER**, to taste

12 ¾-inch slices **PEASANT BREAD**, grilled or toasted

1 pound purple **KALE**, cut into chiffonade

1 tablespoon fresh **LEMON JUICE**

WARM LAMB'S TONGUE

in a BLACK TRUFFLE VINAIGRETTE

WITH PECORINO *and* A THREE-MINUTE EGG

SERVES 4

4 LAMB'S TONGUES

1 ounce BLACK TRUFFLES, thinly sliced

1 sprig of ROSEMARY, leaves only, chopped

¾ cup plus 6 tablespoons extra-virgin OLIVE OIL

3 tablespoons SHERRY VINEGAR

KOSHER SALT and freshly ground BLACK PEPPER, to taste

2 GARLIC cloves, thinly sliced

1 tablespoon ANCHOVY PASTE

1 tablespoon BALSAMIC VINEGAR

½ pound CHANTERELLE mushrooms

1 tablespoon WHITE VINEGAR

4 EGGS

½ pound baby SPINACH

½ cup OVEN-ROASTED TOMATOES (page 146), cut into thin strips

4 tablespoons extra-virgin OLIVE OIL

PECORINO DI PIENZA, for shaving

The velvety texture of lamb's tongue is pure luxury, especially when paired with earthy black truffles. Add the soft cooked yolk of a perfectly poached egg and we have Babbo on the plate. Lamb's tongue is the kind of thing you can get only if you have made yourself a good customer of a good butcher. Calf's tongue does not have the delicate flavor but makes a good substitute here.

1. Place the tongues in a pot just large enough to hold them and cover with water. Cover the pot and bring to a boil, then lower the heat and simmer until the tips of the tongues are tender, 1 to 1½ hours. Remove from the heat and allow to cool in the cooking liquid just until cool enough to handle. These are much easier to peel while still very warm.

2. Peel the tongues and, using a sharp paring knife, remove the fatty parts from the lower portion of muscle. Slice the tongues into ⅛-inch pieces and set aside.

3. In a large bowl, combine the truffles, rosemary, ¾ cup of the oil, 2 tablespoons of the sherry vinegar, and salt and pepper. Add the tongue slices and set aside.

4. Preheat the oven to 400° F.

5. In a medium bowl, combine the sliced garlic, anchovy paste, balsamic vinegar, and salt and pepper. Gently whisk in 3 tablespoons of the oil and pour the mixture over the mushrooms. Toss the mushrooms well, then dump out onto a 12 x 20-inch sheet of aluminum foil. Make a packet of the foil, folding the top and sides well, and roast until soft, about 25 minutes. Allow the mushrooms to cool, then cut them into ⅛-inch slices. Set aside.

6. Bring 2 quarts of water, the white vinegar, and a pinch of salt to a simmer. Prepare a cool water bath nearby. One at a time, carefully crack the eggs onto a saucer, then slide them into the water, making sure not to break the yolks. Poach the eggs for 3 minutes, just until opaque. Remove with a slotted spoon and transfer to the cool water bath until ready to serve.

7. In a 12- to 14-inch sauté pan, combine the marinated tongue slices, the mushrooms, and enough of their combined liquids to keep them moist but not swimming. Heat over medium-high heat to warm through. Adjust the seasoning with salt and pepper if necessary.

8. In a medium bowl, combine the spinach leaves, roasted tomatoes, the remaining tablespoon of sherry vinegar, the remaining 3 tablespoons of olive oil, and salt and pepper to taste and toss well. Mound some of the salad on the center of each of four dinner plates. Divide the mushroom and tongue mixture evenly among the four plates, loosely arranging the hot mixture around the spinach. Remove the poached eggs from their water bath and gently pat dry, then season aggressively with salt and pepper. Nestle one egg into the center of each mound of spinach. Drizzle the oil around the plate. Using a vegetable peeler, shave two or three slices of cheese over each plate, and serve immediately.

LAMB TARTARE

with Mint Crostini

and a QUAIL EGG

SERVES 4

1 pound **LAMB SHOULDER**, trimmed of all fat and sinew

½ tablespoon **DIJON MUSTARD**

¼ cup extra-virgin **OLIVE OIL**

½ small **RED ONION**, finely chopped into tiny dice

½ teaspoon chopped **CAPERS**

2 tablespoons fresh **LEMON JUICE**

3 tablespoons **JALAPEÑO PESTO** (page 220)

1 **BAGUETTE**, cut into ½-inch slices

1 cup **MINT AND ONION JAM** (see sidebar)

4 **QUAIL EGGS**

Da Vero **OLIVE OIL**, for drizzling

I love steak tartare and I love lamb, so this dish was a no-brainer. I have not seen a lot of raw lamb dishes, but this certainly seems lighter and yet more intensely flavored than the classic. Keep the ground meat very cold until ready to serve; it tastes better that way.

1. Preheat the grill or broiler.

2. Run the meat through the second-smallest setting on a meat grinder. If you do not have a meat grinder, chop the meat very fine with a very sharp knife.

3. In a small bowl, combine the mustard, olive oil, diced onion, capers, and lemon juice and stir well.

4. In a large bowl, combine the ground lamb, mustard mixture, and the jalapeño pesto, and mix well with your perfectly clean hands.

5. Grill or broil the bread slices for 2 minutes on one side.

6. Divide the meat mixture into four portions and mound in the center of four chilled dinner plates. Spread the baguette slices with the mint-onion jam and arrange around the tartare. Make a small indentation with your thumb in the center of each mound of meat. Crack one egg into each indentation, drizzle the plates with the Da Vero oil, and serve immediately.

Mint and Onion Jam
Makes 1 cup

1 tablespoon plus 1½ cups
    extra-virgin **OLIVE OIL**
1 medium **RED ONION**, sliced into
    rings, plus ½ onion, finely
    chopped
KOSHER SALT and freshly ground
    BLACK PEPPER
2 tablespoons **SUGAR**
1 teaspoon hot **RED PEPPER FLAKES**
2 cups **MINT** leaves, packed

In a 12- to 14-inch sauté pan, heat
1 tablespoon of oil over medium
heat. Add the onion rings, season
with salt, pepper, and 1 tablespoon
of the sugar, and cook over
medium-low heat until the onions
are soft and translucent, about
10 minutes; do not brown. Cool to
room temperature.

    In a blender or food processor,
combine the cooked onions, the
remaining tablespoon of sugar,
1 teaspoon of salt, the red pepper
flakes, and the remaining 1½ cups of
olive oil. Blend until the mixture is a
coarse puree. Add the mint leaves in
batches, pureeing after each addition. When all of the mint leaves
have been incorporated, add the
chopped onion and puree again. The
jam can be kept, in an airtight container in the refrigerator, for up to
1 week.

WARM TRIPE
alla Parmigiana

Tripe used to be a difficult sell, but at Babbo this stuff flies out of the kitchen. An initial cooking in water flavored with vinegar and vanilla takes away the uric smell most people find objectionable and makes the tripe so tender it doesn't need a long cooking time.

1. Place the tripe in a large pot and fill with water to cover. Add the vinegar and vanilla, cover, and bring to a boil. Reduce the heat to a simmer and cook for 1 hour, or until the tripe is tender. Be careful, it can overcook; it should have the texture and weight of a wet swim cap, but give easily when bitten. Remove from the heat and refrigerate the tripe in the cooking liquid until the liquid and tripe are both very cold.

2. Remove the tripe from its cooking liquid and slice into ½-inch-thick strips. Heat 3 tablespoons of the olive oil in a 14- to 16-inch sauté pan until just smoking. Add the carrots, onion, celery, and chopped garlic and sauté over medium heat until tender and light golden brown, 8 to 10 minutes, then add the wine and crushed tomatoes. Bring to a boil, then add the tripe, sage leaves, and salt and pepper. Cook 15 to 20 minutes, adding up to a cup of the tripe cooking liquid if necessary to keep the mixture from getting too thick.

3. Rub each slice of grilled bread with the cut side of the halved garlic clove, and brush one side with the remaining 2 tablespoons of olive oil. Halve each slice diagonally.

4. Divide the tripe evenly among six warmed bowls. Grate a generous amount of Parmigiano-Reggiano over each and serve immediately with the toast.

SERVES 6

1 pound **HONEYCOMB TRIPE**

¼ cup **WHITE VINEGAR**

½ tablespoon **VANILLA EXTRACT**

5 tablespoons extra-virgin **OLIVE OIL**

2 **CARROTS**, cut on the diagonal into ¼-inch slices

1 **RED ONION**, cut into ¼-inch slices

1 **CELERY** rib, cut into ¼-inch slices

2 **GARLIC** cloves, roughly chopped, plus 1 clove cut in half

1 cup **WHITE WINE**

1 cup canned **TOMATOES**, crushed, with their juice

4 **SAGE** leaves

KOSHER SALT and freshly ground **BLACK PEPPER**, to taste

6 slices crusty **PEASANT BREAD**, grilled or toasted

PARMIGIANO-REGGIANO, for grating

capocollo with DANDELIONS
AND FIDDLEHEAD PICKLES

SERVES 4

Pickles

3 cups WHITE WINE VINEGAR

2 tablespoons SEA SALT

15 BLACK PEPPERCORNS

2 GARLIC cloves, peeled

½ tablespoon FENNEL SEEDS

¼ cup SUGAR

2 cups young FIDDLEHEAD
FERNS

¼ pound young DANDELION
GREENS

Juice of 1 LEMON

3 tablespoons extra-virgin
OLIVE OIL

KOSHER SALT and freshly ground
BLACK PEPPER, to taste

1 pound *CAPOCOLLO*, thinly sliced

PARMIGIANO-REGGIANO, for
shaving

We used to buy our *capocollo* from the great *salumi* producer Alps, in Queens, but now we make our own, and I think it's even better. The combination of the bitter dandelions and the tangy and crunchy fiddleheads is an excellent foil for the sweet, fatty meat. Extra pickles can be stored in the refrigerator for up to a month.

1. To make the pickles: In a large nonreactive saucepan, combine the vinegar, 2 cups water, the sea salt, peppercorns, garlic, fennel seeds, and sugar and bring to a boil. Place the fiddleheads in a large heat-proof bowl and pour the hot marinade over them. Cool to room temperature.

2. In a medium bowl, combine the dandelions, lemon juice, olive oil, and salt and pepper and toss well.

3. Divide the *capocollo* evenly among four chilled dinner plates. Mound some of the salad on each plate. Remove the cooled fiddleheads from their pickling bath with a slotted spoon and place a few on each plate. Top with a few shavings of Parmigiano-Reggiano, and serve immediately.

DUCK BRESAOLA

with BORLOTTI *and* RED ONION JAM

Here is an excellent introduction to curing meat at home: It is simple and virtually foolproof. The best kind of duck breast, called magret, is thick and very meaty. A breast will lose about half of its original volume by the time it is cured. If you don't want to make the duck the main event, it adds some adult fun to salads or pastas, cut into thin julienne.

1. To make the *bresaola:* In a small bowl, combine the salt, pepper, sugar, red pepper flakes, rosemary, and thyme. Rub the duck breast with this mixture, wrap it loosely in wax paper, and refrigerate for 4 days. Unwrap the breast, then wrap like a package with string, leaving one long end. Suspend the breast from a shelf in your refrigerator for 3 weeks.

2. To assemble the dish, make the onion jam. In a 12- to 14-inch sauté pan, heat 2 tablespoons of the olive oil over high heat until hot but not smoking. Add the onions and cook over low heat until softened and just slightly golden brown. Season with salt and pepper and add the orange juice. Continue to cook, stirring occasionally, until the juice has reduced and completely coats the onions and they are falling apart, adding a little water if necessary to keep the onions from sticking. This should take about 20 minutes. Season again with salt and pepper if necessary and set aside to cool.

3. In a mixing bowl, gently stir together the beans, the remaining 4 tablespoons of olive oil, the garlic, red pepper flakes, and vinegar until well mixed, and set aside for 1 hour.

4. Slice the *bresaola* very thin with a sharp knife or on a slicer. Arrange some of the slices on each of four chilled dinner plates. Remove the beans from their bath with a slotted spoon and divide them evenly among the plates. Finish each plate with a dab of the onion jam and sprinkle with the parsley. Serve immediately.

SERVES 4

Bresaola

3 tablespoons KOSHER SALT

3 tablespoons freshly ground BLACK PEPPER

1 tablespoon SUGAR

1 tablespoon hot RED PEPPER FLAKES

1 tablespoon chopped fresh ROSEMARY leaves

1 tablespoon chopped fresh THYME leaves

1 whole (2-pound) DUCK BREAST

6 tablespoons extra-virgin OLIVE OIL, plus more for drizzling

2 RED ONIONS, cut into ¼-inch dice

KOSHER SALT and freshly ground BLACK PEPPER

1 cup fresh ORANGE JUICE

1 (10-ounce) can BORLOTTI BEANS, rinsed and drained

2 GARLIC cloves, thinly sliced

½ teaspoon hot RED PEPPER FLAKES

¼ cup RED WINE VINEGAR

10 flat-leaf PARSLEY leaves, finely shredded

WARM TESTA

with **WAXY POTATOES**

SERVES 16

Testa

½ **PIG'S HEAD**

½ cup **KOSHER SALT**, plus more
    to taste

2 **CELERY** stalks

2 **CARROTS**, peeled

2 envelopes unflavored **GELATIN**

Freshly ground **BLACK PEPPER**,
    to taste

KOSHER SALT

3 waxy **POTATOES**, peeled and
    sliced into ¼-inch rounds

Leaves from 1 bunch of **THYME**

1 teaspoon finely minced
    SHALLOT

1 teaspoon **DIJON MUSTARD**

3 tablespoons **BALSAMIC**
    VINEGAR

6 tablespoons extra-virgin
    OLIVE OIL

½ cup **SHALLOT PICKLES** (see
    sidebar)

1 teaspoon **MUSTARD SEEDS**

PARSLEY OIL (page 50)

Freshly ground **BLACK PEPPER**,
    to taste

Testa translates as "head cheese" in English, but it tastes a lot better than it sounds. This will hold for 2 weeks in the fridge well wrapped and also makes a killer sammie. You can really test your butcher on this. The real ones buy whole pigs on occasion and can save a head for a regular customer. The rest just buy hog quarters and portion them. They will not be able to help you.

1. To make the *testa:* Place the pig's head in a large pot with water to cover by 2 inches. Add the salt, celery, and carrots and bring to a boil over medium-high heat. Turn down the heat to a high simmer and cook for 3 hours, or until the meat is tender enough to fall off the bone and the liquid is gelatinous. Skim the surface occasionally as it simmers. Discard the vegetables, add the gelatin, and stir to dissolve. Let the head cool in the liquid for 30 minutes.

2. Pull all of the meat pieces and gristle off the bones and chop them roughly. Season the meat with salt and pepper to taste. Pack the meat into 2 terrine molds or loaf pans, filling them right up to the top. (If there is not enough meat to fill the second pan, the meat is excellent to serve as rillettes; put the extra in a little crock and cover with the cooking liquid.) Ladle some of the cooking liquid over the terrines to cover the meat. Wrap tightly in plastic wrap, then allow to cool overnight in the refrigerator. To turn out of the mold, run a warm table knife around the edges and turn out onto an oval plate.

3. Bring about 3 quarts of water to a boil and add 1 tablespoon salt. Blanch the potatoes until tender, 1 to 2 minutes. Drain the potatoes and place in a medium bowl.

4. In a small bowl, combine the thyme leaves, shallot, mustard, and balsamic vinegar. Gently whisk in the olive oil until emulsified. Pour the vinaigrette over the potatoes and toss gently to coat.

5. Using a sharp knife or a meat slicer, cut the *testa* in thin slices. Arrange 2 slices on each warmed dinner plate, then top with the potato slices. Garnish with shallot pickles, mustard seeds, parsley oil, and pepper. Serve immediately.

Shallot Pickles

Makes about 1 cup

1 cup **RED WINE VINEGAR**

½ cup **SUGAR**

½ cup **KOSHER SALT**

½ cup fresh **BEET JUICE**

10 **SHALLOTS**, peeled and sliced into
    ⅛-inch-thick rounds

In a deep bowl, combine the vinegar,
1 cup water, the sugar, salt, and beet
juice. Add the shallot rings and make
sure they are completely covered by
pickling liquid. Cover and refrigerate
for at least 24 hours.

This shallot pickles may be held
in an airtight container, refrigerated,
for up to 2 weeks.

PROSCIUTTO san daniele
with BLACK PEPPER *fett' unta*
AND WINESAP APPLE *MARMELLATA*

San Daniele prosciutto comes from Friuli and, with Parma and Carpegna, it is one of Italy's triumvirate of perfect hams. It is expensive, but a little bit goes a long way. Buy it from a busy store, with high turnover; when it sits wrapped in plastic for a while it loses its exceptional color and some of the porky quality that makes it so good.

1. In a heavy-bottomed saucepan, combine the sugar and 2 cups of water and bring to a boil. Add the apples and cook over high heat for 10 minutes, or until they are tender but not falling apart.

2. While the fruit is cooking, place the dry mustard in a small bowl and add water to form a thin paste, or slurry. Add the mustard oil, black mustard seeds, and salt and pepper to taste. Add this mixture to the fruit and cook over high heat until the mixture is thick and syrupy, about 20 minutes. Remove from the heat and allow to cool.

3. Place the spinach in a large salad bowl and toss with the lemon juice, 3 tablespoons of the olive oil, and salt and pepper to taste.

4. In a small bowl, combine the remaining 4 tablespoons of olive oil and the 2 tablespoons of black pepper and mix well.

5. Divide the prosciutto evenly among four chilled dinner plates, spreading the slices across the plate. Top each serving with a mound of spinach. Place a generous dollop of the marmalade on each plate. Cut the toasts in half on the diagonal and drizzle with the pepper oil. Serve immediately.

SERVES 4

1 cup SUGAR

4 WINESAP APPLES, cored and cut into ¼-inch half-moon slices

3 tablespoons Colman's dry MUSTARD

1 teaspoon MUSTARD OIL (available at specialty stores)

2 tablespoons BLACK MUSTARD SEEDS

KOSHER SALT

2 tablespoons freshly ground BLACK PEPPER, plus more to taste

1 bunch of baby SPINACH

Juice of 1 LEMON

7 tablespoons extra-virgin OLIVE OIL

½-pound PROSCIUTTO SAN DANIELE, thinly sliced

4 1-inch slices of crusty PEASANT BREAD, toasted in a 400°F. oven for 2 minutes

CHAPTER TWO

Pasta

Few things are simpler, yet more difficult to perfect, than a plate of pasta.

At Babbo, as in Italy, pasta falls primarily into two camps: hard and fresh. Hard pasta is served everywhere and every day in Italy and is part of the culture. It is made from hard durum wheat flour and water and in the best places is extruded through bronze die, then dried in temperature- and humidity-controlled rooms until very hard. It is most often served with oil-, tomato-, or vegetable-based condiments and also with seafood cooked in oil and wine, as well as with butter and cheese.

Fresh pasta is generally made with flour ground from the softer wheat of northern-central Italy. This is most often mixed with eggs and then kneaded and rolled out with a wooden *mattarello* (rolling pin) or between two metal dowels in a pasta machine to form sheets. These sheets are cut into strands, such as tagliatelle or pappardelle, or into shapes that are stuffed with a filling.

Soft pasta is much more porous and absorbent, and when tossed with an oil-based sauce it tends to soak up the oil and become a slick, greasy rag. For that reason the strands are generally served with butter, as are the stuffed pastas, or with meat sauces, the most famous being ragù Bolognese. When tossed with the correct amount of ragù (most often less than you'd think), it becomes the dreamy poetry that Petronius lived, a harmonic convergence of just-firm noodles and properly rich yet spare meat sauce of properly extracted intensity. Hard pasta is less porous and more resilient. Tossed with an oil-based condiment of slow-cooked vegetables, it slithers in with it and yet remains itself, retaining the firm texture that is the hallmark of great pasta while dancing the shaka with the condiment.

For both hard and soft pasta, the most critical element is the proportion of condiment, or sauce, to pasta, and achieving the proper consistency for that condiment. I can't stress enough that it is far better to have too little of the condiment and "loosen" it in the pan with a splash of pasta-cooking water (or even warm tap water) than to have too much. Condiment that is *too* loose can be "tightened" in the sauté pan with more cooking time.

At Babbo we serve both types of pasta, and so should you. We have two cooks who work fifty-hour weeks making fresh pasta—all day, every day. Each morning they make dough in the ten-gallon mixer, then roll out the pasta and cut pappardelle or tagliatelle, form the love letters and beef cheek ravioli and all of the other stuffed shapes. These all go in the freezer, neatly arranged on cookie sheets and covered with dish towels. As soon as the shapes freeze they are bagged in individual portions and stored in the freezer. This makes it easier for us to keep up with the pace during hectic dinner-service hours, but this technique can easily be adapted to the home kitchen—with a few caveats. First, our pasta freezer at Babbo is emptied to zero every two days. If stored for longer than a week or so, frozen pasta will dry out, crack, or take on unpleasant refrigerator/freezer smells or tastes. Don't crowd the pasta, as the corners chip off easily if mishandled. Pastas with a very wet filling (such as the goat cheese tortelloni) will crack more quickly than those with a drier filling (such as the beef cheek ravioli).

When choosing a pasta to make, consider the season. I think of soft pasta most often in the cooler months, when braised foods fill my tub and get me to my happy place. In the early summer at the sea, I want *linguine fine* or *bavette* (ribbon-shaped pasta) with my clams or rock shrimp, and make it spicy; in the late summer with tomatoes and eggplants knocking, I dream of thick spaghetti. I never think of cappellini, or angel hair—they just rub me the wrong way. But make pasta the way *you* like it. Your guests can tell if you're faking.

PAPPARDELLE *bolognese*

¼ cup extra-virgin **OLIVE OIL**

2 medium **ONIONS**, finely chopped

4 **CELERY** stalks, finely chopped

2 **CARROTS**, peeled and finely chopped

5 **GARLIC** cloves, sliced

1 pound ground **VEAL**

1 pound ground **PORK**

¼ pound **PANCETTA** or slab bacon, ground

1 can **TOMATO PASTE**

1 cup **MILK**

1 cup dry **WHITE WINE**

1 teaspoon fresh **THYME** leaves

KOSHER SALT and freshly ground **BLACK PEPPER**, to taste

1½ recipes **BASIC PASTA DOUGH** (page 102)

PARMIGIANO-REGGIANO, for serving

Purists first pooh-poohed the idea of dressing pappardelle with what is perhaps Italy's best-known and loved ragù, claiming that the cooks of Bologna would pair this sauce with nothing but tagliatelle. They were actually correct, but since it was my kitchen, and I love pappardelle, I prevailed. This recipe makes enough ragù to sauce 12 servings of pasta, so there will be ample leftovers. It holds well in the fridge for 4 days and can be frozen for months.

1. In a 6- to 8-quart, heavy-bottomed saucepan, heat the olive oil over medium heat. Add the onions, celery, carrots, and garlic and sweat over medium heat until the vegetables are translucent but not browned, about 5 minutes. Add the veal, pork, and pancetta and stir into the vegetables. Brown over high heat, stirring to keep the meat from sticking. Add the tomato paste, milk, wine, and thyme, bring just to a boil, then simmer over medium-low heat for 1 to 1½ hours. Season with salt and pepper.

2. Roll the pasta dough to the thinnest setting on a pasta machine. Cut the pasta sheets crosswise into 1½-inch-wide strips. Set aside on a baking tray, with the layers of pasta separated by wax or parchment paper.

3. Bring 6 quarts of water to a boil and add 2 tablespoons of salt.

4. Transfer 2 cups of the ragù to a 12- to 14-inch sauté pan and heat gently over medium heat. Cook the pappardelle in the boiling water until tender, about 1 minute. Drain the pasta, then add it to the pan with the ragù and toss over medium heat until it is coated and the sauce is dispersed, about 1 minute. Divide evenly among six to eight warmed bowls. Grate Parmigiano-Reggiano over each bowl and serve immediately.

MINT TAGLIATELLE
WITH LAMB AND OLIVES

Mint pasta is a natural with this lusty lamb and olive ragù. I love the firm texture and the almost-green flavor of arbequina olives, but you may substitute any olive except for the flavorless pitted "ripe olives" of my childhood.

1. In a large, heavy-bottomed casserole or Dutch oven, heat the olive oil over high heat until smoking. Season the lamb chunks with salt and pepper and add to the pan, working in batches if necessary to avoid overcrowding the pan. Sear the meat on all sides to a dark golden brown. Once the meat is well browned, remove to a plate and set aside. Add the carrot, onion, celery, garlic, and thyme and cook over medium-high heat until the vegetables are tender and browned, about 5 minutes. Stir in the red wine and tomatoes, scraping the bottom of the pan with a wooden spoon to dislodge any browned bits. Bring to a boil and return the meat to the pan. Reduce the heat to a simmer and cook over low heat, covered, for 1½ hours, or until the meat is extremely tender.

2. Remove the meat from the pan and, when it is cool enough to handle, shred it with a fork. Return it to the pan, add the olives, and simmer for an additional 30 minutes. The mixture should be a thick ragù. Season with salt and pepper and remove the thyme sprigs. Transfer the ragù to a 12-inch sauté pan and keep hot.

3. Bring 6 quarts of water to a boil and add 2 tablespoons of salt. Cook the pasta in the boiling water until tender yet al dente, about 1 minute. Drain the pasta, add it to the pan with the ragù, and toss over high heat for 1 minute to coat. Divide evenly among four warmed dinner plates, top with grated Parmigiano-Reggiano, and serve immediately.

SERVES 4

¼ cup extra-virgin **OLIVE OIL**

1 pound **LAMB SHOULDER**, cut into 1-inch chunks

KOSHER SALT and freshly ground **BLACK PEPPER**, to taste

1 **CARROT**, peeled and finely chopped

1 **ONION**, finely chopped

1 **CELERY** stalk, finely chopped

4 **GARLIC** cloves, thinly sliced

½ bunch of **THYME**, leaves left on stem

2 cups dry **RED WINE**

1 16-ounce can peeled **TOMATOES**, crushed by hand, plus their juices

¼ pound arbequina or other **OLIVES**, pitted

MINT TAGLIATELLE (page 102)

PARMIGIANO-REGGIANO, for serving

Basic Pasta Dough
Makes 1 pound

3½ to 4 cups all-purpose **FLOUR**
4 extra-large **EGGS**
1/2 teaspoon extra-virgin **OLIVE OIL**

Mound 3½ cups of the flour in the center of a large wooden cutting board. Make a well in the middle of the flour and add the eggs and the olive oil. Using a fork, beat together the eggs and oil, then begin to incorporate the flour, starting with the inner rim of the well.

As you expand the well, keep pushing the flour up from the base of the mound to retain the well shape. The dough will come together when half of the flour has been incorporated.

Start kneading the dough with the heels of your hands. Once you have a cohesive mass, remove the dough from the board and scrape up and discard any leftover bits. Lightly reflour the board and continue kneading for 6 more minutes. The dough should be elastic and a little sticky. Wrap the dough in plastic and allow to rest for 30 minutes at room temperature before rolling or shaping as desired.

Variations:

Black Pasta Dough Add 2 packets (2 tablespoons) of squid ink along with the eggs and oil.

Black Pepper Pasta Dough Add 2 tablespoons of ground black pepper along with the eggs and oil.

Green Pasta Dough Bring 3 quarts of water to a boil and add 1 tablespoon salt. Set up an ice bath next to the stove. Blanch 1 cup spinach leaves, packed, in the boiling water for 45 seconds, then remove it with tongs or a slotted spoon and immediately plunge it into the ice bath. Remove the spinach from the ice bath after 2 minutes and squeeze very dry in a clean, dry kitchen towel, removing as much moisture as possible. Chop the spinach very fine and place in a medium bowl with the eggs and olive oil. Stir well to make as homogenized a mixture as possible.

Mint Tagliatelle Bring 3 quarts of water to a boil. Place a bowl filled with water and ice next to the stove. Plunge 1 cup mint leaves into the boiling water and blanch for 45 seconds. Remove from the boiling water with a slotted spoon and immerse in the ice water. When cool, remove from the water, squeeze in a towel to dry, and place in the bowl of a food processor. Puree to form a very fine paste.

In a bowl, combine the mint puree and the eggs and stir well to combine.

Basic Gnocchi

Serves 12

3 pounds russet **POTATOES**
2 cups all-purpose **FLOUR**
1 extra-large **EGG**
1 teaspoon **KOSHER SALT**
½ cup **CANOLA OIL**

Place the whole potatoes in a saucepan with water to cover. Bring to a boil and cook at a low boil until they are soft, about 45 minutes. While still warm, peel the potatoes and pass them through a vegetable mill onto a clean pasta board.

Bring about 6 quarts of water to a boil. Set up an ice bath with 6 cups of ice and 6 cups of water nearby.

Make a well in the center of the potatoes and sprinkle all over with the flour. Break the egg into the center of the well, add the salt, and, using a fork, stir into the flour and potatoes as if you were making pasta. Once the egg is mixed in, bring the dough together, kneading gently until a ball is formed. Knead gently for another 4 minutes, until the ball is dry to the touch.

Divide the dough into 6 balls. Roll one ball at a time into a rope ¾ inch in diameter and cut the rope into 1-inch pieces. Flick the pieces off of a fork or along the concave side of a cheese grater to score the sides. Drop the dough pieces into the boiling water and cook until they float to the surface, about 1 minute. Use a slotted spoon to transfer the gnocchi to the ice bath. Meanwhile, continue with the remaining dough, forming ropes, cutting 1-inch pieces, and flicking them off a fork. Continue until all the gnocchi have been cooked and allow them to sit for several minutes in the ice bath.

Drain the gnocchi and transfer to a mixing bowl. Toss with the canola oil and store covered in the refrigerator for up to 48 hours or until ready to serve.

GREEN *fazzoletti*

with BOAR SAUSAGE RAGÙ

SERVES 4

¼ cup extra-virgin **OLIVE OIL**

1 pound fresh **BOAR**, pork, or
   venison sausage, cut into
   chunks

1 medium **SPANISH ONION**, cut
   into ¼-inch dice

1 medium **CARROT**, peeled and
   finely chopped

2 **GARLIC** cloves, thinly sliced

1 **CELERY** stalk, cut into ¼-inch
   dice

4 whole fresh **SAGE** leaves

2 cups dry **WHITE WINE**

1 16-ounce can peeled whole
   PLUM TOMATOES, crushed by
   hand with juices

1 cup **BROWN CHICKEN STOCK**
   (page 141)

GREEN PASTA DOUGH
   (page 102)

KOSHER SALT

The word *fazzoletti* literally means "face towels," a homely name for a mouthful of pasta. This is a fast and easy way to cut pasta shapes and they will hold a pretty heavy sauce quite well. It is better to remove the pasta shapes from the boiling water one by one with tongs and toss them immediately into the pan with the ragù; they have a tendency to stick together in a ball when drained en masse in a colander.

1. In a heavy-bottomed casserole or Dutch oven, heat the olive oil over medium-high heat until almost smoking. Cook the sausage in the olive oil until it is browned, 10 to 12 minutes.

2. Remove the meat to a plate and add the onion, carrot, garlic, celery, and sage to the casserole. Cook over low heat until softened, 7 to 9 minutes. Add the wine, crushed tomatoes and their juices, and chicken stock and bring to a boil. Return the meat to the pan, then lower the heat, partially cover, and simmer for 1 hour. Keep warm.

3. Divide the pasta dough into 4 equal portions and roll each out to the thinnest setting on a pasta machine. Lay each sheet of pasta on a work surface and cut into 4-inch squares. Place the squares on sheet trays that have been liberally sprinkled with semolina flour, and cover with clean towels until ready to cook.

4. Bring 6 quarts of water to a boil and add 2 tablespoons of salt. Cook the pasta in the boiling water until tender yet al dente, 1½ to 2 minutes. Add the cooked pasta to the hot ragù, reserving some of the pasta cooking water. Toss over high heat for 1 minute to coat the pasta and add a little of the pasta water if necessary to keep the sauce from becoming too "tight." Divide evenly among four warmed pasta bowls and serve immediately.

CALF'S BRAINS *francobolli*
WITH SAGE AND LEMON

Francobolli translates as "postage stamps" in English, a reference to the diminutive size of these delicate and sweet ravioli. Some people find the "brain issue" challenging, but once you get past that you'll see why this is one of my favorite dishes on the menu.

1. In a large, heavy-bottomed pot, bring about 6 quarts of water to a simmer and add 2 tablespoons of salt. Add the brains and poach for about 15 minutes. Drain and set aside to cool.

2. Meanwhile, in a 12- to 14-inch sauté pan, heat the olive oil over medium heat. Add the onions and cook slowly, stirring occasionally to avoid burning or sticking. Remove from the heat and cool.

3. When the brains have cooled, chop them fine and place them in a large bowl. Chop the onions fine and add them to the bowl along with the ricotta, nutmeg, and salt and pepper. Mix well.

4. Divide the pasta dough into 4 equal portions and roll each out to the thinnest setting on a pasta machine. Lay 1 sheet of pasta on a work surface and use a pastry cutter to make 12 2½- by 1-inch rectangles. Place 1 rounded tablespoon of the brain filling on one side of each rectangle and fold the dough in half to form a square. Press firmly around the edges to seal. Continue with the remaining pasta and filling. These can be set aside on a baking tray, the layers separated by dish towels, and refrigerated, for up to 6 hours.

5. Bring about 6 quarts of water to a boil and add 2 tablespoons of salt. Melt the butter in a 12-inch sauté pan and keep warm. Gently drop the ravioli into the boiling water and cook at a gentle simmer for 3 minutes. Drain, reserving some of the cooking water.

6. Add about 4 tablespoons of the pasta cooking water to the melted butter and shake the pan until the liquids are emulsified. Add the *francobolli* to the pan with the sage and lemon zest and toss over medium heat to coat. Divide the *francobolli* evenly among four warmed pasta bowls, grate some cheese over each bowl, and serve immediately.

MAKES ABOUT 48 RAVIOLI; SERVES 4

KOSHER SALT

2 pounds CALF'S BRAINS, soaked in cold water to cover for 2 hours, outer filament removed

2 tablespoons extra-virgin OLIVE OIL

3 large ONIONS, sliced

1 pound fresh RICOTTA

½ teaspoon freshly grated NUTMEG

Freshly ground BLACK PEPPER, to taste

1 recipe BASIC PASTA DOUGH (page 102)

8 tablespoons (1 stick) unsalted BUTTER

8 SAGE leaves, finely chopped

4 tablespoons LEMON ZEST

PARMIGIANO-REGGIANO, for serving

TAGLIATELLE

WITH PARSNIPS AND PANCETTA

SERVES 4

BLACK PEPPER PASTA DOUGH
(page 102)

KOSHER SALT

¼ pound **PANCETTA** or slab
bacon, cut into ½-inch cubes

1 tablespoon unsalted **BUTTER**

½ pound **PARSNIPS**, peeled,
halved, and cut into ¼-inch
half-moons

Freshly ground **BLACK PEPPER**

1 bunch of flat-leaf **PARSLEY**,
finely chopped to yield
¼ cup

PARMIGIANO-REGGIANO, for
serving

Almost everything is improved by the addition of pancetta, and parsnips are no exception. Their sweet flavor can be further enhanced by cooking the 'snips in small batches in really hot oil to produce a crispy, deep golden-brown coin.

1. Roll out the pasta dough to the thinnest setting on a pasta machine. Cut the dough crosswise into ¼-inch-wide strips. Place the tagliatelle on a sheet tray that has been dusted with semolina flour, cover with a clean dish towel, and set aside.

2. Bring 6 quarts of water to a boil and add 2 tablespoons of salt.

3. In a 12- to 14-inch sauté pan, cook the pancetta over high heat until it is browned and the fat has been rendered, about 10 minutes. With a slotted spoon, remove the pancetta to a plate lined with paper towels and set aside. Add the butter and parsnips and sauté over high heat without shaking the pan too much until they are golden brown and slightly crispy, 5 to 6 minutes. Season with salt and pepper, add the parsley, and cook 1 minute longer.

4. Cook the tagliatelle in the boiling water until tender yet al dente, about 2 minutes. Drain the pasta, reserving some of the cooking water, and add the pasta to the pan with the parsnips and pancetta. Toss over high heat to coat the pasta, adding pasta cooking water if necessary to keep the sauce from getting too tight. Divide equally among four heated pasta bowls, grate Parmigiano-Reggiano over each bowl, and serve immediately.

BLACK & WHITE
strichetti
WITH BACCALÀ AND MARJORAM

A combination of two pasta doughs, half tinted black with squid ink, makes for a very dramatic presentation. *Strichetti* translates as "bow ties," and these are a bit longer than *farfalle,* which translates as "butterflies." Note: The *baccalà* must be soaked for 48 hours prior to using in this recipe.

1. Place the *baccalà* in a bowl and add water to cover. Cover and refrigerate for 48 hours, changing the water at least once daily.

2. Drain the cod and pat it dry with paper towels. Break the flesh into small chunks. In a heavy-bottomed saucepan, combine the cod, 2 tablespoons of the marjoram, the tomato sauce, and white wine and mix well with a wooden spoon. Cook over medium-low heat until it has reduced to a thick ragù, about 30 minutes. Season with salt and pepper and set aside. This may be made up to 2 days in advance and refrigerated.

3. Divide the white and black pasta doughs into 2 equal portions each and roll out each portion in a pasta machine on the thinnest setting. Cut the sheets into 3-inch by 2-inch rectangles, pinching the centers of the rectangles to form bow tie shapes as you cut. Place the bow ties on a baking sheet and cover with a damp towel until ready to cook.

4. In a 12- to 14-inch sauté pan, reheat the cod ragù almost to a boil.

5. Bring about 6 quarts of water to a boil and add 2 tablespoons of salt. Drop the *strichetti* into the boiling water and cook for 1 minute. Drain and add to the ragù. Add the scallions and remaining 2 tablespoons of marjoram and toss over high heat for 1 minute. Divide among four warmed pasta bowls and serve immediately.

MAKES ABOUT 120;
SERVES 4 TO 6

1 pound BACCALÀ (dried salt cod)

4 tablespoons fresh MARJORAM leaves

2 cups BASIC TOMATO SAUCE (page 220)

1 cup WHITE WINE

KOSHER SALT and freshly ground BLACK PEPPER, to taste

½ recipe BASIC PASTA DOUGH (page 102)

½ recipe BLACK PASTA DOUGH (page 102)

2 SCALLIONS, sliced on the bias

mint LOVE LETTERS
with SPICY LAMB SAUSAGE

**MAKES 70 TO 80 RAVIOLI;
SERVES 8**

KOSHER SALT

1 pound **SWEET PEAS**, fresh or
frozen (about 3 pounds in the
pod if using fresh)

2 cups **MINT** leaves, 16 reserved
for garnish

1 cup **PARMIGIANO-REGGIANO**,
grated

½ cup **HEAVY CREAM**

Freshly ground **BLACK PEPPER**,
to taste

1 recipe **BASIC PASTA DOUGH**
(page 102)

1 recipe **BASIC TOMATO SAUCE**
(page 220)

1 pound **MERGUEZ** (spicy lamb
sausage), cut into ½-inch
chunks

¼ pound **PECORINO ROMANO**,
for grating

"Love letters" is a bit of menu poetry, but this has been one of the most popular dishes we've served since day one. The inspiration was the natural affinity between lamb and mint, but I also love the Moroccan flavors of mint tea and merguez sausage.

1. Bring 3 quarts of water to a boil and add 1 tablespoon of salt. Set up an ice bath nearby. Submerge the shelled peas into the boiling water and cook until tender yet still bright green, 1 to 2 minutes. Remove the peas with a slotted spoon, reserving the boiling water, and plunge them into the ice bath to refresh and cool. Using the same water, blanch the mint leaves for just 10 to 15 seconds. Transfer immediately to the ice bath. Drain well.

2. In the bowl of a food processor, combine the peas, mint, Parmigiano-Reggiano, heavy cream, and salt and pepper and pulse to form a smooth paste.

3. Using a pasta machine, roll out the pasta to the thinnest setting and then cut the sheets into 3-inch squares. Place 1 tablespoon of the pea filling on each square and fold over to form rectangles. Continue filling and shaping until all the pasta and filling are used. Cover and refrigerate until needed or place on baking sheets between layers of dish towels and freeze overnight. The next day, place in freezer bags and store up to 1 week.

4. In a medium saucepan, bring the tomato sauce to a boil. Add the sausage, reduce the heat to a simmer, and cook for 1 hour, skimming off the fat as it is rendered from the meat. Remove the sauce from the heat, cool briefly, and then pulse it in a food processor until smooth. Transfer to a 12-inch sauté pan and keep warm.

5. Bring 6 quarts of water to a boil and add 2 tablespoons of salt.

6. Cook the pasta in the boiling water until tender and cooked through, 2 to 3 minutes. Drain the pasta and add to the pan with the sauce. Toss gently over high heat for 1 minute, add the reserved mint leaves, toss 1 minute more, then divide evenly among eight warmed dinner plates. Grate the Pecorino Romano over each plate and serve immediately.

BEEF CHEEK *ravioli*

**MAKES 60 TO 70 RAVIOLI;
SERVES 8**

3 tablespoons extra-virgin
    OLIVE OIL

1 **WHITE ONION**, cut into ¼-inch
    dice

½ **CELERY** stalk, cut into
    ¼-inch dice

2 pounds **BEEF CHEEKS**, brisket,
    or beef chuck, trimmed and
    cut into 1-inch chunks

2 cups **RED WINE**

1 cup chopped fresh or canned
    TOMATOES

1 teaspoon fresh **ROSEMARY**,
    chopped

1 recipe **BASIC PASTA DOUGH**
    (page 102)

KOSHER SALT

1 cup (2 sticks) unsalted **BUTTER**

1 recipe **CHICKEN LIVERS
    TOSCANI** (page 79)

2 tablespoons **BLACK TRUFFLES**,
    sliced

1 bunch of flat-leaf **PARSLEY**,
    chopped to yield ½ cup

¼ cup grated **PECORINO
    ROMANO**, plus more for
    serving

Of all the pasta dishes—indeed of *all* the dishes—on the menu, this is probably the one most associated with Babbo. When we first opened there were not that many restaurants celebrating alternative cuts of meat like these incredibly flavorful cheeks. I'm happy to say that's no longer the case.

At the restaurant we make the filling with squab livers, although I have substituted more readily available chicken livers here. If you can get the squab livers, by all means use them—the livers toscani would be made exactly the same way. I would consider doubling the filling recipe and freezing some for a later use; it holds very well in the freezer and I guarantee you will want more immediately.

1. Preheat the oven to 400°F.

2. In a large, ovenproof skillet with a lid, heat the olive oil over medium heat. Add the onion and celery, lower the heat, and cook until very soft but not browned, about 10 minutes. Increase the heat to high and add the beef cheeks. Brown on all sides, working in batches if necessary to avoid overcrowding the pan. Add the wine and stir in with a wooden spoon, scraping the bottom of the pan to dislodge browned bits of vegetable and meat. Bring to a boil, stir in the tomatoes and rosemary, and allow the mixture to return to a boil. Cover, place in the oven, and cook for 1 hour, or until the meat is stringy and very tender.

3. Remove the meat mixture from the oven, allow to cool, and skim off the excess fat. Transfer the mixture to a food processor and pulse until smooth.

4. Using a pasta machine, roll out the dough on the thinnest setting. Cut the sheets into 4-inch squares. Place 1 tablespoon of the beef filling in the center of each square, bring two opposite corners together to form a triangle, and press the edges together firmly to seal. At this point you may freeze the ravioli on cookie sheets between layers of wax paper or parchment.

5. Bring 6 quarts of water to a boil and add 2 tablespoons of salt.

6. In a 12- to 14-inch sauté pan, heat the butter over high heat and cook until it begins to brown but not scorch. Add the chicken livers toscani and cook for 1 minute. Add a few tablespoons of the hot pasta water to create an emulsion in the pan. Add the truffles and cook for 1 minute more.

7. Meanwhile, drop the ravioli in the boiling water and cook for 2 minutes or until they float to the surface. Using a slotted spoon, drain the ravioli and add them to the sauté pan.

8. Add half of the chopped parsley and the ¼ cup of grated Pecorino to the pan. Toss gently for 1 minute over medium heat to coat. Place three ravioli on each of eight warmed dinner plates, removing them carefully from the sauté pan with a spoon. Spoon the extra sauce over each serving, top with the remaining parsley, grate Pecorino over each plate, and serve immediately.

baccalà mezzalune

with GOLDEN TOMATOES and GREEN OLIVES

The filling in these *mezzalune* (half-moon-shaped ravs) is very reminiscent of the brandade I love to eat in French restaurants. Note: The *baccalà*, or dried salt cod, must soak for 48 hours before it can be added to the filling.

1. Place the *baccalà* in a bowl with water to cover. Cover and refrigerate for 48 hours, changing the water at least once daily.

2. Drain the *baccalà*, pat dry with paper towels, and break or cut the flesh into small chunks. In a heavy-bottomed saucepan, combine the cod, potatoes, pesto, 1 cup water, and the milk, and mix well with a wooden spoon. Cook over medium-low heat, stirring occasionally to break up the fish, until the sauce has reduced to a thick ragù, about 45 minutes. Season with salt and pepper and set aside to cool.

3. Roll out the pasta dough to the thinnest setting on a pasta machine. Using a biscuit cutter or water glass, cut out 3-inch circles. Place a scant tablespoon of the cod mixture on one half of each circle, then fold them in half to form a half-moon. Seal the edges with your fingers, pressing to make sure there is no air trapped inside the "package."

4. Bring 6 quarts of water to a boil and add 2 tablespoons of salt.

5. In a 12- to 14-inch sauté pan, heat ¼ cup of the olive oil over medium-high heat. Add the tomatoes and olives and season with salt and pepper. Cook over medium-high heat until the tomatoes begin to burst and the olives are softened, about 1 minute. Add the tomato sauce and bring to a boil, then remove from the heat and set aside.

6. Cook the *mezzalune* in the boiling water until tender and cooked through, about 4 minutes. Drain the pasta and add it to the pan with the tomatoes and olives. Toss over high heat for 1 minute, remove from the heat, and drizzle with the remaining ¼ cup of olive oil. The sauce will more closely resemble a broken vinaigrette than a smooth tomato puree. Divide evenly among eight warmed plates, sprinkle with the parsley, and serve immediately.

MAKES 80 *MEZZALUNE;*
SERVES 6

1 pound **BACCALÀ** (dried salt cod)

1 pound **POTATOES**, peeled and cubed

¼ cup **JALAPEÑO PESTO** (page 220)

1 cup **MILK**

KOSHER SALT and freshly ground **BLACK PEPPER**, to taste

1 recipe **BASIC PASTA DOUGH** (page 102)

½ cup extra-virgin **OLIVE OIL**

1 pint golden **PEAR TOMATOES**, halved lengthwise

¼ pound arbequina or other small green **OLIVES**, pitted

1 cup **BASIC TOMATO SAUCE** (page 220)

10 flat-leaf **PARSLEY** leaves, finely shredded

DUCK LIVER *ravioli*

MAKES 80 RAVIOLI; SERVES 8

¼ cup extra-virgin **OLIVE OIL**

½ medium **RED ONION**, thinly
sliced

1 pound **DUCK LIVERS** or
chicken livers

1 tablespoon hot **RED PEPPER
FLAKES**

1 cup dry **RED WINE**

KOSHER SALT and freshly ground
BLACK PEPPER, to taste

4 tablespoons unsalted **BUTTER**,
chilled and cubed, plus
4 more tablespoons
(1 stick total)

1 lobe (about 1½ pounds)
grade-B duck **FOIE GRAS**

1 recipe **BASIC PASTA DOUGH**
(page 102)

4 tablespoons best-quality
BALSAMIC VINEGAR

1 bunch of flat-leaf **PARSLEY**,
finely chopped to yield ¼ cup

PARMIGIANO-REGGIANO, for
serving

The opulent filling for these ravioli incorporates both duck livers and fresh foie gras. Although we use the lesser, grade-B foie gras, it is still quite costly and difficult to come by; you can substitute high-quality foie gras terrine or canned pâté de foie gras with very good results. When we serve this at Babbo we like to serve a glass of Italian dessert wine like vin santo or passito alongside, much as the French serve foie gras with Sauternes.

1. In a 10- to 12-inch sauté pan, heat the olive oil slowly over medium heat. Add the onion and cook slowly until soft but not brown, about 10 minutes. Add the duck livers and red pepper flakes and cook until lightly browned, about 8 minutes. Add the wine and cook until only 3 to 4 tablespoons of liquid remain, about 8 minutes.

2. Transfer the liver mixture to a food processor and pulse on and off until blended but still lumpy—it should not be a smooth puree. Season with salt and pepper and remove to a large mixing bowl. Cool to room temperature. Fold in the 4 tablespoons of cubed butter with a spatula and mix until incorporated. Set aside. Cut the foie gras into ½-inch dice and stir into the chilled liver mixture.

3. Roll the pasta dough to the thinnest setting on a pasta machine. Cut the sheets into 3-inch by 2-inch rectangles. Place a scant tablespoon of the liver mixture onto one of the rectangles. Cover with a second rectangle, pressing around the edges with your thumb to seal. Repeat with the remaining pasta and filling. Place the ravioli on sheet trays and cover with a clean kitchen towel. The ravioli may be frozen for up to a week.

4. Bring 6 quarts of water to a boil and add 2 tablespoons of salt.

5. In a 12- to 14-inch sauté pan, heat the remaining 4 tablespoons of butter over medium-high heat until the foam subsides. Add the balsamic vinegar and stir with a wooden spoon to incorporate.

6. Drop the ravioli in the boiling water and cook for 2 minutes. Drain the ravioli, reserving a bit of the cooking water, and add them to the pan with the balsamic and butter mixture. Toss gently over high heat to coat, adding some of the pasta cooking water if necessary to keep the sauce from becoming too "tight."

7. To assemble the dish, divide the ravioli evenly among eight warmed dinner plates. Top each plate with some of the pan sauce, then sprinkle with the chopped parsley. Grate Parmigiano-Reggiano over each portion and serve immediately.

GOAT CHEESE
tortelloni
WITH DRIED ORANGE AND FENNEL POLLEN

The trick to this dish is making sure that the filling is quite moist. Once cooked and plated, the soft filling should ooze out of the cut tortelloni like ripened Brie that has spent hours on the counter. Fennel pollen was very difficult to find when I first tasted it at Macelleria Cecchini in Panzano, but now it seems ubiquitous.

1. In a large bowl, mash the goat cheese with the milk until soft. Add the herbs, nutmeg, ¼ cup of the Parmigiano, and salt and pepper, and stir well. Cover the mixture and refrigerate until firm, about 30 minutes.

2. Using a pasta machine, roll out the pasta to the thinnest setting and then cut the sheets into 4-inch squares. Place 1 tablespoon of the goat cheese filling in the center of each 4-inch square. Fold two opposite corners together to form a triangle and press the edges together firmly to seal. Bring the long points of the triangle together in a ring and join with firm finger pressure. Continue filling and shaping tortelloni until all the pasta and filling are used. At this point you may freeze the tortelloni on cookie sheets between layers of wax paper. Transfer to plastic bags and store in the freezer for up to a week.

3. Bring 6 quarts of water to a boil and add 2 tablespoons of salt. Drop the tortelloni into the boiling water and cook until tender, 3 to 5 minutes. Carefully drain the tortelloni, reserving about 1 cup of the pasta water.

4. Meanwhile, in a sauté pan, heat the butter and ¼ cup of the pasta water together, whisking to form an emulsified sauce. Add the cooked tortelloni, fennel fronds, and orange zest to the pan to heat gently and coat with the sauce, about 1 minute. Divide among six warmed plates, topping the tortelloni with fennel fronds and orange zest. Finish with a sprinkling of fennel pollen and the remaining ¼ cup of Parmigiano-Reggiano and serve immediately.

MAKES 60 TORTELLONI; SERVES 6

2 cups fresh GOAT CHEESE, preferably Coach Farm brand

1 cup MILK

1 tablespoon finely chopped flat-leaf PARSLEY

10 SAGE leaves, finely chopped

1 teaspoon finely chopped fresh ROSEMARY

1 tablespoon finely chopped fresh THYME

½ teaspoon freshly grated NUTMEG

½ cup freshly grated PARMIGIANO-REGGIANO

KOSHER SALT and freshly ground BLACK PEPPER, to taste

1½ recipes BASIC PASTA DOUGH (page 102)

½ cup (1 stick) unsalted BUTTER

12 to 14 clean, beautiful FENNEL fronds

2 teaspoons narrow ORANGE ZEST strips, dried in a 200°F. oven for 30 minutes

1 tablespoon FENNEL POLLEN or ground fennel seeds

**MAKES 40 TO 50 RAVIOLI;
SERVES 8**

3 tablespoons extra-virgin
  OLIVE OIL

½ pound young **DANDELION
  GREENS**, stemmed and
  chopped

½ pound young **SORREL**,
  stemmed and chopped

½ pound **SWISS CHARD**,
  stemmed and chopped

KOSHER SALT and freshly ground
  BLACK PEPPER, to taste

1 cup fresh **RICOTTA**

¼ cup freshly grated
  PARMIGIANO-REGGIANO

Several gratings of **NUTMEG**

1 recipe **BASIC PASTA DOUGH**
  (page 102)

8 tablespoons (1 stick) unsalted
  BUTTER

2 tablespoons fresh **THYME**
  leaves

Zest of 1 **LEMON**

3 **ESCAROLE** leaves, finely
  shredded

¼ pound aged **GOAT CHEESE**,
  for grating

The tangy flavor of sorrel is like a spring tonic to my palate. Many do not appreciate its bitter edge, but here it works really well as a counterpoint to the sweet, creamy ricotta.

1. In a 14- to 16-inch sauté pan, heat the olive oil over high heat. Add the dandelions, sorrel, and chard and cook over medium heat, stirring often, until they have cooked down and are very tender, about 20 minutes. Season with salt and pepper, remove from the heat, and set aside until cool enough to handle. Squeeze the greens firmly to remove as much moisture as possible, then chop finely.

2. In a large bowl, combine the chopped greens, ricotta, Parmigiano-Reggiano, and nutmeg. Season with salt and pepper and stir well to combine. Set aside.

3. Roll out the pasta dough to the thinnest setting on a pasta machine. Cut 4-inch squares from the pasta dough and place a scant tablespoon of the filling in one corner of each square. Pat the filling down to flatten it slightly and fold each square over the filling to form an isosceles triangle. Press the edges together to seal. Place the finished ravioli on a sheet tray covered with a damp towel until ready to cook.

4. Bring 6 quarts of water to a boil and add 2 tablespoons of salt.

5. In a 12- to 14-inch sauté pan, heat the butter over medium-high heat until the foam subsides. Add the thyme, lemon zest, and escarole. Remove from the heat.

6. Meanwhile, cook the ravioli in the boiling water until tender and cooked through, about 5 minutes. Drain the ravioli and add them to the pan with the hot butter. Toss over high heat for 1 minute, then divide evenly among eight warmed pasta bowls. Grate the goat cheese over each portion and serve immediately.

ASPARAGUS *and* RICOTTA
ravioli

In the world of noodles these are the first taste of spring—a simple ode to the end of winter produce and poetry to the palate. We all eat several plates of these the first week in April.

1. Bring 3 quarts of water to a boil and add 1 tablespoon of salt. Set up an ice bath nearby. Cook the asparagus spears in the boiling water until very tender, about 3 minutes. Drain and immediately refresh in the ice bath. Once the asparagus spears are cooled, drain and pat dry. Slice each spear very thin on the diagonal, reserving ¼ cup for garnish.

2. In a medium bowl, combine the asparagus, ricotta, Parmigiano-Reggiano, olive oil, and salt and pepper and stir well to combine.

3. Roll out the pasta dough to the thinnest setting on a pasta machine. Cut the pasta sheets into 4-inch rectangles. Place a scant tablespoon of the ricotta filling on one half of each rectangle, then fold them over like a book to enclose the filling. Press the edges of each ravioli with your fingers to seal. The ravioli can now be frozen between sheets of parchment until ready to cook.

4. Bring 6 quarts of water to a boil and add 2 tablespoons of salt.

5. In a 14- to 16-inch sauté pan, heat the butter over high heat until the foam subsides. Add the reserved asparagus and remove from the heat. Cook the ravioli in the boiling water until they are tender and cooked through (you should taste one to test it), about 3 minutes. Drain the ravioli and add them to the pan with the butter. Add 3 tablespoons of the pasta cooking water and toss gently over high heat for 1 minute. Season with salt and pepper. Divide evenly among eight warmed pasta bowls and serve immediately with Parmigiano-Reggiano grated over the top.

MAKES ABOUT 60 RAVIOLI; SERVES 8

KOSHER SALT

20 medium **ASPARAGUS** spears, tough ends trimmed

1½ cups fresh **RICOTTA**, drained

½ cup freshly grated **PARMIGIANO-REGGIANO**, plus more for serving

2 tablespoons extra-virgin **OLIVE OIL**

Freshly ground **BLACK PEPPER**, to taste

1 recipe **BASIC PASTA DOUGH** (page 102)

1 cup (2 sticks) unsalted **BUTTER**

CLASSIC TORTELLINI
in Brodo

**MAKES 80 TORTELLINI;
SERVES 8**

2 tablespoons unsalted **BUTTER**

7 ounces boneless, skinless **CHICKEN BREAST**

½ cup dry **WHITE WINE**

3-ounce piece of **PANCETTA**, chilled

3-ounce piece of **MORTADELLA**, chilled

1 cup **PARMIGIANO-REGGIANO**, grated, plus more for grating over

Several gratings of fresh **NUTMEG**

¼ cup **MILK**

1 large **EGG**, beaten

KOSHER SALT

1½ recipes **BASIC PASTA DOUGH** (page 102)

6 cups **CAPON STOCK** (see sidebar)

Freshly ground **BLACK PEPPER**

Along with *tagliatelle al ragù* and *lasagne*, *tortellini* are one of the cornerstones of Bolognese pasta heaven. If capons are hard to find, turkey makes great stock, too.

1. In a 12- to 14-inch sauté pan, melt the butter over medium heat until it just starts to foam. Slice the raw chicken very thin across the grain, and cook it over medium heat, stirring constantly, until very lightly browned. Add the wine, cover, and cook for 3 minutes. Uncover and cook until the liquid evaporates, 5 more minutes. Set aside to cool.

2. Cut the pancetta and mortadella in ¼-inch dice and place in a food processor. Add the cooled chicken and pulse just until coarsely ground. Transfer to a large mixing bowl and add the Parmigiano-Reggiano, nutmeg, milk, and egg. Fold together carefully, season with salt, cover, and refrigerate for 1 hour.

3. Roll out the pasta dough to the thinnest setting on a pasta machine. Cut it into 2-inch squares and place 1 teaspoon of the chicken filling on the center of each square. Bring two opposite corners together to form a triangle, pressing the edges firmly together to seal. Bring the ends of the triangle together in a ring and join with firm finger pressure. Continue until all of the pasta and filling are used up.

4. Bring the capon stock to a boil. Drop the tortellini in the boiling stock and simmer for 8 to 10 minutes, or until tender. Season with salt and pepper, if necessary, and divide the pasta and broth evenly among eight warmed pasta bowls. Grate Parmigiano-Reggiano over each portion and serve immediately.

Capon Stock
Makes 2 quarts

2 tablespoons extra-virgin **OLIVE OIL**

1 whole **CAPON** (5 to 8 pounds), cut
   in pieces, excess fat removed

3 **CARROTS**, peeled and coarsely
   chopped

2 **ONIONS**, coarsely chopped

4 **CELERY** stalks, coarsely chopped

1 tablespoon **TOMATO PASTE**

1 tablespoon **BLACK PEPPERCORNS**

Stems from 1 bunch of flat-leaf
   PARSLEY

In a large, heavy-bottomed
saucepan, heat the oil until smoking.
Add the capon pieces and brown all
over, stirring to avoid burning.
Transfer the browned capon parts to
a bowl, then add the carrots, onions,
and celery to the pan and cook until
soft and browned. Return the bird to
the pan and add 4 quarts of water,
the tomato paste, peppercorns, and
parsley, stirring to dislodge the
browned meat and vegetable bits
from the bottom of the pan. Bring
almost to a boil, reduce the heat,
and cook at a low simmer for 2
hours, until reduced by half, occasionally skimming off the fat. Strain
the stock, pressing the solids with
the bottom of a ladle to extract all
the liquid. Cool, then refrigerate or
freeze until ready to use.

PUMPKIN *lune*

with BUTTER *and* SAGE

Traditional to Mantova, these *lune* (little moons) often have crushed amaretti cookies inside the filling. We like to grate an oversized cookie over the top in addition to the cheese.

1. Preheat the oven to 350°F.

2. Cut the squash in half, remove the seeds, drizzle with the olive oil, and place on a baking sheet. Roast for 25 to 35 minutes, or until the squash is very soft. Remove from the oven, let cool, then scoop the flesh from the skin.

3. In a large bowl, combine the cooled squash, cheese, nutmeg, balsamic vinegar, and salt and pepper. Stir well to combine.

4. Roll out the pasta dough to the thinnest setting on a pasta machine. Using a biscuit cutter or water glass, cut out 2-inch circles. Pipe or carefully spoon a rounded tablespoon of filling onto the center of half of the rounds and cover the filling with a second pasta round. Press the edges together firmly to seal.

5. Bring 6 quarts of water to a boil and add 2 tablespoons of salt. Drop the *lune* in the boiling water and cook for 2 minutes. While the pasta cooks, melt the butter in a 12- to 14-inch sauté pan until it foams and subsides. Add 2 to 4 tablespoons of the pasta cooking water to the butter and whisk to emulsify. Drain the pasta and add it to the butter. Add the sage leaves and toss gently for 1 minute over medium heat to coat the pasta with sauce. Divide the *lune* among four warmed plates, grate the Parmigiano-Reggiano and amaretti over each plate, and serve immediately.

MAKES 35 TO 40 *LUNE;* SERVES 4

1 small **PUMPKIN**, or butternut or acorn squash (about 1 pound)

2 tablespoons extra-virgin **OLIVE OIL**

½ cup grated **PARMIGIANO-REGGIANO**, plus more for serving

½ teaspoon freshly grated **NUTMEG**

2 tablespoons **BALSAMIC VINEGAR**

KOSHER SALT and freshly ground **BLACK PEPPER**, to taste

½ recipe **BASIC PASTA DOUGH** (page 102)

8 tablespoons (1 stick) unsalted **BUTTER**

8 fresh **SAGE** leaves

1 large **AMARETTI COOKIE** (page 318)

ANGEL'S PYRAMIDS
WITH BUTTER AND SAGE

In Babbo's world of pasta, all novice cooks start with morning pasta production as their introduction to the kitchen. Each has a pasta named after him or her (Angel followed Jacob) and the fillings vary with the season. These seem to be the faves.

1. In a large, heavy-bottomed skillet, combine the olive oil, lamb's tongue, and pancetta and cook over medium heat until it begins to brown, about 10 minutes. Add the scallions and 2 tablespoons of the thyme and continue to cook over medium heat until the pancetta is cooked through and the meat is browned. Transfer to a large bowl and cool to room temperature. Stir in the egg and Parmigiano-Reggiano, and season with salt and pepper.

2. Roll out the pasta dough to the thinnest setting on a pasta machine. Cut the pasta sheets into 3-inch squares. Using a pastry bag fitted with a medium-small tip or a tablespoon, place a scant tablespoon of the filling into the center of each square. Bring the four corners of each square together over the filling to form a pyramid. Press the edges together tightly with your fingers to seal. Arrange the pyramids on baking sheets and hold in the refrigerator or freezer until ready to cook. (The pasta can be frozen for up to 1 week at this point.)

3. Bring 6 quarts of water to a boil and add 2 tablespoons of salt.

4. In a 14- to 16-inch sauté pan, heat the butter over high heat until the foam subsides, add the remaining 2 tablespoons of thyme, and then lower the heat to medium, continuing to cook the butter until it browns.

5. Drop the pasta in the boiling water and cook until tender yet al dente, about 3 minutes. Carefully remove the pyramids from the boiling water with a slotted spoon and transfer them to the pan with the browned butter. Toss very gently for 1 minute. Immediately divide among eight warmed pasta bowls and serve with Parmigiano-Reggiano grated over the top.

Note: Cook raw lamb's or calf's tongue in simmering water to cover for 1 hour.

MAKES 45 TO 50 PYRAMIDS; SERVES 8

2 tablespoons extra-virgin OLIVE OIL

½ pound ground cooked LAMB'S TONGUE, calf's tongue, or turkey breast (see Note)

¼ pound PANCETTA, ground or chopped very fine by hand

2 whole SCALLIONS, finely chopped

4 tablespoons fresh THYME leaves

1 EGG

¼ cup PARMIGIANO-REGGIANO, plus more for grating

KOSHER SALT and freshly ground BLACK PEPPER, to taste

1 recipe BASIC PASTA DOUGH (page 102)

1 cup (2 sticks) unsalted BUTTER

16 fresh SAGE leaves

SPAGHETTINI

with SPICY ARTICHOKES,

SWEET GARLIC, AND LOBSTER

SERVES 4

8 baby **ARTICHOKES**, trimmed
and quartered

1 cup extra-virgin **OLIVE OIL**

Leaves from 1 bunch of **MINT**,
about ½ cup, packed

1 tablespoon hot **RED PEPPER
FLAKES**

2 **GARLIC** cloves, thinly sliced

4 1-pound **LOBSTERS**

KOSHER SALT

1 pound dry **SPAGHETTINI**

2 cups **BASIC TOMATO SAUCE**
(page 220)

12 **SWEET GARLIC CLOVES**
(see sidebar)

Freshly ground **BLACK PEPPER**,
to taste

This is called a Saturday-night special because for some reason we sell twice as many orders on Saturday as any other day of the week. The artichokes are quick-marinated in mint- and chile-flavored oil. After you've served the 'chokes, save the oil for a deliciously spicy vinaigrette.

1. In a 12- to 14-inch sauté pan, combine the artichokes, oil, mint, red pepper flakes, and the sliced garlic. Place over medium heat until the center of the pan has reached a full boil; the artichokes should be submerged in oil. Remove from the heat and let cool for 15 to 20 minutes. Set aside.

2. Fill a pot large enough to hold the lobsters three-quarters full with water and bring to a boil. Boil the lobsters until done, approximately 12 minutes. Drain, let cool slightly, and remove all the meat from the claws and tails. Cut the tails in half lengthwise and leave the rest as is. (All of the preceding components can be prepared 8 hours in advance and refrigerated.)

3. Bring 6 quarts of water to a boil and add 2 tablespoons of salt. Cook the pasta in the boiling water according to package directions, until tender yet al dente, and drain.

4. While the pasta cooks, in a large sauté pan, heat the tomato sauce to a simmer. Drain the artichokes (reserving the oil for another use) and add them to the pan with the sweet garlic cloves and the lobster meat. Stir over medium heat to just warm through. Season with salt and pepper.

5. Drain the pasta and add to the sauté pan. Toss over medium heat to coat with the sauce, about 30 seconds. Divide among four heated bowls and serve immediately.

Sweet Garlic Cloves

2 tablespoons extra-virgin **OLIVE OIL**
1 head of **GARLIC**, separated into
    peeled cloves
1 cup Cinzano or other **SWEET WHITE**
    WINE

In a 12- to 14-inch sauté pan, heat
the olive oil over high heat until
almost smoking. Add the garlic
cloves and sauté until lightly
browned. Add the Cinzano and continue to cook over high heat until the
garlic is soft and the wine is reduced
to a syrupy consistency and coats
the garlic.

    Sweet garlic cloves can be
stored for up to 1 week, in an airtight
container in the refrigerator.

linguine fine WITH BABY EELS, HOT CHILES, AND GARLIC

SERVES 4

KOSHER SALT

6 tablespoons extra-virgin
OLIVE OIL

4 GARLIC cloves, thinly sliced

1 teaspoon hot RED PEPPER
FLAKES

½ pound BABY EELS or tiny
whitebait

¼ cup WHITE WINE

Freshly ground BLACK PEPPER,
to taste

1 pound dried *LINGUINE FINE*

¼ cup fresh BREAD CRUMBS,
toasted for 2 minutes in a
400°F. oven

2 tablespoons flat-leaf PARSLEY,
roughly chopped

This is a classic example of the product being the whole dish. When baby eels are in season we can sell up to 20 orders per night. The baby eels are easier to find in Chinatown, where they are sold as elvers.

1. Bring 6 quarts of water to a boil and add 2 tablespoons of salt.

2. In a 12- to 14-inch sauté pan, heat 2 tablespoons of the olive oil until just smoking. Add the garlic and red pepper flakes and sauté over high heat until the garlic is lightly toasted, about 2 minutes. Add the eels and toss over high heat for 1 minute. Add the white wine, remove from the heat, and season with salt and pepper.

3. Cook the linguine in the boiling water according to package directions until tender yet al dente. Drain the pasta, reserving ½ cup of the water, and add the pasta to the sauté pan with the eels. Toss over high heat for 1 minute, adding a scant splash of the pasta water if necessary to keep the condiment from getting too "tight." Drizzle with the remaining 4 tablespoons of olive oil and toss it through. Divide evenly among four warmed pasta bowls, top with the bread crumbs, sprinkle with the parsley, and serve immediately.

bavette

with BABY OCTOPUS,

GREEN CHILES, AND MINT

If you can't find the baby octopuses, a large one will be just fine; you'll just need to cook it whole (for up to an hour or until it's tender) and then cut it into ½-inch pieces before tossing into the pan. The combo of hot chiles and mint adds sexiness to anything with tomato sauce.

1. In a medium saucepan, combine the baby octopuses, vinegar, cork, and water to cover. Bring to a boil and cook uncovered for 15 minutes. Drain and allow the octopus to cool.

2. Bring 6 quarts of water to a boil and add 2 tablespoons of salt.

3. In a 12- to 14-inch sauté pan, heat the olive oil over high heat until hot but not smoking. Add the garlic cloves and cook until light golden brown, about 3 minutes. Add the jalapeño pesto, tomato sauce, and octopuses and cook over high heat for 5 minutes.

4. Meanwhile, cook the *bavette* in the boiling water until tender yet al dente. Drain the pasta and add it to the pan with the sauce. Add the mint leaves and toss over high heat for 1 minute, season with salt and pepper, and serve immediately.

SERVES 4

2 pounds **BABY OCTOPUS**, 8 to 10 per pound

3 tablespoons **RED WINE VINEGAR**

1 **WINE CORK**

KOSHER SALT

¼ cup extra-virgin **OLIVE OIL**

4 **GARLIC** cloves, thinly sliced

¼ cup **JALAPEÑO PESTO** (page 220)

1 cup **BASIC TOMATO SAUCE** (page 220)

1 pound dried *BAVETTE* (thin, ribbon-shaped pasta) or linguine

12 fresh **MINT** leaves

Freshly ground **BLACK PEPPER**, to taste

perciatelli

with CARDOONS, GARLIC, *and* PECORINO

Cardoons have such a distinct and delicate flavor that I like to show-case them in this simple dish. We do the same thing with wild spring garlic as well as ramps.

1. In a large pot, combine the cardoons, lemon juice, and water to cover. Bring to a boil and cook until the cardoons are tender and easily pierced with the point of a paring knife, about 45 minutes. Drain, allow to cool, and slice into matchsticks. Set aside.

2. Bring 6 quarts of water to a boil and add 2 tablespoons of salt. Add the *perciatelli* and cook until tender yet al dente, about 10 minutes.

3. Meanwhile, in a 12- to 14-inch sauté pan, heat the olive oil until almost smoking. Add the garlic and toast until light golden brown. Add the cardoons and toss over high heat. Drain the pasta, reserving ½ cup of the pasta water, and add the pasta to the sauté pan. Toss over high heat to coat the pasta with oil, adding some of the pasta water if necessary to "loosen" the sauce. Add the chives, season aggressively with salt and pepper, and divide evenly among four warmed pasta bowls. Grate Pecorino over each bowl and serve immediately.

SERVES 4

1 pound **CARDOONS**, stalks only, peeled

Juice of 4 **LEMONS**

KOSHER SALT

1 pound dried *PERCIATELLI* (hollow strands of pasta)

4 tablespoons extra-virgin **OLIVE OIL**, plus more for drizzling

6 **GARLIC** cloves, thinly sliced

1 bunch of **CHIVES**, finely sliced

Freshly ground **BLACK PEPPER**, to taste

PECORINO ROMANO, for grating

RIGATONI

WITH FIVE LILIES

and RICOTTA SALATA

SERVES 4

3 tablespoons extra-virgin
 OLIVE OIL

1 pound **VIDALIA ONIONS**, cut
 into ¼-inch rings

4 tablespoons (½ stick) unsalted
 BUTTER

5 **GARLIC** cloves, finely chopped

½ pound **LEEKS**, cut into
 ⅛-inch rings and washed

½ pound **RED ONIONS**, peeled
 and cut into ½-inch chunks

1 bunch of **SCALLIONS**, trimmed
 and cut into 3-inch lengths

½ cup **BROWN CHICKEN STOCK**
 (see sidebar) or water

KOSHER SALT and freshly ground
 BLACK PEPPER, to taste

1 pound **RIGATONI**

¼ pound **RICOTTA SALATA**, for
 serving

¼ cup finely chopped flat-leaf
 PARSLEY

1 bunch of **CHIVES**, cut into
 1-inch lengths

The allium family, of which these onions are all members, is actually part of the lily family, hence the provocative name.

1. In a 12- to 14-inch sauté pan, heat the olive oil over medium heat until hot but not smoking. Add the Vidalia onions and lower the heat. Cook over medium-low heat until deeply brown and caramelized, 8 to 10 minutes. When the onions are very soft, remove from the heat and set aside.

2. Meanwhile, in a 12- to 14-inch sauté pan, heat the butter over medium heat until the foam subsides. Add the garlic, leeks, red onions, and scallions and cook over medium-high heat until all the onions and garlic are softened and golden brown, about 6 minutes. Add the chicken stock or water and cook until the liquid evaporates. Season with salt and pepper. Remove from the heat. Stir in the Vidalia onions.

3. Bring 6 quarts of water to a boil and add 2 tablespoons of salt. Cook the rigatoni in the boiling water according to package directions, until tender yet al dente. In the last minute of cooking, return the onion mixture to medium-high heat. Drain the pasta and add it to the onion mixture, tossing over high heat for 1 minute. Divide the pasta and onions evenly among four warmed pasta bowls, top with plenty of grated ricotta salata, the parsley, and the chives, and serve immediately.

Brown Chicken Stock

Makes 2½ quarts

2 tablespoons extra-virgin **OLIVE OIL**
Bones, wings, and scraps of 3 whole
    CHICKENS, excess fat removed
3 **CARROTS**, peeled and coarsely
    chopped
2 **ONIONS**, coarsely chopped
4 **CELERY** stalks, coarsely chopped
2 tablespoons **TOMATO PASTE**
1 tablespoon **BLACK PEPPERCORNS**
Stems of 1 bunch of flat-leaf **PARSLEY**

In a large, heavy-bottomed saucepan, heat the oil until smoking. Add
the chicken bones and scraps and
brown all over, stirring to avoid
burning. Remove the chicken parts
and reserve. Add the carrots, onions,
and celery and cook until soft and
browned. Return the chicken bones
to the pot and add 3 quarts of water,
the tomato paste, peppercorns, and
parsley, stirring to dislodge the
browned chicken and vegetable
bits from the bottom of the pan.
Bring almost to a boil, reduce the
heat, and cook at a low simmer for
2 hours, until reduced by half, occasionally skimming excess fat. After
cooking, remove from heat and
strain out all solids, pressing them
with the bottom of a ladle to extract
all liquids. This can be frozen for up
to 1 month.

SPAGHETTI

with SWEET 100 TOMATOES,

GARLIC CHIVES, AND LEMON BASIL

This pasta celebrates the month of September, when tomatoes are truly in full season and just exploding. It's our favorite take on *pasta al pomodoro.*

1. Bring 6 quarts of water to a boil and add 2 tablespoons of salt.

2. In a 12- to 14-inch sauté pan, heat the olive oil over high heat until almost smoking. Lower the heat to medium-high and add the garlic cloves. Cook for 2 minutes, or until softened and slightly browned. Add the tomatoes, chives, and basil and cook over high heat until the tomatoes are just beginning to burst. Season with salt and pepper.

3. Meanwhile, cook the spaghetti in the boiling water according to package directions until it is tender yet al dente. Drain the pasta and add it to the pan with the tomatoes. Toss over high heat for 1 minute, then divide evenly among four warmed pasta bowls and serve immediately.

SERVES 4

KOSHER SALT

¼ cup extra-virgin OLIVE OIL

4 GARLIC cloves, thinly sliced

1 pint SWEET 100 TOMATOES or other tiny tomatoes

½ bunch of GARLIC CHIVES, cut into 1-inch lengths

12 fresh LEMON BASIL leaves, finely shredded

Freshly ground BLACK PEPPER, to taste

1 pound SPAGHETTI

PENNE *with* ZUCCA,

ONIONS, ANCHOVIES, AND BREAD CRUMBS

SERVES 4

KOSHER SALT

4 tablespoons extra-virgin
  OLIVE OIL

1 RED ONION, finely chopped

4 GARLIC cloves, thinly sliced

6 salt-packed ANCHOVY fillets,
  soaked in milk for 20 minutes,
  rinsed, and drained

1 pound BUTTERNUT SQUASH,
  peeled, seeded, and cut into
  ½-inch cubes

Freshly ground BLACK PEPPER,
  to taste

1 pound PENNE RIGATE

¼ cup finely chopped flat-leaf
  PARSLEY

½ cup toasted fresh BREAD
  CRUMBS

I love simple pastas based on vegetables and anchovies, and this is one of my heroes. The sweetness of the *zucca* (butternut squash) combines exquisitely with the briny anchovies and makes this a great candidate to be matched with a powerful young southern Italian red wine, such as a Taurasi or a Cirò.

1. Bring 6 quarts of water to a boil and add 2 tablespoons of salt.

2. In a 12- to 14-inch sauté pan, heat 2 tablespoons of the olive oil over medium heat. Add the onion, garlic, and anchovies and cook over medium heat, stirring occasionally, until the onion and garlic are softened and the anchovies have begun to break up. Turn the heat up to high and add the squash cubes. Toss over high heat for 5 minutes, or until the cubes are tender and browned at the edges. Season with salt and pepper and remove from the heat.

3. Cook the penne in the boiling water according to the package directions, until tender yet al dente. Return the squash mixture to the heat, drain the pasta, and add it to the pan. Add the parsley and remaining 2 tablespoons of olive oil and toss over high heat for 1 minute. Divide the pasta and squash evenly among four warmed pasta bowls, top with bread crumbs, and serve immediately.

Oven-Roasted Tomatoes

Makes 1 cup

1 pound **ROMA TOMATOES**
1 teaspoon **SUGAR**
1 tablespoon extra-virgin **OLIVE OIL**
KOSHER SALT and freshly ground
    BLACK PEPPER

Preheat the oven to 200°F.

Cut the tomatoes in half lengthwise, squeeze out the seeds, and remove the membrane. In a medium bowl, combine the sugar, oil, salt, and pepper and toss the tomatoes with the mixture to coat.

Place the tomatoes, cut side down, on a baking sheet lined with parchment paper. Roast for 4 hours, or until the tomatoes are very soft and have lost about half of their liquid. Store in the refrigerator in a tightly sealed container for up to 4 weeks.

maccheroni alla chitarra

with HOT PEPPER, ROASTED TOMATOES, AND ***bottarga***

The unusual flavor of *bottarga*—the pressed roe of tuna or red mullet—is the star of this show. I first discovered the roe at a tasting by Manicaretti, but now it is much easier to find and a little less expensive. Because I really like this dish on the incendiary side, I use habaneros. Be very careful when working with habaneros; until they are cooked they are nearly lethal. You may sub dried red pepper flakes and lessen your risk.

1. Bring 6 quarts of water to a boil and add 2 tablespoons of salt.

2. In a 12- to 14-inch sauté pan, combine the olive oil, chile, and garlic and sauté until the garlic is almost brown, about 3 minutes. Add the tomatoes and tomato sauce and bring to a simmer.

3. Cook the pasta according to the package directions, until tender yet al dente, about 6 minutes. Drain the pasta and add it to the tomato mixture with the parsley. Toss over high heat for 1 minute. Divide among four heated bowls, scatter the shaved *bottarga* over each bowl like a dusting of cheese, sprinkle with bread crumbs, and serve immediately.

SERVES 4

KOSHER SALT

2 tablespoons extra-virgin OLIVE OIL

1 HABANERO CHILE, seeded and thinly sliced

3 GARLIC cloves, thinly sliced

1 cup OVEN-ROASTED TOMATOES (see sidebar)

¼ cup BASIC TOMATO SAUCE (page 220)

1 pound *MACCHERONI ALLA CHITARRA* or spaghettini

¼ cup whole flat-leaf PARSLEY leaves

BOTTARGA, for grating

¼ cup toasted fresh BREAD CRUMBS

BUCATINI ALL'AMATRICIANA

SERVES 4

¾ pound *GUANCIALE* (page 75) or pancetta, thinly sliced

3 GARLIC cloves, thinly sliced

1 RED ONION, halved and sliced ½-inch thick

1½ teaspoons hot RED PEPPER FLAKES

KOSHER SALT and freshly ground BLACK PEPPER, to taste

1½ cups BASIC TOMATO SAUCE (page 220)

1 pound *BUCATINI*

1 bunch of flat-leaf PARSLEY, leaves only

PECORINO ROMANO, for grating

Bucatini are sometimes referred to as "garden hoses," not only for their tubular shape but because they are hard to control on the fork. I love their very chewy texture and the fact that guys with ties usually have to lose the tie after eating these. We make *guanciale*—bacon made from pig's jowls or cheeks—in-house, but you could substitute pancetta, or good slab bacon. There is a cool organization called Bacon-of-the-Month Club, which I highly recommend (see Sources, "Grateful Palate").

1. Bring 6 quarts of water to a boil and add 2 tablespoons of salt.

2. Place the *guanciale* slices in a 12- to 14-inch sauté pan in a single layer and cook over medium-low heat until most of the fat has been rendered from the meat, turning occasionally. Remove the meat to a plate lined with paper towels and discard half the fat, leaving enough to coat the garlic, onion, and red pepper flakes. Return the *guanciale* to the pan with the vegetables, and cook over medium-high heat for 5 minutes, or until the onion, garlic, and *guanciale* are light golden brown. Season with salt and pepper, add the tomato sauce, reduce the heat, and simmer for 10 minutes.

3. Cook the *bucatini* in the boiling water according to the package directions, until al dente. Drain the pasta and add it to the simmering sauce. Add the parsley leaves, increase the heat to high, and toss to coat. Divide the pasta among four warmed pasta bowls. Top with freshly grated Pecorino cheese and serve immediately.

ZITI

WITH TUSCAN-STYLE CAULIFLOWER

We call all vegetables cooked in this manner "Tuscan-style," fitting, as I learned this blanch-free method in Faith Willinger's Florentine kitchen, perhaps one of the most Tuscan in Italy.

1. Bring about 6 quarts of water to a boil and add 2 tablespoons of salt.

2. In a 12- to 14-inch sauté pan, heat the olive oil over high heat until almost smoking. Add the onion, mint, red pepper flakes, and garlic, and sauté over medium-high heat until the garlic is just golden, 1 to 2 minutes. Add the cauliflower and cook until tender, about 7 minutes.

3. Cook the ziti in the boiling water according to the package directions, until tender yet al dente. Drain the pasta and add it to the pan with the cauliflower. Toss over high heat for 1 minute, then divide the pasta evenly among four heated bowls, grate Pecorino over each bowl, and serve immediately.

SERVES 4

KOSHER SALT

¼ cup extra-virgin OLIVE OIL

1 RED ONION, finely chopped

½ bunch of fresh MINT, leaves only

1 teaspoon hot RED PEPPER FLAKES

2 GARLIC cloves, thinly sliced

2 heads of CAULIFLOWER, cut into 1-inch chunks

1 pound ZITI

PECORINO ROMANO, for grating

THE QUARTINO

We knew right from the start that we wanted to revisit the custom of serving wine by the glass at Babbo. In our experience by-the-glass programs left too many gaps for the serious wine drinker. When I order an expensive glass of wine many questions occur to me: How much wine will I get? Can I see the bottle it comes from? Will the wine fill the glass, eliminating the "space" both the wine and I need to best appreciate its flavors? From these concerns and the staid Italian tradition of hosteria-style consumption, the practice of serving by the quartino was born at Babbo. This mini wine decanter holds exactly a quarter liter of wine, or a third of a traditional 750-milliliter bottle.

The quartino enhances the wine-drinking experience on many levels. First and foremost it gives the drinker control over the amount of wine in his glass. Personally I prefer to have very little wine in my glass when I drink, and I would rather refill from my quartino after every sip than have a large quantity of juice creating a top-heavy situation in my stem. I like to roll the wine around and slosh it from side to side, tilting my glass to catch rays of light as I swirl and smell, twirl and tip, invert and inhale. In many respects the quartino allows the customer to enjoy the romance and circumstance of by-the-bottle wine service. He can share the quartino with a lover or friend or consume it all by himself with calculated precision.

—J.B.

GNOCCHI
with oxtail ragù

This is our variation on the recipe my grandma served and one my dad still serves at his shop in Seattle, Salumi. The meat in the flavorful ragù is just about the most succulent there is. This recipe makes enough ragù for two meals. Freeze the rest for a cold day.

1. Preheat the oven to 375°F.

2. Trim the excess fat from the oxtails and season liberally with salt and pepper.

3. In a 6- to 8-quart, heavy-bottomed casserole or Dutch oven, heat the olive oil over high heat until it is just smoking. Quickly dredge the oxtails in the flour and sear them on all sides until browned, turning with long-handled tongs. This should take 8 to 10 minutes. Remove the browned oxtails to a plate and set aside.

4. Add the onions to the same pan and, stirring constantly with a wooden spoon, cook them until lightly browned, 5 to 7 minutes. Add the wine, stock, tomato sauce, and thyme and bring the mixture to a boil. Return the oxtails to the pot, submerging them in the liquid, and return the pot to a boil. Cover the casserole and cook in the oven for 1 to 1½ hours, or until the meat is falling off the bone.

5. Remove the pan from the oven and carefully remove the oxtails with long-handled tongs. When they are cool enough to handle, remove the meat from the bones and shred it into small pieces with a fork. Discard the bones.

6. With a small ladle, skim the fat from the surface of the sauce. Return the shredded meat to the casserole. Place the casserole over medium-high heat, bring to a boil, then reduce to a simmer and allow to reduce to a very thick ragù. Season with salt and pepper.

7. Bring 6 quarts of water to a boil and add 2 tablespoons of salt. Add the gnocchi and cook until they float. Drain well.

8. In a 12- to 14-inch sauté pan, heat about 3 cups of the ragù. Add the gnocchi to the sauté pan with the ragù. Toss very gently over medium heat to coat the gnocchi with the ragù, 1 to 2 minutes. Divide among six heated bowls and grate Pecorino over each bowl. Serve immediately.

SERVES 6

5 pounds **OXTAIL**, cut into 2-inch pieces

KOSHER SALT and freshly ground **BLACK PEPPER**

6 tablespoons extra-virgin **OLIVE OIL**

FLOUR, for dredging

2 medium **ONIONS**, sliced ¼-inch thick

4 cups **RED WINE**

2 cups **BROWN CHICKEN STOCK** (page 141)

2 cups **BASIC TOMATO SAUCE** (page 220)

2 tablespoons fresh **THYME** leaves

½ recipe **BASIC GNOCCHI**, cooked and cooled (page 103)

PECORINO ROMANO, for grating

GNOCCHI

with VENISON and ROSEMARY

Sweet, rich venison makes a great ragù, but any wild game you can get—like boar or rabbit—will work just as well. In fact, this recipe (and the recipe for oxtail ragù) is a good basic road map for creating a ragù with any ingredient you choose, even poultry or fish.

1. In a 6- to 8-quart, heavy-bottomed casserole or Dutch oven, heat the olive oil over high heat until it is just smoking. Season the venison chunks with salt and pepper and sear the pieces on all sides until browned, turning with long-handled tongs. You may have to work in batches to avoid overcrowding the pan. Remove the browned meat to a plate and set aside.

2. To the same pan, add the onion, carrot, celery, and garlic and, stirring constantly with a wooden spoon, cook them until lightly browned, 5 to 7 minutes. Add the tomato paste, stir through, and cook until rusty red brown, about 7 minutes. Add the wine, stock, and rosemary and bring the mixture to a boil. Return the meat to the pot, submerging it in the liquid, and bring to a boil. Reduce the heat to a simmer and cook, uncovered, until the meat is tender and falling apart, about 1½ hours.

3. Remove the meat from the ragù and, when it is cool enough to handle, shred it with a fork. With a small ladle, skim the fat from the surface of the sauce. Return the shredded meat to the pot, bring to a boil over medium-high heat, then reduce to a simmer and cook until reduced to the consistency of a very thick sauce. Adjust the seasoning with salt and pepper.

4. Bring 6 quarts of water to a boil and add 2 tablespoons of salt. Add the gnocchi and cook until they float. Drain well.

5. Ladle 2 to 3 cups of the ragù into a 12- to 14-inch sauté pan, and stir for 1 minute over high heat. Add the gnocchi to the sauté pan with the ragù. Toss very gently over medium heat to coat the gnocchi with ragù, 1 to 2 minutes. Divide among six heated bowls and grate Asiago over each bowl. Serve immediately.

SERVES 6

¼ cup extra-virgin **OLIVE OIL**

1 pound **VENISON SHOULDER**, cut into 1-inch chunks

KOSHER SALT and freshly ground **BLACK PEPPER**

1 **ONION**, finely chopped

1 **CARROT**, finely chopped

1 **CELERY** stalk, finely chopped

6 **GARLIC** cloves, roughly chopped

1 6-ounce can **TOMATO PASTE**

2 cups dry **RED WINE**

2 cups **BROWN CHICKEN STOCK** (page 141)

3 sprigs of fresh **ROSEMARY**

½ recipe **BASIC GNOCCHI**, cooked and cooled (page 103)

ASIAGO cheese, for grating

CHAPTER THREE

Mare

(From the Sea)

When I order a piece of fish in Italy, I am generally in a town on the water, and the food I order was certainly caught that day because that is the Italian way. Fish from foreign or distant waters rarely make it to the market or the table except in big-shot towns like Roma, Milano, or Torino. In cooking and in serving, Italians do not mess with their fish too much. They understand that the less fish has been touched, the more likely that it is recently from the sea. If I order linguine with seafood, the clams, scampi, mussels, lobster, or whatever always come in the shell, a testament to the fact that it was alive up to the moment it was cooked, not prepared in advance. Likewise, fin fish are generally roasted or grilled and served whole in all their splendor, sauced with nothing more than lemon and good extra-virgin olive oil and perhaps a sprinkling of good sea salt.

This is not to say Italians don't appreciate their fish. In Italy, the notion of *terroir* is not restricted to products from the land, and each region is firmly convinced of its own superiority. Venetians will wax poetic about the local sole and rant and rave about the difference in flavor between a lagoon sole and a pothole sole from a deep spot four hundred yards beyond the edge of the lagoon. The Pugliese rave about the *zuppa di pesce* (fish soup) made from a particular scorpionfish (and from the sweet peppers from outside of Bari), but they shun a similar-looking fish from Cesanatico.

Americans, however, tend to be a little skittish about bones in our fish and mollusk shells in our pasta. We prefer that the kitchen do most of the work of separating that which is edible from that which is not. We don't insist on seeing the whole fish, and because our seas offer so many varieties of large fish, portion sizing is not frowned upon. In addition, we have such high expectations of our national distribution system that Alaskan spot prawns in New Jersey or Pacific halibut in Leelanau, Michigan, do not strike us as

the least bit risky. Yet instinctively we know that these so-called fresh foods must be days or weeks out of the water. Consequently, we may not always be enjoying fish and seafood as fresh as our Italian friends.

So what do you do? I suggest you find a fishmonger and shop there often. Only after a human relationship has been formed can you be certain of getting the very best on a consistent basis. This is how Italian cooks shop; they know the sea and the merchant and accept no compromises. At Babbo, we send a team of three people to the fish market every morning at three A.M. to spend the entirety of my best sleeping time finding the best the market has to offer. Together with my partner Dave Pasternack, who has elevated reverence for fish to a poetic level, they search out the most exquisite fish available. If the fish was in the water less than thirty hours ago, and has been on ice and treated like royalty ever since, the cook's job is made easy: Our objective is simply to accentuate and celebrate the flavor and texture of each specimen without masking anything we like about it. Different species can take different levels of flavor intensity; we often cook bream whole at Babbo and serve it simply with great oil and lemon, while we get aggressive with cooking calamari in the style of a Sicilian lifeguard, taking it to another level.

I personally love the big mouth-feel of wild king salmon grilled and served with a little balsamic vinegar and black pepper, or the wild striped bass that comes into the market just as the ramps pop up, both of them grilled and drizzled with the very best oil—or nothing. These are truly seasonal delicacies; much like strawberries and quince, they are perfect only for a short time each year. That is the celebration of fish in the Italian style and the way we try to do fish at Babbo.

SNAPPER *in cartoccio*
with SUGAR SNAPS **AND ARTICHOKES**

This is a summer variation on the fish-in-a-packet (*in cartoccio*) theme with sweet snap peas that are further sweetened by the addition of Cinzano to the garlic. The clams add another layer of flavor and the acidity contributed by the golden tomatoes knits the whole thing together.

1. Preheat the oven to 450°F.

2. In a 12- to 14-inch sauté pan, combine the artichokes, 1 cup of the oil, the mint, red pepper flakes, and the sliced garlic and place over medium heat until the center of the pan has reached a full simmer. The artichokes should be submerged in oil. Remove from the heat and let cool 15 to 20 minutes. Set aside.

3. Season the red snapper fillets aggressively with salt and pepper on both sides. Cut 4 pieces of parchment paper 24 by 48 inches each.

4. In the center of each piece, place 1 tablespoon of the remaining olive oil. Atop the oil, place 2 artichokes, 5 sweet garlic cloves, 5 cockles, 1 snapper fillet, one fourth of the snap peas, one fourth of the tomatoes, and 1 frozen wine and stock cube. Drizzle each packet with an equal amount of the white wine. Fold the paper up around the ingredients to form a packet. Seal the edges of each packet with egg white.

5. Place the packets on a sheet tray and cook in the oven for 12 to 15 minutes. Remove the packets from the oven and slice the paper with a knife, taking care to avoid being burned by the steam. Serve immediately.

SERVES 4

8 baby **ARTICHOKES**, trimmed, outer leaves removed, and quartered

1¼ cups extra-virgin **OLIVE OIL**

1 bunch of fresh **MINT** leaves

1 tablespoon hot **RED PEPPER FLAKES**

2 **GARLIC** cloves, thinly sliced

4 6-ounce fillets **RED SNAPPER** or other firm-fleshed white fish, skin and bones removed

KOSHER SALT and freshly ground **BLACK PEPPER**, to taste

1 recipe **SWEET GARLIC CLOVES** (page 133)

20 New Zealand **COCKLES**, scrubbed

½ pound **SUGAR SNAP PEAS**

¼ pound **SUNGOLD TOMATOES**

4 **FROZEN WINE AND STOCK CUBES** (page 173)

½ cup **WHITE WINE**

1 **EGG WHITE**, lightly beaten

CRISPY
BLACK BASS
with Endive *Marmellata*
AND SAFFRON VINAIGRETTE

SERVES 4

4 heads of **ENDIVE**, cored and
halved

2 cups fresh **ORANGE JUICE**,
strained and pulp reserved
separately

¼ cup **HONEY**

½ cup golden **RAISINS**

KOSHER SALT and freshly ground
BLACK PEPPER, to taste

½ teaspoon **SAFFRON THREADS**

6 tablespoons extra-virgin
OLIVE OIL

1½ tablespoons **CHAMPAGNE**
VINEGAR

4 8-ounce fillets of **BLACK BASS**

¼ cup finely chopped flat-leaf
PARSLEY

Best-quality **OLIVE OIL**, for
drizzling

The single word "crispy" sells more food than a barrage of adjectives describing the ingredients or cooking techniques on a menu. There is something innately appealing about crispy food. For that reason, it is important that the fish go immediately to the table, as it loses its crunch as it cools.

1. In a shallow, heavy-bottomed pan, combine the endive, orange juice (but not the pulp), honey, and raisins and simmer over low heat until the liquid has reduced by half and the endive is very tender, about 30 minutes. Drain the endive, season with salt and pepper, and set aside to cool.

2. Place the orange pulp in a small, nonreactive saucepan and warm over medium heat until it releases its juices, adding water if necessary to keep it from scorching. Add the saffron, cover, and turn off the heat. Steep for 15 minutes. In a nonreactive bowl, combine the pulp, 4 tablespoons of the olive oil, the champagne vinegar, and salt and pepper and whisk well to emulsify. Set aside.

3. In a 14- to 16-inch sauté pan, heat the remaining 2 tablespoons of olive oil over high heat until smoking. Score the skin of each fish fillet twice, season them aggressively with salt and pepper, and place in the pan, skin side down. Cook until crispy on the skin side, about 3 minutes, then turn and finish cooking on the flesh side, about 2 more minutes.

4. Meanwhile, in a 10- to 12-inch sauté pan, heat the endive *marmellata* over high heat until warmed through. Stir in the parsley.

5. Place one portion of the *marmellata* on each of four warmed dinner plates. Place a fillet on top, spoon vinaigrette around the *marmellata*, drizzle with the oil, and serve immediately.

BIG EYE TUNA
al tarocco

SERVES 4

8 tablespoons extra-virgin
  OLIVE OIL

½ pound hen-of-the-woods or
  SHIITAKE mushrooms,
  thinly sliced

1 RED ONION, minced

1 teaspoon fresh THYME leaves

KOSHER SALT and freshly
  ground BLACK PEPPER,
  to taste

4 6-ounce TUNA STEAKS,
  sashimi-quality, about
  1 inch thick

1 cup instant POTATO FLAKES

¼ cup crushed BLACK
  PEPPERCORNS

1 BLOOD ORANGE, cut into
  segments

½ pound MIZUNA

1 recipe SWEET GARLIC
  CLOVES (page 133)

1 head of RADICCHIO, cored,
  leaves cut into 1-inch pieces

2 large RADISHES, thinly sliced

4 SCALLIONS, thinly sliced

4 tablespoons BLOOD ORANGE
  VINAIGRETTE (page 241)

2 tablespoons PARSLEY OIL
  (page 50)

Tarocco translates from the Sicilian as blood orange, and that's what flavors the sauce in this dish. The instant potato flakes add a great texture and flavor to the already very sexy sashimi-grade tuna.

1. Preheat the oven to 350°F.

2. In a 12- to 14-inch sauté pan, heat 2 tablespoons of the oil until just smoking. Add the sliced mushrooms, red onion, thyme, and salt and pepper and sauté until the mushrooms are crispy, 5 to 7 minutes. Remove from the heat and set aside.

3. Season the tuna steaks well with salt and pepper. Combine the potato flakes and crushed peppercorns, slightly moisten one side of each tuna steak with water, and press the moistened side into the potato and peppercorn mixture. In a 12- to 14-inch nonstick sauté pan, heat 4 tablespoons of the olive oil over medium-high heat until just smoking. Sauté the steaks, crust side down, until the crust is crispy, about 3 minutes. Turn the steaks and cook for an additional 2 minutes. The steaks will be medium rare at this point.

4. While the tuna is cooking, in a separate 12- to 14-inch sauté pan, heat the remaining 2 tablespoons of olive oil until just smoking. Add half of the blood orange segments, the mizuna, the sweet garlic cloves, and the radicchio and toss over high heat to wilt the greens and warm through, about 1 minute.

5. Divide the salad mixture among four warmed dinner plates. Place one steak on each salad mound. Garnish with the remaining blood orange segments, the radishes, and the scallions. Drizzle with the vinaigrette and parsley oil.

planked
KING SALMON
with CUCUMBERS *and* BALSAMIC VINEGAR

Italians do not cook their fish on a wood plank, but American Indians in the Pacific Northwest have done so for centuries, as has Larry Forgione. The nearly smoky flavor of the flesh roasted on the board contrasts in a wonderful way with the wet acidity of the almost-pickled cucumbers and the deep sweetness of traditional balsamic vinegar.

You'll need a clean, new cedar plank, 8 inches by 12 inches.

1. Preheat the oven to 475°F. Brush the plank with the ¼ cup of olive oil and place it in the oven for 20 minutes. Season the salmon fillets with salt and pepper and brush with olive oil. Carefully place the fish fillets on the plank skin side down and roast until medium rare, 9 to 10 minutes.

2. Meanwhile, place the cucumbers in a bowl and add the shallots, the remaining 3 tablespoons of olive oil, the red wine vinegar, sugar, scallions, mustard seeds, and pink peppercorns. Season with salt and pepper and stir to mix well.

3. Once the salmon is cooked medium rare, remove the plank from the oven. Divide the cucumbers evenly among four plates, place one fillet atop each portion of cucumbers, skin side up, drizzle with the balsamic vinegar, and serve.

SERVES 4

¼ cup plus 3 tablespoons extra-virgin **OLIVE OIL**

4 **KING SALMON** fillets, about 8 ounces each, skin on

KOSHER SALT and freshly ground **BLACK PEPPER**, to taste

1 **ENGLISH CUCUMBER**, halved, seeded, and cut on the diagonal into ¼-inch half-moons

1 **SHALLOT**, thinly sliced

¼ cup **RED WINE VINEGAR**

2 teaspoons **SUGAR**

2 **SCALLIONS**, white parts only, thinly sliced

1 teaspoon **MUSTARD SEEDS**

1 teaspoon **PINK PEPPERCORNS**

2 tablespoons 12-year-aged **BALSAMIC VINEGAR**

MUSTARD-CRUSTED *salmon*
with ROASTED SCALLIONS
AND PRESSED BEET VINAIGRETTE

Here, the crunchy mustard crust encasing the medium-rare flesh of the sweet salmon makes it feel almost like a peppered steak. I roast the scallions until they are nearly dry and straw-like for added textural counterpoint.

1. Preheat the oven to 400°F.

2. On a large sheet of aluminum foil, drizzle the beets with 1 tablespoon of the olive oil and season with salt and pepper. Wrap the beets tightly in the foil and roast until very tender, about 45 minutes. While the beets roast, drizzle the scallions with 1 tablespoon of the oil and season with salt and pepper. Wrap tightly in aluminum foil and roast until very soft and fragrant, about 25 minutes. Set aside, keeping them warm.

3. When the beets are cooked and cool enough to handle, peel them and cut 2 of them into 4 or 5 pieces. Place the beet pieces in the bowl of a food processor and pulse to form a very coarse puree. Run the remaining beets through a juicer to extract as much liquid as possible. In a small bowl, combine the beet puree, beet juice, sherry vinegar, ½ cup of the olive oil, and salt and pepper, adding more vinegar if necessary to create the desired acidity. Set aside.

4. In a shallow bowl or high-sided plate, combine the mustard seeds and coarse sea salt and stir well to combine. Season the salmon fillets with black pepper and press the skin side of each fillet into the mustard and salt mixture to coat it completely. In a 14- to 16-inch nonstick pan, heat the remaining ¼ cup of olive oil until smoking. Carefully place the fillets in the pan, skin side down, and cook without disturbing for at least 7 minutes, allowing the seeds and salt to form a crust. When you've tested the crust by shaking the pan slightly and are confident that you will not disturb the crust by turning the fish, turn each fillet with a broad spatula and cook on the flesh side for 3 or 4 minutes. Place a few of the scallions on each of four warmed dinner plates, top with a cooked fillet, crust side up, and some of the beet vinaigrette, and serve immediately.

SERVES 4

4 **BEETS**, trimmed

¾ cup plus 2 tablespoons extra-virgin **OLIVE OIL**

KOSHER SALT and freshly ground **BLACK PEPPER**

12 **SCALLIONS**, trimmed to 10-inch length, roots removed

4 tablespoons **SHERRY VINEGAR**, or more to taste

½ cup **MUSTARD SEEDS**

¼ cup coarse **SEA SALT**

4 wild king or North Atlantic **SALMON** fillets, about 8 ounces each

GRILLED
KING SALMON

with FAVETTA, RADISHES,
AND LEMON CELERY CITRONETTE

SERVES 4

Favetta

KOSHER SALT

2 pounds fresh FAVA BEANS

2 tablespoons fresh THYME
leaves

½ cup extra-virgin OLIVE OIL

Freshly ground BLACK PEPPER,
to taste

Citronette

3 tablespoons fresh LEMON
JUICE

1 tablespoon DIJON MUSTARD

¼ cup plus 1 tablespoon extra-
virgin OLIVE OIL

2 tablespoons chopped CHIVES

KOSHER SALT and freshly ground
BLACK PEPPER

4 8-ounce KING SALMON fillets

½ pound RADISHES, thinly sliced

1 CELERY stalk, sliced paper thin
on the bias

12 flat-leaf PARSLEY leaves, finely
shredded

Since I was born and raised in Seattle, no fish is more important or memory-evoking to my primordial crocodile brain than king salmon. Wild king salmon has a depth of flavor and intensity of color that puts the farmed stuff to shame, but it is entirely seasonal, so shop wisely. Here, the inherent earthy sweetness of the *favetta* is furthered by the char off of the grill. At Babbo we always serve salmon and tuna medium rare; it just tastes better that way.

1. To make the *favetta:* Bring a large pot of water to a boil and add 1 tablespoon of salt. Set up an ice water bath nearby. Shuck the fava beans and blanch in the boiling water for 2 minutes; drain and transfer to the ice bath to cool. Drain the beans again and peel off the tough skins.

2. In the bowl of a food processor, combine the peeled fava beans and thyme leaves. Pulse on high speed and slowly incorporate the ½ cup olive oil while blending, until the *favetta* has a consistency similar to that of guacamole. Season with salt and pepper. Transfer the *favetta* to a small bowl, cover tightly, and set aside.

3. In a medium, nonreactive bowl, combine the lemon juice, mustard, and ¼ cup of the olive oil and whisk well. Add the chives and season with salt and pepper.

4. Preheat the grill or broiler. Season each salmon fillet with salt and pepper and grill until medium rare, about 5 minutes on each side.

5. In a 10- to 12-inch sauté pan, heat 1 tablespoon of the olive oil over high heat. Add the *favetta* and toss over high heat until warmed through.

6. To assemble the dish, spoon the *favetta* onto four warmed dinner plates. Place one piece of fish atop each dollop of *favetta*. Toss the radishes and celery with the citronette, and spoon some onto each fillet. Drizzle the remaining citronette around the fish, sprinkle with parsley, and serve immediately.

HALIBUT
in cartoccio
with PUNTARELLA *and* GRAPEFRUIT

SERVES 4

½ cup extra-virgin OLIVE OIL

4 salt-packed ANCHOVY fillets,
  rinsed and drained

4 GARLIC cloves, thinly sliced

1 pound PUNTARELLA, chicory, or
  frisée, cut into 1-inch pieces,
  soaked in cold water for
  15 minutes, and drained

KOSHER SALT and freshly ground
  BLACK PEPPER

4 6-ounce boneless, skinless
  HALIBUT fillets (or other
  firm-fleshed white fish)

4 FROZEN WINE AND STOCK
  CUBES (see sidebar)

1 GRAPEFRUIT, cut into segments
  with no pith attached

1 teaspoon fresh THYME leaves

½ cup dry WHITE WINE

1 EGG WHITE, lightly beaten

Cooking fish *in cartoccio,* that is, in a parchment packet, is an excellent way to retain its moisture and flavor, and it also creates a dramatic presentation. The trick is to slash the swollen package as it comes out of the oven to forestall the inevitable deflation. This is a winter variation with bitter *puntarella* (wild chicory) played against the sunny sweetness of pink grapefruit.

1. Preheat the oven to 450°F.

2. In a 12- to 14-inch sauté pan, heat ¼ cup of the olive oil. Add the anchovies and garlic and cook over medium-low heat until the anchovies are falling apart and the garlic is browned, about 1 minute. Add the greens, increase the heat to high, and sauté for 2 minutes. Season with salt and pepper and set aside.

3. Season the fish fillets aggressively with salt and pepper on both sides.

4. Cut 4 pieces of parchment paper 24 inches by 48 inches each. Drizzle a tablespoon of the oil in the center of each piece and top with one quarter of the cooked *puntarella* and 1 frozen stock cube. Add 1 fish fillet to each packet and top it with a few grapefruit sections and the thyme. Drizzle each packet with 2 tablespoons of the white wine. Fold the paper up around the ingredients to form a packet. Brush the edges of the parchment with the beaten egg white, then fold tightly to seal.

5. Place the packets on a sheet tray and bake in the oven for 15 minutes. Remove the packets from the oven and slice the paper with a knife, taking care to avoid being burned by the steam. Serve immediately.

Frozen Wine and Stock Cubes
Makes 12 cubes

4 cups **BROWN CHICKEN STOCK**
    (page 141)
1 cup **WHITE WINE**

Combine the chicken stock and
white wine in a saucepan. Boil
uncovered over high heat until
reduced by half, about 12 minutes.
Pour the mixture into plastic ice
cube trays and freeze, covered with
plastic wrap. When the cubes are
firm, transfer the cubes to a plastic
bag for storage.

Puntarella

Puntarella, a member of the chicory family, is synoynmous with Roman
cooking. It has a bitter flavor with an amazing crunchy yet tender texture and is generally available in the spring and early summer, although
it can produce in the mild winter climates. It is best used and tastiest
when young, and its twisted, succulent stems are often dressed with
anchovies, lemon juice, and extra-virgin olive oil. High-end greengro-
cers or markets will carry *puntarella,* and the seeds are now also available through a number of garden supply companies.

WINE SERVICE

Traditionally, decanting was performed to separate an older wine from the sediment in its bottle. Although this style of decanting, candle and all, is appropriate sometimes, most of the decanting we do at Babbo is actually the splashing or oxidizing of young white and red wines. To splash a wine is to freely pour it from the bottle at a height of ten inches or so above an open-mouthed receptacle, such as a glass pitcher or traditional decanter. This rigorous pouring serves to agitate, oxidize, and excite the wine. Remember that wine is a living and evolving thing and treat it accordingly. You may need to get physical with a burly young Barolo; seduce a silky, sexy super Tuscan from the seventies; or caress and convince a shy and gentle Carmignano.

The temperature at which a wine is served is the most important and controllable variable in wine service. We tend to serve our white wine a little bit warmer and our red wines a bit cooler than is the norm elsewhere, and in fact very few of our white wines are stored in refrigerators. With the exception of sparkling wines and certain high-volume bottles, all white wines are stored in our cellar with the red wines at 58°F., and effectively both red and white wines are presented to the customer at that temperature. If requested by the customer, whites can be chilled at the center table to maintain the cellar temp, but we encourage diners to follow the evolution of their red wine in the glass as it moves through various temperatures and levels of oxidation over the course of the evening.

—J.B.

HALIBUT
with Carciofini al mattone
AND TOMATO ANCHOVY VINAIGRETTE

SERVES 4

1 cup **BASIC TOMATO SAUCE** (page 220)

2 salt-packed **ANCHOVY** fillets, rinsed and patted dry

½ small **RED ONION**, minced

1 tablespoon finely chopped fresh **ROSEMARY** leaves

2 tablespoons fresh **THYME** leaves

KOSHER SALT and freshly ground **BLACK PEPPER**, to taste

1 pound baby **ARTICHOKES** with stems, outer leaves discarded

2 cups **WHITE WINE**

Juice of 1 **LEMON**

4 **GARLIC** cloves, sliced

10 tablespoons extra-virgin **OLIVE OIL**

4 8-ounce **HALIBUT** fillets, skin scored with a sharp paring knife

2 cups (about ¾ pound) baby **ARUGULA**

2 tablespoons **SHERRY VINEGAR**

¼ cup **TAPENADE** (see sidebar)

4 fresh marinated **ANCHOVY** fillets (page 46)

Halibut is very meaty on the palate, so in creating its condiment we like to get jiggy with strong flavors like the anchovies and black olives. The artichoke technique, literally cooked under a brick, is one I picked up from one of my favorite cookbooks of all time, Faith Willinger's *Red, White & Greens*.

1. In a small saucepan, combine the tomato sauce, anchovy fillets, onion, rosemary, and 1 tablespoon of the thyme. Bring to a boil, reduce heat to a simmer, and cook until reduced to the consistency of chutney, stirring occasionally. Season with salt and pepper and set aside.

2. Halve the artichokes lengthwise and place in a 12- to 14-inch sauté pan with the wine, lemon juice, garlic, and the remaining tablespoon of thyme. Add water to cover the artichokes. Place over medium heat and cook until the center of the pan has begun to simmer. Remove from the heat, cover, and set aside for 15 to 20 minutes, or until the artichokes are somewhat tender but not fully cooked. Remove the artichokes from the liquid and gently pat them dry.

3. Heat a grill pan over high heat until smoking. Brush lightly with oil and place the artichokes in the pan, cut side down. Place another heavy pan or brick directly on top of the artichokes and sear for 1 to 2 minutes. Remove from the heat and set aside.

4. Season the fish fillets aggressively with salt and pepper. In a 12- to 14-inch sauté pan, heat 4 tablespoons of the olive oil over high heat until smoking. Place the fillets in the pan, skin side down, and cook without moving them over high heat for 5 minutes. Carefully turn the fish over to the flesh side and cook for an additional 2 minutes.

5. Meanwhile, in a large mixing bowl, combine the arugula and artichokes. Add the sherry vinegar, the remaining 6 tablespoons of olive oil, and salt and pepper and toss to combine.

Tapenade

Makes 1½ cups

¼ **RED ONION**, finely chopped
¼ cup **RED WINE VINEGAR**
2 tablespoons **CAPERS**, rinsed and
    drained
2 tablespoons **DIJON MUSTARD**
6 tablespoons **BLACK OLIVE PASTE**
6 tablespoons extra-virgin **OLIVE OIL**
KOSHER SALT and freshly ground
    BLACK PEPPER, to taste

In the bowl of a food processor, combine the onion, vinegar, capers, mustard, and olive paste and pulse to mix but not completely puree. Leaving the machine running on a constant setting, slowly drizzle in the olive oil until the mixture is emulsified. Season with salt and pepper. The tapenade may be stored for up to 1 week, refrigerated, in an airtight container.

6. When the fillets are cooked through, place one on each of four warmed dinner plates. Drizzle each fillet with tomato anchovy vinaigrette and tapenade. With tongs, place some of the artichokes on each plate. Divide the arugula salad into four equal portions and, forming tight bunches, wrap each portion of arugula with an anchovy and place one bunch on top of each fillet. Drizzle again with tapenade and tomato anchovy vinaigrette and serve immediately.

wild STRIPED BASS

with CHARRED LEEKS *and* SQUID VINAIGRETTE

Wild striped bass is an incredible delicacy on the order of wild king salmon. To complement its robust flavor and steak-like texture, we serve it with a beautiful and aggressive squid vinaigrette. This is not a dish for people who are on the fence about eating fish.

1. Bring 3 quarts of water to a boil and set up an ice bath nearby. Plunge the calamari into the boiling water and cook for 30 seconds. Remove the calamari with a slotted spoon or strainer and immediately plunge it into the ice bath. Allow it to cool for 1 minute, then drain and set aside. Blanch the leeks in the same water for 8 to 9 minutes, until just tender. Refresh in the ice bath, then cut in half lengthwise.

2. Preheat the grill or broiler. Brush the leek halves with 2 tablespoons of the olive oil and season with salt and pepper. Grill or broil the leeks, cut side toward the heat, until charred, 8 to 10 minutes. Resist the temptation to move them more than once.

3. In a 12- to 14-inch sauté pan, heat 3 tablespoons of the oil over high heat until smoking. Season the fish fillets with salt and pepper and cook, skin side down, for 5 to 7 minutes, or until the flesh is crispy and moves easily without tearing.

4. While the fish cooks, combine the wine, lemon juice, and squid ink in another sauté pan and bring to a boil. Turn off the heat and whisk in the mustard, then the remaining 4 tablespoons of olive oil. Season with salt and pepper and add the calamari. Keep warm.

5. Turn the fish over and add the leeks to the pan. Cook the fish on the other side for 2 to 3 minutes and heat the leeks through. Place two leeks in the center of each of four warmed plates. Place one fillet atop each bed of leeks, flesh side up. Drizzle each fillet with some of the squid vinaigrette and garnish with the tentacles and lemon zest. Serve immediately.

SERVES 4

1 pound cleaned CALAMARI tentacles or cuttlefish tentacles

4 large LEEKS, whites only, cleaned and cut into 5-inch lengths

9 tablespoons extra-virgin OLIVE OIL

KOSHER SALT and freshly ground BLACK PEPPER

4 6-ounce WILD STRIPED BASS fillets, skinned

¼ cup dry WHITE WINE

Juice and zest of 1 LEMON

2 packets (2 tablespoons) of SQUID INK (see Sources)

1 teaspoon DIJON MUSTARD

monkfish piccata

with CAPERBERRIES and PRESERVED LEMONS

SERVES 4

1½ pounds **MONKFISH**, bone
removed and cut into
8 medallions

KOSHER SALT and freshly ground
BLACK PEPPER

1 cup **FLOUR**

½ cup extra-virgin **OLIVE OIL**

¾ cup dry **WHITE WINE**

Pinch of **TURMERIC**

½ cup fresh **LEMON JUICE**

4 ounces **CAPERBERRIES**

1 **LEMON**, cut into pithless
segments

2 **PRESERVED LEMON** quarters
(page 223), sliced paper thin

1 bunch of **PARSLEY**, finely
shredded

Cooking firm monkfish pieces like this mimics the texture of veal scaloppine and also makes for a fun presentation. This is a good way to introduce fish to people who might otherwise prefer chicken.

1. Season the fish slices well with salt and pepper. Season the flour with salt and pepper and place it in a shallow bowl or on a plate. Dredge each piece of fish in the flour, patting off the excess.

2. In a 12- to 14-inch sauté pan, heat ¼ cup of the olive oil over high heat until smoking. Working in batches if necessary to avoid overcrowding the pan, cook the fish in the hot oil, turning once to brown both sides evenly and cook through, about 4 minutes per side. Remove the fish to a plate lined with paper towels. When all the fish is done, keep warm and add the wine, the turmeric, lemon juice, and caperberries to the pan. Swirl over high heat for 2 minutes. Season the sauce with salt and pepper and add the lemon segments, preserved lemons, and parsley and swirl them over high heat for 1 minute. Add the remaining ¼ cup of olive oil and swirl again.

3. Divide the fish evenly among four warmed dinner plates and pour some of the sauce over each plate. Serve immediately.

SAUTÉED SKATE
and rock shrimp
in a SAFFRON SWEET CLAM CITRONETTE

SERVES 4

4 small **SKATE WINGS**, cleaned and skinned, about 3 pounds total

KOSHER SALT and freshly ground **BLACK PEPPER**

1 cup Wondra **FLOUR**

5 tablespoons extra-virgin **OLIVE OIL**

6 **SHALLOTS**, finely chopped

1 bunch of **ARUGULA**

½ pound **ROCK SHRIMP** or medium shrimp, peeled and deveined

½ pound New Zealand **COCKLES**, scrubbed

1 cup **SAFFRON CITRONETTE** (page 241)

½ cup dry **WHITE WINE**

2 tablespoons chopped flat-leaf **PARSLEY**

I like to cook skate wing on the bone, as it stays much juicier and doesn't shrink as much. If you prefer it easier to eat, have the fishmonger take it off the bone, as it's tricky to do at home.

1. Season the skate wings with salt and pepper and dredge both sides in the Wondra flour. In a 14- to 16-inch sauté pan, heat 3 tablespoons of the olive oil over high heat until just smoking. Add the skate and cook 4 to 5 minutes. Turn the fish, add half the shallots, and cook until the fish is golden brown and cooked through, 4 to 5 minutes more.

2. Once all the fish has been cooked, add the remaining 2 tablespoons of olive oil to the pan and add the arugula. Season with salt and pepper and toss over high heat for 1 minute to wilt but not cook completely. Divide the arugula among four warmed bowls, and place one skate wing atop each bed of arugula.

3. Meanwhile, in a separate pan with a cover, combine the rock shrimp, cockles, citronette, white wine, and the remaining shallots. Cover, bring to a boil, and cook until the shrimp are cooked through and the cockles have opened, about 4 minutes. Season with salt and pepper. Divide the shellfish and broth evenly among the four bowls, pouring the broth over the skate. Sprinkle with the parsley and serve immediately.

TILEFISH
IN A
sungold tomato and
COOL CUCUMBER GAZPACHO

I love the bright acidity of cool gazpacho in the summer and it goes well with a hot afternoon and a piece of beautifully cooked fish. Half portions of the tilefish could easily be an appetizer that, followed by a pasta, would make a perfect light meal.

1. Cut a 3-inch section of cucumber, unpeeled, into ¼-inch dice and set aside. Peel and seed the remaining cucumbers, cut into chunks, and place in a food processor. Pulse the cucumbers until they are liquefied but still retain some chunkiness (you may need to work in batches). Remove to a large bowl and stir in 4 tablespoons of the olive oil, the vinegar, jalapeño, and salt and pepper. Set the gazpacho aside.

2. In a 12- to 14-inch sauté pan, heat the remaining 3 tablespoons of olive oil over high heat until just smoking. Score each fish fillet on the skin side, season aggressively with salt and pepper on both sides, and place them in the pan, skin side down, working in batches if necessary. Cook, undisturbed, until the skin is crispy and moves from the bottom of the pan without tearing, about 5 minutes. Carefully turn the fillets and cook on the flesh side for 1 to 2 minutes. Add the tomatoes to the hot pan and toss gently until they are heated through and just beginning to burst.

3. Divide the gazpacho evenly among four pasta bowls. Place a fillet atop each puddle of gazpacho, scatter a few tomatoes and the diced cucumbers around and over each fillet, sprinkle with red pepper flakes, and serve immediately.

SERVES 4

2 ENGLISH CUCUMBERS

7 tablespoons extra-virgin OLIVE OIL

2 tablespoons CHAMPAGNE VINEGAR

1 JALAPEÑO PEPPER, seeded and finely chopped

KOSHER SALT and freshly ground BLACK PEPPER, to taste

4 6-ounce TILEFISH fillets, skin on

1 pint mixed SUNGOLD and RED CHERRY TOMATOES

Pinch of hot RED PEPPER FLAKES

BLACK BASS
in a **lemon brodetto**
with TAYLOR BAY SCALLOPS *and* **HUBBARD SQUASH**

Taylor Bay scallops are practically heat-and-serve in their simple perfection. They are in season from November to March and need virtually no prep time or cooking time. The Hubbard is one of my favorite squashes, but any hard winter squash will work out just as well.

1. In a medium saucepan, combine the capon stock and white wine and bring to a boil. Reduce to a simmer and add the preserved lemons and lemon oregano jam, stirring to incorporate. Season with salt and pepper and keep warm.

2. In a 12- to 14-inch sauté pan, heat 3 tablespoons of the olive oil over high heat until almost smoking. Add the squash cubes and sauté over high heat until they are browned, crispy, and tender, about 7 minutes. Add the marjoram leaves and salt and pepper, toss over high heat for 1 more minute, then set aside, keeping hot.

3. Season the fish fillets with salt and pepper. Heat ¼ cup of the olive oil over high heat in a 14- to 16-inch sauté pan until smoking. Cook the fish fillets, skin side down, for 5 minutes, or until the skin is nicely crispy and the flesh is cooked through about three quarters of the way. Carefully turn the fillets with a wide spatula and cook on the flesh side for 2 to 3 minutes.

4. Bring the broth to a boil, add the scallops, cover, and steam until they open, about 2 minutes. Divide the scallops among four warmed bowls, add a scant cup of the hot *brodetto* and some of the squash, and top with a bass fillet. Sprinkle with the scallions and serve immediately.

SERVES 4

4 cups **CAPON STOCK**
(page 127)

1 cup dry **WHITE WINE**

2 **PRESERVED LEMON** quarters
(page 223), thinly sliced

½ cup **LEMON OREGANO JAM**
(page 189)

KOSHER SALT and freshly ground
BLACK PEPPER, to taste

¼ cup plus 3 tablespoons
extra-virgin **OLIVE OIL**

1 pound **HUBBARD SQUASH**,
peeled, seeded, and cut into
½-inch cubes

1 tablespoon fresh **MARJORAM**
leaves

4 **BLACK BASS** fillets, skin on,
about 6 ounces each

20 **SCALLOPS**, preferably Taylor
Bay, in the shell

2 **SCALLIONS**, thinly sliced

whole roasted BRANZINO
WITH BRAISED FENNEL AND
LEMON OREGANO JAM

SERVES 4

4 1-pound whole **BRANZINO**, scaled and gutted

3 **FENNEL** bulbs, one shaved to yield 2 cups and two cut into ¼-inch slices

2 tablespoons fresh **THYME** leaves

2 tablespoons fresh **OREGANO** leaves

1 cup pitted **BLACK OLIVES**

KOSHER SALT and freshly ground **BLACK PEPPER**, to taste

1 cup dry **WHITE WINE**

7 tablespoons extra-virgin **OLIVE OIL**

1 tablespoon **SUGAR**

2 cups **LEMON OREGANO JAM** (see sidebar)

This is how Italians cook their fish most often. The quality and type of fish you use is even more important than in other dishes because there is nothing to mask an off flavor if the fish is less than perfectly fresh. The best way to eat the fillets is with a tablespoon of the lemon jam and a drizzle of good oil. You may substitute any beautiful fresh whole fish; my faves are bream and black bass.

1. Preheat the oven to 450°F.

2. Rinse each fish and use kitchen shears to remove the top and bottom fins and gills. In a mixing bowl, combine the shaved fennel, thyme, oregano, olives, and salt and pepper. Season each fish inside and out with salt and pepper. Stuff each fish with one quarter of the shaved fennel mixture and place the fish in a shallow casserole just large enough to hold them. Cover and refrigerate until needed.

3. Arrange the fennel quarters in a single layer in a large, oven-proof saucepan. Pour in the white wine to cover and season with salt and pepper. Bring to a boil over high heat. Remove from the heat and transfer to the oven to braise, uncovered, until tender, 15 to 20 minutes. Remove from the oven and set aside. Allow to cool.

4. In a 12- to 14-inch sauté pan, heat 3 tablespoons of the olive oil until smoking. Add the braised fennel quarters and sugar and cook, stirring often, until light golden brown, 8 to 10 minutes. Season with salt and pepper and set aside.

5. Drizzle each fish with 1 tablespoon of the olive oil. Arrange on a baking sheet and roast until the fish are just cooked through, 15 to 20 minutes, or until the flesh is opaque at the skeleton near the gills, which will give a reading of approximately 130°F. on an instant-read thermometer.

6. To assemble the dish, place one fish on each of four warmed dinner plates. Serve the caramelized fennel and lemon oregano jam family style so everyone can help themselves.

Lemon Oregano Jam
Makes 2½ cups

10 **LEMONS**, seeded and cut into
    8 pieces

2 tablespoons **KOSHER SALT**

1 tablespoon freshly ground **BLACK
    PEPPER**

1 cup **SUGAR**

½ cup extra-virgin **OLIVE OIL**

2 tablespoons **OREGANO** leaves

2 tablespoons **MARJORAM** leaves

Working in batches, in the bowl of a
food processor, combine the lemon
pieces, salt, pepper, and sugar and
pulse to break down but not completely puree. Slowly drizzle in the
olive oil to emulsify into a honey-like
consistency. Just before using, blend
in the oregano and marjoram leaves.
The jam may be held for up to 1
week, refrigerated, in an airtight container.

calamari

SICILIAN LIFEGUARD STYLE

I have never actually met a Sicilian lifeguard, but if one were to cook up a pot of calamari, this is how he or she might make it. Geographically, Sicily is much closer to Tunisia, Morocco, and the Moorish world than it is to Milano, so the influences on traditional cooking are very Northern African. I love the way currants, caperberries, pine nuts, and chiles combine to create a sweet, hot, and sour Arabic kiss on the delicate tentacles.

1. Bring 3 quarts of water to a boil and add 1 tablespoon of salt. Set up an ice bath nearby. Cook the couscous in the boiling water for 2 minutes, then drain and immediately plunge it into the ice bath. Once cooled, remove and set aside to dry on a plate.

2. In a 12- to 14-inch sauté pan, heat the oil until just smoking. Add the pine nuts, currants, and red pepper flakes and sauté until the nuts are just golden brown, about 2 minutes. Add the caperberries, tomato sauce, and couscous and bring to a boil. Add the calamari, stir to mix, and simmer for 2 to 3 minutes, or until the calamari is just cooked and completely opaque. Season with salt and pepper, pour into a large warm bowl, sprinkle with scallions, and serve immediately.

SERVES 4

KOSHER SALT

1 cup ISRAELI COUSCOUS

¼ cup extra-virgin OLIVE OIL

2 tablespoons PINE NUTS

2 tablespoons CURRANTS

1 tablespoon hot RED PEPPER FLAKES

¼ cup CAPERBERRIES

2 cups BASIC TOMATO SAUCE (page 220)

1½ pounds cleaned CALAMARI, tubes cut into ¼-inch rounds, tentacles halved

Freshly ground BLACK PEPPER, to taste

3 SCALLIONS, thinly sliced

CRISPY BREAM
in Zupetta Pugliese

SERVES 4

Peperonata

6 tablespoons extra-virgin
   OLIVE OIL

1 **RED ONION**, finely chopped

4 **BELL PEPPERS**, 2 red and
   2 yellow, trimmed and cut
   into ½-inch dice

1 teaspoon hot **RED PEPPER
   FLAKES**

1 tablespoon **SUGAR**

½ cup **BASIC TOMATO SAUCE**
   (page 220)

KOSHER SALT and freshly ground
   BLACK PEPPER, to taste

4 **BELL PEPPERS**, 2 red and
   2 yellow, roasted, peeled, and
   seeded

4 8-ounce **BREAM** *(orata)* fillets,
   skin scored twice

¼ cup **RED PEPPER OIL**
   (page 51)

½ bunch of fresh **CHIVES**, cut
   into 3-inch lengths

Each region of the Italian coastline has its own special take on *zuppa di pesce,* or fish soup. In Puglia, particularly Bari, the fish soup is always made with sweet peppers. This little soup is the Babbo variation.

Known as *orata* at Babbo and *sparus aurata* to piscatologists, bream is a delicately flavored white fish, related to the porgy, that is distinguished by a golden band behind its eyes and a large black spot on its gill cover. It is native to both the Mediterranean and Caribbean seas and can grow to up to thirty-two inches, but we prefer the one- to one-and-a-half-pound size.

1. In a 10- to 12-inch sauté pan, heat 2 tablespoons of the extra-virgin olive oil over high heat until just smoking. Add the onion and diced bell peppers and sauté over high heat for 5 minutes. Add the red pepper flakes, sugar, tomato sauce, and salt and pepper and cook over low heat until tender, about 10 minutes. Keep warm.

2. Meanwhile, combine the roasted peppers with ½ cup water in a blender. Puree, then season with salt and pepper and stir into the *peperonata.*

3. In a 12- to 14-inch sauté pan, heat the remaining 4 tablespoons of olive oil over high heat until smoking. Season the fish fillets with salt and pepper on both sides and cook skin side down until very crispy, 2 to 3 minutes. Turn carefully with a wide spatula and cook on the other side for 1 to 2 minutes. You may need to cook the fish in batches to avoid overcrowding.

4. Divide the *peperonata* evenly among four warmed bowls and place one fillet in each bowl. Drizzle with the red pepper oil, top with the chives, and serve immediately.

SWORDFISH
involtini alla siciliana

Sicilians love to roll stuff up; they make *involtini* out of *everything*. My favorite part of this recipe is the bread crumb mixture inside the fillet. It creates a mouthful of dry yet rich textures that really accentuate the tender smoothness of the slow-cooked swordfish.

1. Preheat the oven to 450°F.

2. In a 12-inch ovenproof skillet, combine the tomato sauce, 2 tablespoons of the olive oil, the olives, capers, red pepper flakes, pine nuts, currants, and wine and bring to a boil over medium heat. Remove from the heat and set aside.

3. In a small bowl, combine the bread crumbs, parsley, the remaining 2 tablespoons of olive oil, and salt and pepper and mix well.

4. Rinse the fish slices and pat dry. Season each piece with salt and pepper and place flat on the work surface. Spread the bread crumb mixture evenly across each of the fish pieces and carefully roll like a jellyroll, securing it with string or toothpicks. Place the rolls in the skillet with the sauce. Transfer the skillet to the oven and bake for 10 to 12 minutes, or until cooked through.

5. Place a roll on each of four warmed dinner plates, spoon some of the sauce over each, and serve.

SERVES 4

1½ cups **BASIC TOMATO SAUCE** (page 220)

4 tablespoons extra-virgin **OLIVE OIL**

½ cup **GAETA OLIVES**

¼ cup salt-packed **CAPERS**, rinsed and drained

1 tablespoon hot **RED PEPPER FLAKES**

2 tablespoons **PINE NUTS**

¼ cup **CURRANTS**

1 cup dry **WHITE WINE**

1 cup fresh **BREAD CRUMBS**

¼ cup finely chopped flat-leaf **PARSLEY**

KOSHER SALT and freshly ground **BLACK PEPPER**, to taste

1½-pound piece of **SWORDFISH**, cut into 4 ⅓-inch-thick slices by your fishmonger

CONTORNI

Perhaps nowhere are the differences between Italian and American meals more apparent than in the matter of *contorni,* or side dishes. Many of my customers and friends were brought up in families in which every single dinner consisted of meat, two kinds of vegetables, and a starch, usually a potato or rice. In Italy they eat a little differently. Antipasto, particularly in the south, consists of several kinds of vegetables and perhaps some *salumi.* This is regularly followed by a plate of pasta, sometimes as simple as *aglio, olio e peperoncino* (garlic, oil, and chile pepper), or sometimes with tomato sauce or even shellfish. Next comes the *secondo,* usually a comparatively small portion of meat or fish that is almost always served by itself, no potatoes in evidence. The written menu at most restaurants in Italy will have a section of *contorni* that offers little more than salads, or sliced tomatoes or maybe some roasted peppers or cooked greens—that's it.

At Babbo we think we have combined the best of both traditions. As a nod to our customers' preferences and our desire to simplify the dining experience, we generally accompany a piece of fish, meat, or bird with the vegetable or grain that complements it, yet doesn't challenge the appetite so much as to overstuff.

The best thing to do if you are having trouble deciding what to serve with a dish is to go to the local greenmarket, find out what is in season, and buy it. Take it home, cut it into one- or two-inch pieces, put it into a roasting pan, drizzle it with olive oil, and toss it into a 475°F. oven. Cook it until it's cooked through and maybe starting to get a little dark on the outside edges. Remove it from the oven and allow it to cool for 5 minutes. Squeeze a little lemon juice on it, season it with sea salt and pepper, and just serve it as it is. If, on the other hand, you want to get a tiny bit fancier, the following are some of our favorite *contorni.*

CLOCKWISE FROM TOP:
Spring Scafata; *Escarole with Roasted Shallots; Cardoons with Lemon and Onions*

SPRING *SCAFATA*

10 to 12 CARDOON stalks

Juice of 1 LEMON

3 tablespoons extra-virgin
   OLIVE OIL

2 LEEKS, white parts only, halved
   and cut into 1-inch pieces

3 GARLIC cloves, thinly sliced

2 tablespoons finely shredded
   MINT leaves

Pinch of hot RED PEPPER
   FLAKES

12 baby ARTICHOKES, trimmed
   and quartered

½ pound medium ASPARAGUS,
   bottoms trimmed by 1 inch

½ pound SUGAR SNAP PEAS

2 CARROTS, peeled and cut into
   ½-inch chunks

1 FENNEL bulb, cored and cut
   into ½-inch strips

1 cup dry WHITE WINE

KOSHER SALT and freshly ground
   BLACK PEPPER, to taste

PECORINO ROMANO, for grating

1. Peel the fibrous outer skin from the cardoons and slice each stem into ¼-inch by 3-inch matchsticks. Place in a medium saucepan with water to cover and add the lemon juice. Bring to a boil over high heat, then reduce the heat to medium and cook until tender, about 30 minutes. Drain and allow to cool.

2. In a 12- to 14-inch sauté pan, heat the olive oil over medium-high heat and add the leeks and garlic. Cook for 5 minutes, until softened and slightly golden. Add the mint, red pepper flakes, artichokes, asparagus, peas, carrots, and fennel and cook for 5 minutes. Add the wine, bring to a boil, season with salt and pepper, and cook, covered, for 20 minutes, or until the vegetables are very tender. Adjust the seasoning, sprinkle with Pecorino, and serve.

ESCAROLE *with roasted shallots*

1. Preheat the oven to 400°F. Drizzle the shallots with 2 tablespoons of the olive oil, season with salt and pepper, and place in a small roasting pan. Roast until very soft and golden brown, about 25 minutes. Remove from the oven and, when cool enough to handle, cut each shallot in half. Do not worry if the shallots start to come apart a little.

2. In a 12- to 14-inch sauté pan, heat the remaining ¼ cup of olive oil over high heat. Add the escarole and shallots and sauté over high heat until tender, about 7 minutes. Season with salt and pepper and serve immediately

SERVES 4 AS A SIDE DISH

4 **SHALLOTS**, trimmed and peeled

2 tablespoons plus ¼ cup extra-virgin **OLIVE OIL**

KOSHER SALT and freshly ground **BLACK PEPPER**

1 head of **ESCAROLE**, cored and roughly chopped

CARDOONS *with lemon and onions*

1. Peel the fibrous outer skin from the cardoons and slice each stem into ¼-inch by 3-inch sticks. Place in a medium saucepan with water to cover and add the lemon juice. Cook over high heat until tender, about 45 minutes. Drain and allow to cool.

2. In a 12- to 14-inch sauté pan, heat the olive oil over medium-high heat. Add the preserved lemons and onions, season with salt and pepper, and cook over medium-high heat for 5 minutes. Add the cardoons, balsamic vinegar, honey, red pepper flakes, and wine and cook over high heat for 5 minutes. Serve immediately.

SERVES 4 AS A SIDE DISH

10 to 12 **CARDOON** stalks

Juice of 1 **LEMON**

2 tablespoons extra-virgin **OLIVE OIL**

2 **PRESERVED LEMON** quarters, cut into thin slices (page 223)

2 **RED ONIONS**, cut into ½-inch rings

KOSHER SALT and freshly ground **BLACK PEPPER**, to taste

2 tablespoons **BALSAMIC VINEGAR**

1 tablespoon **HONEY**

Pinch of hot **RED PEPPER FLAKES**

¼ cup dry **WHITE WINE**

NINE-HERB SALAD

½ bunch each, leaves only: **MINT, ROSEMARY, PARSLEY, THYME, OREGANO, MARJORAM, BASIL** and **CHIVES**

Fronds from 1 **FENNEL** bulb

¼ pound baby **SPINACH**

1 tablespoon fresh **LEMON JUICE**

3 tablespoons extra-virgin **OLIVE OIL**

KOSHER SALT and freshly ground **BLACK PEPPER**, to taste

In a large bowl, combine the herbs and spinach. Add the lemon juice, olive oil, and salt and pepper and toss well to coat the greens. Divide among four chilled dinner plates and serve immediately.

SCALLION *BARLOTTO*

SERVES 4 AS A SIDE DISH

2 bunches **SCALLIONS**, trimmed and cut into ¼-inch pieces

1 **GARLIC** clove

½ cup extra-virgin **OLIVE OIL**

KOSHER SALT and freshly ground **BLACK PEPPER**

1 cup **BARLEY**

¼ cup unsalted **BUTTER**

1 cup **BROWN CHICKEN STOCK** (page 141)

1. In the bowl of a food processor, combine the scallions and garlic and pulse until coarsely pureed. Continue pulsing and slowly drizzle in olive oil to form an emulsion. Season with salt and pepper to taste and set aside.

2. Bring 3 quarts of water to a boil and add 1 tablespoon salt. Add the barley and cook until somewhat tender but not cooked through, about 10 minutes. Drain and set aside.

3. In a 12- to 14-inch sauté pan, heat the butter over high heat until it foams and subsides. Add the cooked barley and cook, stirring over medium-high heat, for 10 minutes, adding the chicken stock in small increments and allowing it to be absorbed by the barley. Stir in the scallion puree, season with salt and pepper, and serve.

TOP TO BOTTOM:
Nine-Herb Salad; Scallion Barlotto;
Polenta

POLENTA

SERVES 4 AS A SIDE DISH

1 cup quick-cook **POLENTA** or cornmeal

½ cup **MASCARPONE** cheese

In a medium saucepan, bring 5 cups of water to a boil. Add the polenta in a thin stream, whisking constantly, until it is all incorporated. Stir with a wooden spoon until the mixture is thick and dense, 3 to 5 minutes. Remove from the heat and stir in the cheese. Serve immediately.

Charred sweet corn FREGULA

SERVES 4 AS A SIDE DISH

KOSHER SALT

1½ cups *FREGULA* pasta

2 ears **CORN**, shucked

2 tablespoons extra-virgin **OLIVE OIL**

Freshly ground **BLACK PEPPER,** to taste

¾ cup **BROWN CHICKEN STOCK** (page 141)

¼ cup freshly grated **PARMIGIANO-REGGIANO**

1. Bring 3 quarts of water to a boil and add 1 tablespoon of salt. Set up a small ice bath nearby. Cook the *fregula* in the boiling water until somewhat tender but not cooked through, 10 to 12 minutes. Drain the *fregula*, refresh it in the ice bath, and spread it on a tray lined with paper towels to dry.

2. Preheat the grill.

3. Brush the ears of corn with the olive oil, season with salt and pepper, and place on the grill, turning every 2 minutes until all sides are nicely charred and the kernels are just beginning to burst. Remove the corn from the grill with tongs and, when the ears are cool enough to handle, cut the kernels off the cob with a sharp knife.

4. Combine the blanched *fregula,* the sweet corn, and the chicken stock in a 12- to 14-inch sauté pan and cook over high heat until the stock boils and is mostly absorbed into the grain, about 5 minutes. Add the grated Parmigiano-Reggiano and salt and pepper and toss over high heat for 1 minute more.

Roasted beet FARROTTO

1. Preheat the oven to 400°F.

2. Trim the tops off the beets and drizzle them with the olive oil. Season the beets with salt and pepper, wrap them in aluminum foil, and roast until tender, about 40 minutes. When cool enough to handle, peel the beets and cut each in half, then cut into half-moon slices about ¼ inch thick. Place the slices in a bowl and gently toss with the pomegranate molasses and salt and pepper. Set aside.

3. Bring 3 quarts of water to a boil and add 1 tablespoon of salt. Set up an ice bath nearby, and cook the farro in the boiling water until tender yet not completely cooked, about 20 minutes. Drain the farro and place it in a sauté pan with the chicken stock. Add the sliced beets and toss over high heat until most of the chicken stock has been absorbed and the farro is completely cooked through, about 3 minutes. Adjust the seasoning with salt and pepper, grate the Parmigiano over, and serve immediately.

SERVES 4 AS A SIDE DISH

2 large **RED BEETS**

2 tablespoons extra-virgin **OLIVE OIL**

KOSHER SALT and freshly ground **BLACK PEPPER**, to taste

2 tablespoons **POMEGRANATE MOLASSES** (available in specialty stores)

1½ cups **FARRO** (spelt) (page 216)

½ cup **BROWN CHICKEN STOCK** (page 141)

PARMIGIANO-REGGIANO, for grating

FAGIOLI AL TOSCANO

1. Trim the beans and cut them into 3-inch lengths.

2. In a 12- to 14-inch sauté pan, heat the olive oil over high heat until hot but not smoking. Add the onion, garlic, red pepper flakes, and anchovy paste and stir over medium-high heat until the vegetables have begun to brown and become translucent, about 5 minutes. Add the beans and cook over medium heat until the beans are tender and deep brown, about 15 minutes. Season with salt and pepper and serve immediately.

SERVES 4 AS A SIDE DISH

1 pound green, wax, or romano **BEANS**

¼ cup extra-virgin **OLIVE OIL**

1 small **RED ONION**, finely chopped

4 **GARLIC** cloves, thinly sliced

½ tablespoon hot **RED PEPPER FLAKES**

2 tablespoons **ANCHOVY PASTE**

KOSHER SALT and freshly ground **BLACK PEPPER**, to taste

BROCCOLI RABE

with roasted garlic

1 head of **GARLIC**

2 tablespoons plus ¼ cup extra-virgin **OLIVE OIL**

KOSHER SALT and freshly ground **BLACK PEPPER**

3 salt-packed **ANCHOVY** fillets, rinsed and drained

1 pound **BROCCOLI RABE**, tough stems trimmed

Pinch of hot **RED PEPPER FLAKES**

1. Preheat the oven to 400°F.

2. Remove the first few papery layers from the garlic. Drizzle the garlic with 2 tablespoons of the olive oil, season with salt and pepper, and wrap tightly in aluminum foil. Roast until the garlic is very soft, about 40 minutes. Remove from the oven and, once cool enough to handle, separate the cloves and squeeze half of them from their skins into a small bowl. Set aside the remaining unpeeled cloves. Add the anchovy fillets to the squeezed garlic and gently mash together. Set aside.

3. Bring 4 quarts of water to a boil and add 2 tablespoons of salt. Set up an ice bath nearby. Blanch the broccoli rabe in the boiling water for 3 minutes, then remove with a slotted spoon and immediately refresh in the ice bath. Once cooled, drain and squeeze dry in a clean kitchen towel. Roughly chop the broccoli rabe and set aside.

4. In a 12- to 14-inch sauté pan, heat the remaining ¼ cup of olive oil over high heat and stir in the garlic and anchovy mixture. Cook over high heat for 2 minutes, then add the broccoli rabe, remaining cloves of roasted garlic, and red pepper flakes. Sauté over high heat until the broccoli rabe starts to brown at the edges. Season with salt and pepper and serve.

PUMPKIN ORZO

1. Cut the squash or pumpkin into 3 or 4 evenly sized pieces. Season with salt and pepper, drizzle with the olive oil, and wrap in foil. Roast in the oven for 30 to 45 minutes, or until very soft. Remove from the oven and allow to cool for 5 minutes, then place the cooked squash in the bowl of a food processor. Add the honey, balsamic vinegar, and salt and pepper and pulse to form a relatively smooth puree. Set aside.

2. Bring 3 quarts of water to a boil and add 2 tablespoons of salt. Set up an ice bath nearby. Cook the orzo in the boiling water for 3 minutes, to blanch but not cook through. Drain the orzo and plunge it into the ice bath. Once cooled, drain it and lay it out on a baking sheet to dry.

3. Bring the chicken stock to a boil in a 12-inch sauté pan. Add the orzo and squash puree and cook over high heat, stirring frequently, until the chicken stock is fully absorbed by the orzo. Season with salt and pepper and serve.

SERVES 4 TO 6 AS A SIDE DISH

½ pound **BUTTERNUT SQUASH** or pumpkin, seeded and peeled

KOSHER SALT and freshly ground **BLACK PEPPER**

2 tablespoons extra-virgin **OLIVE OIL**

2 tablespoons **HONEY**

2 tablespoons **BALSAMIC VINEGAR**

1 cup **ORZO**

1 cup **BROWN CHICKEN STOCK** (page 141)

RADICCHIO *and lemon*

In a 12- to 14-inch sauté pan, heat the olive oil over high heat until almost smoking. Add the onion and lemon and sauté over high heat for 3 to 5 minutes, until the lemon and the onion are soft and golden brown. Add the radicchio and toss to just wilt, 1 minute. Season with salt and pepper, add the vinegar, and serve.

SERVES 4 AS A SIDE DISH

¼ cup extra-virgin **OLIVE OIL**

½ **RED ONION**, finely chopped

Rind of 2 **LEMONS**

4 heads of **RADICCHIO DI TREVISO**, rinsed and cored

KOSHER SALT and freshly ground **BLACK PEPPER**

¼ cup **RED WINE VINEGAR**

ARTICHOKES *cooked in olive oil*

In a 12- to 14-inch sauté pan, combine the artichokes, oil, mint, red pepper flakes, and the sliced garlic and place over medium heat until the center of the pan has reached a boil. The artichokes should be submerged in oil. Remove from heat and let cool for 15 to 20 minutes. Season with salt and pepper and serve at room temperature. The oil that remains after the artichokes are eaten can be used to make a wonderful vinaigrette.

SERVES 4 AS A SIDE DISH

1 pound baby **ARTICHOKES**, trimmed and quartered

1½ cups extra-virgin **OLIVE OIL**

1 bunch of fresh **MINT**, leaves only

1 tablespoon hot **RED PEPPER FLAKES**

3 **GARLIC** cloves, thinly sliced

KOSHER SALT and freshly ground **BLACK PEPPER**

BRUSSELS SPROUTS
with pancetta

1. Bring 6 quarts of water to a boil and add 2 tablespoons of salt. Set up an ice bath nearby. Cook the whole Brussels sprouts in the boiling water for 2 minutes, then drain and plunge into the ice bath. Once they have cooled, drain the sprouts, trim off the tough ends, and cut in half lengthwise.

2. In a 12- to 14-inch sauté pan, heat the pancetta over low heat until most of the fat has been rendered and the cubes are crispy, 8 to 10 minutes. Remove the pancetta from the pan with a slotted spoon and reserve. Drain all but 2 tablespoons of the fat. Add the Brussels sprouts to the pan and cook over medium heat until tender, 6 to 7 minutes. Return the pancetta to the pan and add the thyme, parsley, and salt and pepper and serve immediately.

SERVES 4 TO 6 AS A SIDE DISH

KOSHER SALT

1½ pounds **BRUSSELS SPROUTS**

½ pound **PANCETTA**, cut into ½-inch cubes

1 teaspoon finely chopped fresh **THYME**

1 teaspoon finely chopped fresh flat-leaf **PARSLEY**

Freshly ground **BLACK PEPPER**, to taste

CLOCKWISE FROM TOP LEFT: *Artichokes Cooked in Olive Oil; Radicchio and Lemon; Brussels Sprouts with Pancetta*

CHAPTER FOUR

Terra e Bosco

(From the Earth and Forest)

To understand meat cookery is to understand the science of heat transfer. The seeming sorcery of the fire and the alchemy of marinades and dry rubs, and the anatomy of different cuts and different grades, always strike fear into the novice cook's heart. Once you are familiar with the basic ideas, it will all seem as natural to you as it does to every Italian grandma from Belleville to Bari.

A very important thing to realize is that tougher or fattier meats always have better flavor; this is why the osso buco and the short rib are so delicious and the filet mignon will never be found on a menu where I am chef. Pork shoulder will always taste more "porky" than a pork chop because it comes from a well-used muscle, one that experienced more flow of energy from the food and water the animal consumed.

At Babbo we also use many of the "alternative" cuts and so-called "variety meats" because we adore the tradition of the Italian farm table. In agricultural societies, in which many families still raise a couple of pigs or cows for slaughter every year, the reality of the word "waste" is crystal clear; nothing goes to waste. The ears, face, and nose become *testa;* the hooves become *zampone;* the intestines hold *salumi* made from all the loose scraps; the brains go into ravioli; the leather goes to a tannery; and the tail goes into soup. In this way, great recipes are born out of necessity.

We are also firm traditionalists in that we approach our new dishes with the same spirit that infused the originals, that love of sexy, intuitive, powerful, and evocative flavors that bring up such intense memories when you smell or taste a dish you have not had in a long while. Slow-cooking meat in fragrant liquid, or braising, is one of the best ways to coax huge impact out of what are usually less expensive cuts.

This is not to say that you cannot find a steak or a straightforward plate of grilled lamb chops on the menu or in this book. When we execute these very simple dishes, we tend to invoke a little more of that alchemy I mentioned—perhaps a dry rub of spices and salt or a marinade of milk and bay leaves, to intensify the meat's natural flavor. If I may suggest searching out a source for meat and poultry given antibiotic-free feed and raised as organically as possible, I think you'll start to notice an immediate difference in the way your meat tastes.

Personalizing the flavor and texture of cured meats from family to family is another Italian tradition that is, sadly, rapidly disappearing in busy Italian-American families. At Babbo we have at least one or two sausages on the menu, in addition to the four or five *salumi* in the antipasto department. This is part of the cultural heritage I refuse to give up, and one that can really change your feeling about food. Getting comfortable with the meat grinder and making your own sausages is one of the ways to jump the hurdle from rookie to seasoned (no pun intended) pro.

Bottom line, find a butcher, make a friend, get your hands dirty, and let's have some dinner.

GRILLED
BABY CHICKEN
al mattone
with PANZANELLA

Al mattone translates as "under the brick," which is the traditional Tuscan method for cooking a chicken over hot coals. This is a dish that truly captures the taste of Italy in the summer. It is rarely served in fancy restaurants; you're more likely to find it at one of the many *sagre*, or small country celebrations, held throughout the countryside in Tuscany.

1. Rinse the chickens and pat dry. Remove the giblets and set aside for another use. Season each with salt and pepper, then toss in the olive oil.

2. Make a very hot fire in the grill or heat a large cast-iron skillet or grill pan over high heat until smoking. Working in batches if necessary, place the chickens on the grill or in the pan and weigh them down with the bricks. Cook over high heat until cooked through and crispy, turning every 3 minutes, for a total of 15 minutes.

3. Meanwhile, make the *panzanella*. In a large mixing bowl, combine the onion, tomatoes, cucumber, and bread and toss gently to mix. Add the vinegar and olive oil and toss to coat. Gently mix in the basil and oregano and season with salt and pepper. Set aside for 20 minutes.

4. Once the chickens are cooked, place one on each of four warmed plates. Divide the *panzanella* evenly among the plates and serve.

SERVES 4

4 whole **BABY CHICKENS**, about 1 pound each, backbones removed and flattened

KOSHER SALT and freshly ground **BLACK PEPPER**, to taste

½ cup extra-virgin **OLIVE OIL**

4 clean **BRICKS** wrapped in foil

Panzanella

1 **RED ONION**, cut into ¼-inch slices

2 large beefsteak or heirloom **TOMATOES**, cut into ½-inch cubes

1 Kirby **CUCUMBER**, 6 to 8 inches, seeded and cut into ½-inch cubes

2 cups day-old **ITALIAN BREAD**, cut into ½-inch cubes (or fresh bread, cut into ½-inch cubes and lightly toasted in the broiler for 1 minute)

¼ cup good-quality **RED WINE VINEGAR**

½ cup extra-virgin **OLIVE OIL**

¼ cup torn **BASIL** leaves

2 tablespoons fresh **OREGANO** leaves

KOSHER SALT and freshly ground **BLACK PEPPER**, to taste

GRILLED
guinea hen

with POMEGRANATE VINAIGRETTE

SERVES 4

1 **RED ONION**, diced

2 tablespoons fresh **THYME**
leaves

1 tablespoon freshly ground
BLACK PEPPER, plus more
to taste

½ cup **BALSAMIC VINEGAR**

¼ cup **HONEY**

½ cup extra-virgin **OLIVE OIL**

8 **GUINEA HEN LEGS**, boned
out, skin left on

KOSHER SALT

**CHARRED SWEET CORN
FREGULA** (page 202)

POMEGRANATE VINAIGRETTE
(page 241)

When corn is eaten in Italy, it is usually in the form of polenta. But the sweet corn of New Jersey is so delicious that I cannot imagine any Italian not just loving it served this way. We love guinea hen legs because they are so moist and juicy, but chicken legs would work just as well. Boning the leg-thigh quarters is not difficult (see page 218), but you can have the butcher do it for you if you prefer. *Fregula* is a Sardinian semolina pasta, similar to Israeli couscous.

1. In a large, nonreactive casserole, combine the onion, thyme, black pepper, vinegar, honey, and olive oil. Place the guinea hen legs in the marinade and turn to coat on all sides. Cover and refrigerate for 8 hours or overnight.

2. Preheat the grill or broiler.

3. Remove the guinea hen legs from the marinade and pat them dry. Place them skin side down over the hottest part of the fire and grill until dark brown and crisp on the skin side, 6 to 7 minutes. Season with salt and pepper, turn, and cook on the flesh side until just cooked through, 4 to 5 minutes. Keep warm.

4. Divide the *fregula* among four warmed dinner plates. Place two guinea hen legs on each plate, drizzle with the pomegranate vinaigrette, and serve immediately.

BARBECUED SQUAB
al mattone
with PORCINI MUSTARD

SERVES 4

2 tablespoons **HONEY**

¼ cup **BALSAMIC VINEGAR**

1 cup extra-virgin **OLIVE OIL**

Leaves from ½ bunch of fresh
   THYME

1 large **RED ONION**, thinly sliced

4 whole **SQUAB**, breast and
   backbones removed

4 **BRICKS**, standard garden
   variety, well wrapped foil

SALT and freshly ground **BLACK
   PEPPER**, to taste

ROASTED BEET FARROTTO
   (page 203)

4 tablespoons **PORCINI MUSTARD**
   (page 220)

Here is another example of cooking "under the brick." Weighted with a hot terra-cotta brick the bird cooks a little more quickly, gets a crisp skin, and retains more of its juices. We like to serve squab medium rare. Ask for birds that have been glove- or sleeve-boned.

1. In a nonreactive casserole just large enough to fit all the squab in one layer, combine the honey, vinegar, olive oil, thyme leaves, and onion and mix well. Add the squab and turn to coat, making sure that as much of each bird is in contact with the marinade as possible. Cover and refrigerate for at least 4 hours, or up to 8 hours, turning the squab occasionally.

2. Preheat the grill or broiler. Place the bricks on the grill and heat until very hot.

3. Remove the squab from the marinade and pat them dry with paper towels. Season with salt and pepper. Place the squab breast down on the hottest part of the grill, carefully place a hot brick on top of each, and cook for 6 minutes on one side. Then, using tongs, remove the brick, carefully turn the squab, replace the brick, and grill the other side for 4 to 6 minutes, or until medium rare, about 130°F. on an instant-read thermometer.

4. To assemble the dish, place some of the farrotto in the center of each of four warmed dinner plates. Place a squab atop each mound of farrotto and top with a tablespoon of porcini mustard.

Farro

Farro is a unhybridized form of wheat with its husk intact, which gives it a full-bodied, nutty flavor similar to barley. It is a staple of Tuscan kitchens, as it grows best on dry hillsides far above sea level. Farro is a fantastic source of the antioxidant Vitamin E, and it even purportedly contributes to a person's sexual stamina.

boning a duck leg-thigh quarter

1. Lay the leg quarter skin side down on a cutting board. Starting at the thigh end, locate the bone with your fingertips and use a sharp boning or paring knife to cut the flesh away from either side of the bone.

2. Next, gently work the knife under the bone to release the flesh from the bone completely, carefully cutting through any tendons you may encounter.

3. Pull the flesh down and away from the thigh bone, effectively turning the leg inside out and exposing the leg–thigh joint. Continue to cut the flesh off the leg bone. Do not cut through the joint that holds the thigh and leg bones together; otherwise, you will not have a "handle" and the boning process will be more difficult.

4. Once you have worked the flesh off the bone, use a heavy chef's knife or cleaver to cut off all but the end of the bone, which will help the leg to retain its shape.

duck *braciole*

with FAVAS *and* PECORINO

When the first favas arrive in April, they become the first course on our traditional tasting menu. The rich flavor of the duck leg intensifies as it warms up, so be sure to allow these to come to room temp before serving.

1. Preheat the oven to 450°F.

2. In a mixing bowl, combine the orange zest, bread crumbs, garlic, parsley, and olive oil and mix well.

3. Place the duck legs skin side down on a cutting board and season with salt and pepper. Divide the bread crumb mixture among the legs, filling them as full as possible. Fold the meat up around the mixture and tie tightly with butcher's twine. Place the legs in a small roasting pan, flap side down, and roast for 30 minutes, or until browned and crispy and cooked through. Remove from the oven and allow to cool. (These will hold for up to 3 days wrapped in plastic and refrigerated.)

4. Slice and place one leg on each of four dinner plates. Scatter the beans around the duck, top with several long shavings of cheese, drizzle with olive oil, and serve immediately.

SERVES 4

Zest of 1 ORANGE

½ cup toasted fresh BREAD CRUMBS

4 GARLIC cloves, finely chopped

¼ cup finely chopped flat-leaf PARSLEY

2 tablespoons extra-virgin OLIVE OIL

4 Long Island DUCK LEGS, boned and butterflied open

KOSHER SALT and freshly ground BLACK PEPPER

1 cup raw FAVA BEANS, peeled

PECORINO TOSCANO, for shaving

Best-quality extra-virgin OLIVE OIL, for drizzling

Basic Tomato Sauce

Makes 4 cups

¼ cup extra-virgin **OLIVE OIL**
1 **SPANISH ONION**, finely diced
4 **GARLIC** cloves, peeled and thinly
   sliced
3 tablespoons chopped fresh
   THYME, or 1 tablespoon dried
½ medium **CARROT**, finely shredded
2 28-ounce cans peeled whole
   TOMATOES
KOSHER SALT, to taste

In a 3-quart saucepan, heat the
olive oil over medium heat. Add the
onion and garlic and cook until soft
and light golden brown, 8 to 10
minutes. Add the thyme and carrot
and cook for 5 minutes more, or
until the carrot is quite soft. With
your hands, crush the tomatoes
and add them with their juices.
Bring to a boil, stirring often, and
then lower the heat and simmer for
30 minutes, or until the sauce is as
thick as hot cereal. Season with
salt and serve. This sauce holds for
1 week in the refrigerator or for up
to 6 months in the freezer.

Jalapeño Pesto

Makes 1 cup

6 **JALAPEÑO PEPPERS**, stems
   removed, seeds intact
¼ cup blanched and sliced
   ALMONDS
½ **RED ONION**, diced
¼ cup extra-virgin **OLIVE OIL**

Combine the peppers, almonds,
and onion in the bowl of a food
processor. Pulse until pureed, then
slowly drizzle in the oil until emulsified.

   Jalapeño pesto can be held for
up to 1 week, refrigerated, in an
airtight container.

Porcini Mustard

Makes 2 cups

½ **RED ONION**, finely chopped
1 cup **BALSAMIC VINEGAR**
2 ounces dried **PORCINI**
   mushrooms
¼ cup **DIJON MUSTARD**
¼ cup extra-virgin **OLIVE OIL**
¼ cup canned **BLACK TRUFFLES**,
   finely chopped

In a medium, heavy-bottomed
saucepan, combine the onion,
vinegar, 1 cup water, and the
mushrooms and bring to a boil.
Reduce to a simmer and cook
until the liquid is reduced by half.
Remove from the heat and allow to
cool in a large, clean bowl.

   Place the cooled mixture into
the bowl of a food processor and
puree with the mustard and olive
oil until emulsified. Pass the mixture through a strainer to remove
the mushroom and onion solids,
then stir in the black truffles. This
can be refrigerated for up to 2
weeks in an airtight container.

Chianti Mustard

Makes 1½ cups

1 cup coarse-grained **MUSTARD**
½ cup **CHIANTI**
2 tablespoons extra-virgin **OLIVE OIL**

In a medium bowl, combine the mustard, chianti, and olive oil and whisk well to combine.

Quince Vinegar

Makes 2½ cups

1 10-ounce block of **QUINCE PASTE** (called *membrillo* in Spanish gourmet shops)
1 cup **SHERRY VINEGAR**
2 tablespoons **DIJON MUSTARD**
¼ cup extra-virgin **OLIVE OIL**
¼ cup **APPLE JUICE**

In a heavy-bottomed saucepan, heat the quince paste, vinegar, and 1 cup of water over medium heat until the paste is melted. Remove from the heat and gently whisk in the mustard and olive oil until emulsified. Thin to liquid consistency with apple juice. Allow to cool. The vinegar can be stored, refrigerated in an airtight container, for up to 2 weeks.

Prune Vinegar

Makes 2½ cups

1 cup pitted **PRUNES**
1 cup red wine **VINEGAR**
KOSHER SALT and freshly ground **BLACK PEPPER**, to taste
½ cup **ORANGE JUICE**

In a heavy-bottomed saucepan, combine the prunes, vinegar, and 1 cup water and bring to a boil. Reduce to a simmer and cook, uncovered, until the mixture is thick and jam-like, about 25 minutes. Process until smooth in the food processor. Season with salt and pepper and add the orange juice. The vinegar may be kept up to 2 weeks in the refrigerator, in an airtight container.

DUCK
with CHICORY,
PRESERVED LEMONS, *and* KUMQUAT VINAIGRETTE

SERVES 4

2 whole **LONG ISLAND PEKIN DUCKS**

2 tablespoons hot **RED PEPPER FLAKES**

1 tablespoon **KOSHER SALT**, plus more to taste

1 tablespoon freshly ground **BLACK PEPPER**, plus more to taste

5 tablespoons extra-virgin **OLIVE OIL**

2 cups **CHICORY** or frisée

1 tablespoon fresh **LEMON JUICE**

2 **PRESERVED LEMON** quarters (see sidebar), sliced paper thin

KUMQUAT VINAIGRETTE (page 240)

4 tablespoons **SPANISH PICKLED PUMPKIN** (aropé) or *mostarda di cremona*

I love the sweet-and-sour aspect of this dish, heightened by the presence of the bitter chicory in salad form. You can make the confit legs up to 2 weeks in advance or buy them from D'Artagnan, and use any extras to make duck ragù.

1. Separate the legs and breasts from the duck carcasses. Pull off the loose fat from the duck pieces and carcasses and set it aside. (Save the carcasses for stock.)

2. In a small bowl, combine the red pepper flakes and 1 table-spoon each of salt and pepper. Rub the legs all over with this mixture. Wrap the legs individually in plastic, and refrigerate them, the breasts, and the reserved duck fat overnight.

3. In a small saucepan, combine the reserved duck fat and ¼ cup water and cook over low heat until the water has evaporated and the fat is liquefied, about 1 hour. Preheat the oven to 325°F. Place the duck legs in a shallow, nonreactive casserole and cover with the hot fat. Cover and bake for 2 hours. Remove from the oven and allow to cool. Keep the oven on. (The legs may be stored in the refrigerator, covered in the fat, for up to 4 weeks.)

4. Remove the legs from the cooled fat and wipe off the excess fat with a paper towel. Season the breasts and legs well with salt and pepper. With a sharp paring knife, score the breasts on the skin side with an X, making sure to penetrate the duck's skin and fat but not the flesh.

5. In a 12- to 14-inch ovenproof sauté pan, heat 1 tablespoon of the olive oil over high heat until smoking. Add the legs and sauté them, skin side down, until the skin is crispy. Remove the pan from the heat and place it in the oven to heat through, for about 5 minutes.

6. In a second sauté pan of equal size, heat 1 tablespoon of the olive oil until smoking. Add the breasts, skin side down, and sear them over high heat, draining the excess fat from the pan when

Preserved Lemons
Makes 16 quarters

4 whole **LEMONS**, scrubbed
3 cups **KOSHER SALT**
Juice of 4 **LEMONS**

Make two long perpendicular cuts through one end of each lemon, so that they are partially quartered but still intact (it should resemble, to the active imagination, a tulip).

Salt each lemon liberally and place in a crock or large jar, layering salt and lemons and packing them in tightly so that each lemon is completely surrounded by salt. Top with more salt and pour the lemon juice over all. Cover tightly and store for 1 month, flipping the container every week or so to ensure an even cure.

necessary. When the skin is crispy, turn the breasts and cook on the flesh side until they are medium rare, or approximately 130°F. on a meat thermometer. Transfer the breasts to a cutting board and allow them to rest for 5 minutes; then slice them on the bias.

7. In a medium bowl, combine the chicory, lemon juice, preserved lemon, remaining 3 tablespoons of olive oil, and salt and pepper. Toss well to combine and divide evenly among four warmed dinner plates. Place a leg and sliced breast on each plate, drizzle with the kumquat vinaigrette, and serve immediately with some of the Spanish pickled pumpkin on top.

GRILLED QUAIL
WITH
scorzanera alla romana,
BRAISED DANDELIONS, *and* BLOOD ORANGES

SERVES 4

8 QUAIL, preferably boneless (your butcher can do this for you)

¼ cup BALSAMIC VINEGAR

2 cups extra-virgin OLIVE OIL

2 tablespoons HONEY

Leaves from ½ bunch of THYME

1 tablespoon freshly ground BLACK PEPPER, plus more to taste

¾ pound SALSIFY, peeled, cut into 4-inch lengths, and quartered

Juice of 1 LEMON

8 ounces BLOOD ORANGE CONCENTRATE (see Sources)

1 cup *SABA* (see sidebar, as well as Sources)

SHERRY VINEGAR, to taste

KOSHER SALT, to taste

1 pound DANDELION GREENS

2 cups BROWN CHICKEN STOCK (page 141)

4 GARLIC cloves, thinly sliced

3 tablespoons ANISETTE

1 teaspoon ANCHOVY PASTE

2 BLOOD ORANGES, peeled and segmented

We occasionally use Italian words to describe specific flavors in Italy. *Scorzanera alla Romana* is truly so much more than the words "salsify, roman style" can properly convey. The sweetly marinated quail marry perfectly with the bitter flavor of the dandelions and the haunting licorice scent of the salsify-and-anchovy combination.

1. Check the quail for bones and feathers and place in a large mixing bowl. Add the balsamic vinegar, 1 cup of the olive oil, the honey, thyme, and black pepper and toss to coat. Refrigerate for 2 to 4 hours.

2. Place the salsify in a large bowl, cover with cold water, and add the lemon juice. Set aside until ready to cook.

3. Place the blood orange concentrate in a small saucepan and bring to a boil. Cook over high heat until reduced by half, adjusting the heat to prevent scorching. Stir in the *saba* and ½ cup of the olive oil. Season with sherry vinegar, salt, and pepper. Remove from the heat and set aside.

4. Preheat the grill or broiler.

5. In a 12- to 14-inch sauté pan, combine the dandelion greens, chicken stock, ¼ cup of the olive oil, and half the sliced garlic. Bring to a simmer over medium heat and braise until soft, 10 to 15 minutes. Season with salt and pepper.

6. In a 12- to 14-inch sauté pan, heat the remaining ¼ cup of olive oil over high heat. Drain the salsify, add it to the pan, and sauté until browned, about 8 minutes. Add the remaining sliced garlic, the anisette, and the anchovy paste and toss to coat. Remove from the heat and set aside.

7. Remove the quails from the marinade and pat dry. Place them on the hottest part of the grill or broiler and cook for 4 to 5 minutes on each side, until just pink at the leg bones.

Saba

Saba is the unfermented must of Trebbiano grapes that has been cooked down to a nearly syrupy texture. It is the first stage of what could eventually become balsamic vinegar if treated in the traditional aging methods approved by the consortium of vinegar makers in Modena and Reggio-Emilia. Significantly lighter in color and consistency than balsamic vinegar, it adds a grape-y sweetness and slight bite to roasted or grilled meats, and it is also quite at home in the simple, fruit-based desserts so loved by Italians. We get our *saba* from an importer called Manicaretti (page 329).

8. To assemble the dish, divide the salsify among four warmed dinner plates and arrange into nests. Divide the dandelion greens among the four plates and mound in the center of the salsify nests. Stack two quail over the greens on each plate. Garnish each quail with blood orange sections and drizzle with the blood orange *saba* dressing. Serve immediately.

dry-rubbed
RIB-EYE STEAK
FOR 2

We dry-rub a thick-cut, well-marbled steak to help it form a nice crust while cooking. The effect of the sugar and salt on the meat is similar to dry aging, as it causes some of the steak's water weight to dissipate overnight and intensifies the beefy flavor. Serve with roasted potatoes.

1. In a small bowl, combine the sugar, salt, garlic, red pepper flakes, pepper, mushroom powder, and olive oil and stir well to form a thick, fairly dry paste. Rub the paste all over the steak, coating it evenly, and refrigerate, wrapped in plastic, for 12 hours or overnight.

2. Preheat the grill or broiler.

3. Remove the steak from the refrigerator and brush off the excess marinade with a paper towel. Cook on the hottest part of the grill for 25 minutes, turning every 6 minutes, or to an internal temperature of 120°F. for medium rare.

4. Allow the steak to rest for 10 minutes, then slice against the grain. Drizzle with the olive oil and balsamic vinegar and serve immediately.

SERVES 2

2 tablespoons SUGAR

1 tablespoon KOSHER SALT

5 GARLIC cloves, finely chopped

1 tablespoon hot RED PEPPER FLAKES

1 tablespoon freshly ground BLACK PEPPER

¼ cup dry PORCINI mushrooms, ground to a fine powder in a spice grinder

¼ cup extra-virgin OLIVE OIL

1 28-ounce RIB-EYE STEAK, cut 2 inches thick

Best-quality extra-virgin OLIVE OIL, for drizzling

Best-quality BALSAMIC VINEGAR, for drizzling

BARBECUED
SKIRT STEAK
with ENDIVE *alla piastra*
and SALSA VERDE

SERVES 4

¼ cup finely chopped fresh **ROSEMARY**

¼ cup finely chopped fresh **THYME**

¼ cup finely chopped fresh flat-leaf **PARSLEY**

4 **GARLIC** cloves, finely chopped

¾ cup extra-virgin **OLIVE OIL**

2 pounds **SKIRT STEAK**, trimmed of fibrous fat pieces

KOSHER SALT and freshly ground **BLACK PEPPER**

4 heads of **BELGIAN ENDIVE**, quartered lengthwise

SALSA VERDE (page 234)

RED ONION PICKLES (see sidebar)

PIMENTÓN (Spanish paprika), for sprinkling

Skirt steak is without a doubt one of the most flavorful pieces of beef available. Because it is rarely very thick, a dry rub would cure it like a ham; instead, we put it in a wet marinade. In the spring we sub asparagus for the endive; in the summer we'll use sweet-hot cubanelle peppers.

1. In a nonreactive, medium casserole, combine the rosemary, thyme, parsley, garlic, and ½ cup of the olive oil and stir well to blend. Place the steak in the casserole and turn to coat both sides with the herb mixture. Cover tightly and refrigerate for at least 4 hours or overnight.

2. Preheat the grill or broiler. Remove the steak from the marinade, brush off the excess herb mixture, and season with salt and pepper. Place on the hottest part of the grill. Cook for 3 minutes on one side, then turn carefully with tongs and cook for 2 minutes on the other side. While the second side cooks, brush the endive quarters with the remaining ¼ cup of olive oil, season with salt and pepper, and place on the grill to char well.

3. Remove the steak from the grill and let it rest for 3 minutes. Place 2 tablespoons of salsa verde in the center of each plate. Slice the steak on the bias about ½ inch thick and divide the slices evenly among the plates. Tent 4 endive quarters over each portion, tepee fashion. Top each portion with some of the red onion pickles, sprinkle the plate with *pimentón*, and serve immediately.

Red Onion Pickles
Makes 2 cups

1 cup **RED WINE VINEGAR**
½ cup **SUGAR**
½ cup **KOSHER SALT**
½ cup fresh **BEET JUICE** (for color)
2 **RED ONIONS**, peeled, sliced into
⅛-inch-thick rounds, and
separated into rings

In a deep bowl, combine the vinegar,
1 cup water, the sugar, salt, and beet
juice. Add the onion to the bowl,
making sure they are completely
covered by pickling liquid. Cover and
refrigerate for at least 24 hours.

BRAISED SHORT RIBS
with HORSERADISH GREMOLATA
(brasato al barolo)

SERVES 4

¼ cup extra-virgin **OLIVE OIL**

4 16-ounce **BEEF SHORT RIBS**

KOSHER SALT and freshly ground **BLACK PEPPER**

2 **CARROTS**, peeled and roughly chopped

1 **ONION**, roughly chopped

2 **CELERY** stalks, roughly chopped

5 **GARLIC** cloves, thinly sliced

2 cups **BAROLO** or other full-bodied red wine

1 16-ounce can peeled **TOMATOES**, crushed by hand, with their juices

1 cup **BROWN CHICKEN STOCK** (page 141)

½ bunch of **THYME**

½ bunch of **ROSEMARY**

½ bunch of **OREGANO**

PUMPKIN ORZO (page 205)

Gremolata

Leaves from 1 bunch of flat-leaf **PARSLEY**

Zest of 2 **LEMONS**, cut into julienne strips

¼ pound fresh **HORSERADISH**, grated

We use beef short ribs for this dish and it works out great. You could just as easily use brisket or blade, but I prefer the richness of the rib. Have your butcher cut between and along the length of the bone. The most important step here is the initial browning; do not shorten it or the final braise will not be as intensely flavored or colored.

1. Preheat the oven to 375°F.

2. In a large, heavy-bottomed skillet or Dutch oven, heat the olive oil over high heat until smoking. Season the ribs with salt and pepper and cook them over high heat until deep brown on all sides, about 15 minutes total. Remove the short ribs to a plate and set aside. Add the carrots, onion, celery, and garlic to the pan and cook over high heat until browned and softened, about 4 minutes. Season with salt and pepper and stir in the red wine, tomatoes and juices, chicken stock, and herbs, scraping the bottom of the pan with a wooden spoon to dislodge browned bits. Bring the mixture to a boil and return the short ribs to the pan. Cover with aluminum foil and place in the oven. Cook for 2 hours, or until the meat is very tender and literally falling off the bones.

3. To make the gremolata: In a small bowl, combine the parsley, lemon zest, and horseradish and toss loosely by hand.

4. Divide the pumpkin orzo evenly among four warmed bowls. Place one short rib in each bowl, top with a little of the pan juices and a handful of the gremolata, and serve immediately.

bollito MISTO

There is probably no more satisfying dish during cold weather than this *bollito misto* ("mixed boil"). This is exactly the kind of dish I love to order at a good restaurant. Many restaurants in Italy serve this from an elaborate rolling cart equipped with a perforated plate that lifts the meats out of the simmering broth for carving. Do not be daunted; this is really a one-pot dish that "cooks easy" if you have the time to watch it.

1. Place the tongue in a large pot with water to cover. Bring to a boil, then reduce the heat and simmer for 1 hour. Drain and, when cool, peel off the membrane.

2. In a large stockpot, combine all but 1 cup of the chicken stock and the chopped carrot, onion, and celery and bring to a boil. Add the tongue and brisket, cover, and cook until very tender, about 1½ hours. Remove the meat from the cooking liquid and set aside. Add the capon pieces and cook for 15 minutes, then add the cotechino, Italian sausages, the remaining cup of chicken stock, the carrot and onion chunks, and the potatoes. Cook for an additional 25 minutes.

3. Return the tongue and brisket to the pot to simmer for 20 minutes and warm through. Divide the meats and vegetables into portions and distribute them evenly among six warmed, shallow bowls. Strain the cooking liquid and pour a cupful over each portion of meat. Serve with all of the condiments.

SERVES 6

1 CALF'S TONGUE

2 quarts BROWN CHICKEN STOCK (page 141)

1 CARROT, peeled and coarsely chopped, plus 1 CARROT, peeled and cut into 6 pieces

1 ONION, coarsely chopped, plus 1 ONION, peeled and cut into 6 pieces

1 CELERY stalk, coarsely chopped

1-pound piece of BEEF BRISKET

1 whole CAPON, cut into 6 serving pieces

1-pound piece of COTECHINO SAUSAGE

6 sweet ITALIAN SAUSAGES

6 small new POTATOES

Condiments

½ cup SALSA ROSSA (page 234)

½ cup CRANBERRY MOSTARDA (page 234)

½ cup CHIANTI MUSTARD (page 221)

½ cup SALSA VERDE (page 234)

¼ cup coarse SEA SALT

Salsa Rossa

Makes 1½ cups

4 **RED BELL PEPPERS**, roasted,
  peeled, seeded, and cored
¾ cup extra-virgin **OLIVE OIL**
KOSHER SALT and freshly ground
  BLACK PEPPER, to taste

Place the peppers in the bowl of a
food processor. Puree while slowly
drizzling in the olive oil. Season
with salt and pepper.

Cranberry Mostarda

Makes 3 cups

2 cups granulated **SUGAR**
1 pound **CRANBERRIES**
3 tablespoons Colman's dry
  MUSTARD
1 teaspoon **MUSTARD OIL** (available
  at specialty stores)
2 tablespoons **BLACK MUSTARD
  SEEDS**
KOSHER SALT and freshly ground
  BLACK PEPPER, to taste

In a heavy-bottomed saucepan,
combine the sugar and 2 cups of
water and bring to a boil. Add the
cranberries and cook over high
heat for 10 minutes, or until the
cranberries are just beginning to
burst.

  While the cranberries are cooking, place the mustard in a small
bowl and add water to form a thin
paste. Add the mustard oil, black
mustard seeds, and salt and pepper. Stir this mixture into the
berries and cook over high heat
until the mixture is thick and
syrupy, about 20 minutes. Remove
from the heat and allow to cool.
The mostarda can be refrigerated
in an airtight container for up to 1
week.

Salsa Verde

Makes 1½ cups

1 bunch of flat-leaf **PARSLEY**, leaves
  only
1 bunch of fresh **MINT**, leaves only
1 bunch of fresh **BASIL**, leaves only
½ cup **CAPERS**, rinsed and drained
2 salt-packed **ANCHOVY** fillets, rinsed
  and drained
1 tablespoon **DIJON MUSTARD**
1 teaspoon **KOSHER SALT**
1 teaspoon **SUGAR**
2 tablespoons freshly ground **BLACK
  PEPPER**
1 tablespoon hot **RED PEPPER
  FLAKES**
1 **GARLIC** clove
1 cup extra-virgin **OLIVE OIL**

In the bowl of a food processor,
combine the herbs, capers,
anchovies, mustard, salt, sugar,
pepper, red pepper flakes, and garlic, and pulse to form a coarse
puree. With the motor running,
slowly drizzle in the olive oil to form
a relatively smooth puree that still
has some personality. Season with
salt and pepper. The salsa can be
refrigerated in a covered container
for up to 1 week.

MORE WINE NOTES

As anyone who's tasted a great red wine from a magnum or double magnum can attest, the bigger the bottle the better. Here again, our policy of serving wine by the quartino rather than by the glass has enabled us to expand greatly the parameters of our wine program, making available wines that diners might never otherwise have an opportunity to try. A $59 quartino of Gaja 1985 Sori Tildin Barbaresco served tableside from a double magnum may sound like a pricey accompaniment to braised short ribs and polenta, but at a cost of $600 per double magnum, the quartino allows the diner to experience a historic wine at an accessible price. On any given night the quartino offerings would include six whites ranging in style from flinty and crisp, aromatic and enticing, to fat and explosive; a rose and a cerisuolo; and as many as seven reds varying in regionality, impact, and style. We offer several wines in large format every evening at the restaurant, sometimes paired with dishes on our tasting menus.

Wine pairings are available with both the traditional and the pasta tasting menus at Babbo. Starting with sparkling wine and ending with moscato, these pairings match one or more wines with each dish. Sometimes the wine is a symbiotic pairing that complements and enhances both primary and subtle flavors and textures in the food while maintaining a regional focus. Other times the wines are intended to create dissonance on your palate, exalting a single flavor or texture within the dish while contrasting with and contradicting the others. Our goal is to stimulate the palate and brain, to challenge while satisfying, to nourish the appetite yet continue to question. An example of this type of contrast is the double pairing (two wines served side by side with the same course): Fino sherry and *malvasia* Istriana served side by side with a high-acid citrus-based anchovy appetizer. Or a dry-style solera Marsala, called Vecchio Sanperi, served beside a Sicilian Nero d'Avola with braised short ribs in Barolo. Certainly a Marsala-type wine is not the expected pairing for this dish, yet a sip or two with the first bite and a last sip after the dish has been eaten (with the dry red table wine in between) will cause one to think about the experience of drinking fortified wines with savory foods.

—J.B.

CALF'S LIVER

with SOFT POLENTA *and* FIG VINAIGRETTE

SERVES 4

1½ pounds **CALF'S LIVER**, skin
    removed

1 cup **MILK**

½ pound **CAUL FAT**

Zest of 1 **ORANGE**

12 **SAGE** leaves

KOSHER SALT and freshly ground
    BLACK PEPPER

¾ cup quick-cooking **POLENTA**
    or yellow cornmeal

3 tablespoons extra-virgin
    OLIVE OIL

½ cup **FIG VINAIGRETTE**
    (page 240)

Wrapping these little packets in caul fat is a very traditional preparation for pork liver throughout Italy. I love the way it holds the flavor of the orange zest and sage right against the meat, even as the fat cooks away. If you cannot find caul fat, chop the zest and sage together finely and sprinkle over the dish at the end. The softer the better as far as the polenta goes, so add the cornmeal to the water slowly and use a little less rather than a little more. Don't worry, it will thicken.

1. Cut the liver into twelve 1½-inch cubes and place in a bowl with the milk. Soak for 1 hour.

2. Cut the caul fat into twelve 7-inch squares. Place ½ teaspoon orange zest and 1 sage leaf in the center of each square. Place a piece of liver atop the orange zest and season with salt and pepper. Wrap the liver up into little bundles and set aside.

3. Heat 4 cups of water to a boil in a medium saucepan and add the polenta in a thin stream, whisking constantly. When all of the polenta is added, season with 1 teaspoon salt, cook for 3 minutes, and set aside, covered in plastic.

4. In a nonstick pan, heat the oil over high heat until smoking. Cook the liver bundles in the pan for 4 to 5 minutes per side, working in batches if necessary to avoid overcrowding the pan.

5. Spoon ½ cup of polenta onto the center of each of four warmed dinner plates, place two pieces of liver on top, drizzle with the vinaigrette, and serve.

JOE'S VEAL CHOP

with CHANTERELLES, ROASTED GARLIC, *and* Campari

SERVES 4

2 whole heads of **GARLIC**

12 **RADISHES**

6 tablespoons extra-virgin
OLIVE OIL

KOSHER SALT and freshly ground
BLACK PEPPER

4 bone-in **VEAL CHOPS** from the
center of the loin, about
3 pounds

4 **SHALLOTS**, finely chopped

1 pound **CHANTERELLE**
mushrooms, halved if large

½ cup **CAMPARI**

1 tablespoon chopped fresh
THYME

My partner Joe had been serving veal chops at his first restaurant, Becco, for years when we opened Babbo. I had never had any use for them at my first restaurant because they seemed so expensive. Now that I charge more than fifteen dollars for a main course, they are a staple of the summer menu. For someone who wants big meat and maximum tenderness, a great veal chop is hard to beat. Be sure to ask your butcher for the loin chops, and make sure they are cut one chop per bone so they will be thick and stay nice and juicy.

1. Preheat the oven to 375°F. and preheat the grill or broiler.

2. Slice off the top half of each garlic head, exposing the cloves. Wrap the garlic heads individually in foil and roast in the oven for 1 hour, until soft. Allow to cool, then separate and peel the cloves. Set aside.

3. Meanwhile, toss the radishes in 2 tablespoons of the olive oil and season them with salt and pepper. Roast uncovered in the oven for 20 minutes.

4. Season the chops with salt and pepper. Brush the chops with 2 tablespoons of the olive oil and place on the hottest part of the grill. Cook to medium rare, 6 to 8 minutes per side.

5. Meanwhile, in a 10- to 12-inch sauté pan, heat the remaining 2 tablespoons of olive oil over high heat until smoking. Add the shallots and cook over medium heat for 3 minutes, then add the mushrooms and cook until golden brown and slightly crispy, about 8 minutes. Add the garlic cloves and the Campari and cook until reduced by half. Add the thyme and salt and pepper. Place a chop on each of four warmed dinner plates, pour the sauce over, garnish with the radishes, and serve immediately.

All vinaigrettes can be stored in an airtight container in the refrigerator for up to 1 week.

Cinzano Vinaigrette

Makes about 1 cup

1 cup Cinzano SWEET RED
    VERMOUTH
¼ cup RED WINE VINEGAR
1 tablespoon fresh ROSEMARY
    leaves
KOSHER SALT and freshly ground
    BLACK PEPPER, to taste
¾ cup extra-virgin OLIVE OIL

In a small nonreactive saucepan, combine the Cinzano, vinegar, and rosemary and bring to a boil. Reduce the heat to medium and cook until reduced to ¼ cup, about 10 minutes. Season with salt and pepper and set aside to cool. Once cooled, strain into a medium bowl, discarding the rosemary. Slowly whisk in the olive oil and adjust the seasoning if necessary.

Truffle Vinaigrette

Makes 1 cup

2 tablespoons canned BLACK
    TRUFFLES, thinly sliced
¼ cup SHERRY VINEGAR
⅔ cup extra-virgin OLIVE OIL
KOSHER SALT and freshly ground
    BLACK PEPPER

Combine the black truffles and vinegar in a medium bowl and whisk together to blend and break up the truffle pieces. Slowly whisk in the olive oil and season with salt and pepper.

Fig Vinaigrette

Makes 2¼ cups

2 cups dry FIGS, roughly chopped
2 cups red wine VINEGAR
1/4 cup fresh ORANGE JUICE
KOSHER SALT and freshly ground
    BLACK PEPPER, to taste

In a medium saucepan, combine the figs, vinegar, and ¼ cup water and bring to a boil. Reduce to a simmer, cover, and cook until the consistency is similar to fruit preserves. Remove from the heat and stir in the orange juice and salt and pepper.

Kumquat Vinaigrette

Makes 4 cups

2 cups RED WINE VINEGAR
¼ cup SUGAR
¼ cup HONEY
1½ teaspoons hot RED PEPPER
    FLAKES
1 teaspoon BLACK PEPPERCORNS
1½ teaspoons FENNEL SEEDS
¼ pound KUMQUATS, thinly sliced
1 cup extra-virgin OLIVE OIL
KOSHER SALT and freshly ground
    BLACK PEPPER, to taste

In a nonreactive, medium saucepan, combine the vinegar, sugar, honey, red pepper flakes, peppercorns, and fennel seeds and cook over medium-high heat until reduced by two thirds. Place the kumquats in a shallow casserole and pour the hot mixture over them. Let stand for 1 hour.

Place the mixture in a blender or food processor and process until pureed. Slowly drizzle in the olive oil to form an emulsion. Season with salt and pepper.

Blood Orange Vinaigrette

Makes 2½ cups

1 cup **BLOOD ORANGE JUICE**
1 tablespoon prepared **MUSTARD**
1 tablespoon **BLACK OLIVE PASTE**
1½ cups extra-virgin **OLIVE OIL**
KOSHER SALT and freshly ground
   BLACK PEPPER, to taste

In a small saucepan, cook the orange juice over high heat until reduced to ⅓ cup, about 5 minutes. Transfer to a bowl and whisk in the mustard and black olive paste until well combined. Whisk in the oil until emulsified. Adjust the seasoning with salt and pepper.

Pomegranate Vinaigrette

Makes 1 cup

¼ cup **POMEGRANATE MOLASSES**
   (available at Indian and Middle
   Eastern specialty stores)
4 tablespoons **RED WINE VINEGAR**
1 teaspoon **DIJON MUSTARD**
½ cup extra-virgin **OLIVE OIL**

Whisk all the ingredients together in a small bowl.

Bagna Cauda Vinaigrette

Makes 1 cup

¼ cup salt-packed **ANCHOVY** fillets,
   rinsed, soaked in water for 20
   minutes, and patted dry
¼ cup peeled **GARLIC** cloves
¾ cup extra-virgin **OLIVE OIL**
Juice of 1 **LEMON**
1 tablespoon **WHITE WINE VINEGAR**
1 tablespoon **HEAVY CREAM**
KOSHER SALT and freshly ground
   BLACK PEPPER, to taste

In a 12- to 14-inch sauté pan, simmer the anchovies, garlic, and oil over low heat for 30 minutes, or until the anchovies are falling apart. Remove the pan from the heat, strain out the solids, and chill the oil overnight in a covered container.

Place the chilled oil in a food processor. Add the lemon juice and vinegar and blend until smooth. Mix in the heavy cream and adjust the seasoning with salt and pepper.

Saffron Citronette

Makes 2½ cups

1 cup **CHAMPAGNE VINEGAR**
1 teaspoon Spanish **SAFFRON**
   THREADS
½ medium **RED ONION**, finely
   chopped
2 tablespoons **DIJON MUSTARD**
1 tablespoon **SUGAR**
Zest and juice of 1 **LEMON**
1 cup extra-virgin **OLIVE OIL**
KOSHER SALT and freshly ground
   BLACK PEPPER

In a small saucepan, combine the vinegar, saffron threads, and red onion and bring to a boil. Cook over high heat until reduced to one third of the original volume, remove from the heat, and stir in the mustard, sugar, and the lemon zest and juice. Place the mixture in the bowl of a food processor or blender and, with the motor running, slowly drizzle in the olive oil until the mixture is emulsified. Strain and season with salt and pepper.

OSSO BUCO

with TOASTED PINE NUT GREMOLATA

There is probably nothing more dramatic—or better to eat—than a whole veal shank. It's a showstopper; when we bring this out from the kitchen prior to carving it tableside, every head turns, and for good reason. The succulent meat and the delicious marrow are truly impressive.

1. Preheat the oven to 375°F.

2. Season the shank all over with salt and pepper. In a heavy-bottomed, 6- to 8-quart casserole, heat the olive oil until smoking. Place the shank in the pan and brown all over for 12 to 15 minutes, turning with long-handled tongs to sear every surface. Remove the shank and set aside.

3. Reduce the heat to medium, add the carrot, onion, celery, and thyme, and cook, stirring regularly, until golden brown and slightly softened, 8 to 10 minutes. Add the tomato sauce, chicken stock, and wine and bring to a boil. Return the shanks to the pan, making sure they are submerged at least halfway; if not, add more stock. Cover the pan with a tight-fitting lid of aluminum foil. Braise in the oven for 2 hours, then remove the cover and cook another 30 minutes, until the meat is nearly falling off the bone.

4. Just before the meat is done make the gremolata. In a small bowl, combine the parsley leaves, pine nuts, lemon zest, and horseradish and mix well by hand. Sprinkle with a little salt and pepper and set aside.

5. Remove the casserole from the oven and let stand for 10 minutes before carving the shank and dividing among four warmed dinner plates, topped with the gremolata.

SERVES 4

1 whole **VEAL SHANK**, 3 to 3½ pounds

KOSHER SALT and freshly ground **BLACK PEPPER**

6 tablespoons extra-virgin **OLIVE OIL**

1 medium **CARROT**, cut in ¼-inch-thick coins

1 small **SPANISH ONION**, diced

1 **CELERY** stalk, cut in ¼-inch slices

Leaves from 1 bunch of fresh **THYME**, chopped

2 cups **BASIC TOMATO SAUCE** (page 220)

2 cups **BROWN CHICKEN STOCK** (page 141)

2 cups dry **WHITE WINE**

Gremolata

Leaves from 1 bunch of flat-leaf **PARSLEY**

½ cup **PINE NUTS**, toasted at 400°F. for 2 minutes

Zest of 1 **LEMON**

¼ cup freshly grated **HORSERADISH**

KOSHER SALT and freshly ground **BLACK PEPPER**

VEAL BREAST

with SWEET ONIONS

SERVES 8

3 to 4 pounds **VEAL BREAST**, butterflied and pounded flat by your butcher

KOSHER SALT and freshly ground **BLACK PEPPER**

8 **GARLIC** cloves, peeled

¼ pound **PANCETTA**, very thinly sliced

2 tablespoons finely chopped fresh **ROSEMARY**

3 tablespoons finely chopped fresh **THYME**

3 tablespoons finely chopped flat-leaf **PARSLEY**

¼ cup plus 3 tablespoons extra-virgin **OLIVE OIL**

6 **SPANISH ONIONS**, cut into julienne

3 cups **BROWN CHICKEN STOCK** (page 141)

½ cup dry **WHITE WINE**

Veal breast cooked like this can also be chilled and sliced thin on the slicer to create a delicious antipasto or light main course with some salad on top. The abundance of onions and the absence of tomato in the braising liquid mimic the *carne alla genovesa* of classic Neapolitan cooking.

1. Preheat the oven to 375°F.

2. Lay the meat out on a cutting board and season with salt and pepper. Make 8 evenly spaced slits in the meat, each about 1 inch deep, and shove a garlic clove in each slit. Arrange the pancetta slices on the meat in an even layer. Sprinkle the pancetta evenly with the rosemary, 2 tablespoons of the thyme, and 2 tablespoons of the parsley. Roll the meat up like a jellyroll and tie it tightly with butcher's twine to seal in the stuffing.

3. In a Dutch oven, heat ¼ cup of the olive oil over high heat until smoking. Sear the veal roll in the oil until dark golden brown on all sides; this should take about 20 minutes total. Remove the meat from the pan and set aside. Add the onions and cook over medium-high heat until golden brown and softened, about 10 minutes. Stir in the chicken stock and wine, scraping the bottom of the pan with a wooden spoon to dislodge any browned meat or vegetable bits. Bring to a boil and return the veal to the pan. The liquid should come three quarters of the way up the sides of the meat; if not, add a bit of water. Cover tightly and cook in the oven for 2 hours, or until the meat is very tender.

4. Remove the veal from the braising liquid to a cutting board and allow to rest for 5 minutes. Slice the veal breast into 1-inch-thick medallions. Place one medallion on each of eight warmed dinner plates. Top with the sweet onions and a little of the juices, and sprinkle with the remaining tablespoon of thyme and parsley. Drizzle with the remaining 3 tablespoons of oil and serve immediately.

FENNEL–DUSTED
SWEETBREADS
WITH BACON AND ONIONS

To make sweetbreads truly crispy we dredge them in Wondra flour, which has a percentage of rye flour, in combination with ground roasted fennel seeds. The sweet and complex quince vinegar really adds a great level of acidity that cuts the rich creaminess of the sweetbreads. Sweetbreads are delicious and yet make many diners squeamish. Is there really a difference between eating a muscle and a gland?

1. Bring about 6 quarts of water to a boil and add the vinegar.

2. Rinse the sweetbreads for 5 to 10 minutes under cold running water. Immerse them in the boiling water and blanch for 10 minutes. Carefully remove them from the water and allow to cool.

3. Once the sweetbreads are cool enough to handle, peel off and discard the membrane. Place the sweetbreads in a nonreactive pot or bowl and add cold water to cover. Cover and refrigerate until ready to cook.

4. In a 12- to 14-inch sauté pan, warm 2 tablespoons of the olive oil over medium heat. Add the white onion rings and cook them over medium heat for 4 minutes, stirring often, allowing them to soften but not color. Add the red wine vinegar and sugar and continue sweating until the onions are soft and the liquid is syrupy, about 10 minutes. Add salt and pepper, remove from the heat, and set aside.

5. Preheat the oven to 400°F. Place the shallots in a small roasting pan, drizzle with 1 tablespoon of the olive oil, season with salt and pepper, and roast until very soft, about 30 minutes. Remove from the oven and set aside to cool.

6. In a 12- to 14-inch sauté pan, warm 1 tablespoon of the olive oil over medium heat. Add the red onions and sweat for 4 minutes, allowing the onions to soften but not color. Add the balsamic vinegar and continue to sweat until the onions are soft and the vinegar is reduced, about 10 minutes. Season with salt and pepper, remove from the heat, and set aside.

(continued on next page)

SERVES 4

¼ cup **WHITE VINEGAR**

2 pounds **VEAL SWEETBREADS**

7 tablespoons extra-virgin **OLIVE OIL**

2 medium **WHITE ONIONS**, cut crosswise into ¼-inch rings

¼ cup **RED WINE VINEGAR**

2 tablespoons **SUGAR**

KOSHER SALT and freshly ground **BLACK PEPPER**

4 **SHALLOTS**, peeled

2 medium **RED ONIONS**, quartered lengthwise

2 tablespoons **BALSAMIC VINEGAR**

8 **SCALLIONS**, cleaned and trimmed

½ cup Wondra **FLOUR**

¼ cup **FENNEL SEEDS**, toasted in a 400°F. oven for 4 minutes and ground to a fine powder in a coffee or spice grinder

ROASTED BACON LARDONS (page 248)

2 tablespoons **QUINCE VINEGAR** (page 221)

8 **FENNEL FRONDS**

Roasted Bacon Lardons

2 tablespoons SUGAR

1 tablespoon KOSHER SALT

¼ pound High Hopes BACON, or
    other good-quality, preferably
    organic, bacon, thickly sliced

Preheat the oven to 350°F.

Line a baking tray with parchment paper. Sprinkle the paper evenly with the sugar and salt.

Cut each strip of bacon in half. Place the bacon pieces side by side on the baking sheet, top with another sheet of parchment, and place another pan of the same size on top. Roast in the oven for 18 to 20 minutes, or until the bacon is well browned. Cool slightly, then cut the strips crosswise into thin batons.

7. Bring about 2 quarts of water to a boil. Set up an ice bath nearby. Blanch the scallions in the boiling water for 2 minutes. Remove from the water and immerse the scallions in the ice bath for 2 minutes. Drain on paper towels.

8. Combine the flour and powdered fennel in a small bowl. Divide the sweetbreads into four portions. Season each portion with salt and pepper and dust evenly with the flour and fennel mixture. Heat 2 tablespoons of the olive oil over high heat in a 12- to 14-inch sauté pan until smoking. Sauté the sweetbreads until crispy and golden brown, about 5 minutes on each side, working in batches to avoid overcrowding the pan. You will know that the sweetbreads are cooked through when the juices run clear.

9. Meanwhile, in a 12- to 14-inch sauté pan, heat the remaining tablespoon of olive oil just until smoking. Add the white onions, shallots, red onions, scallions, and bacon and toss over high heat to warm through, about 1 minute.

10. To assemble the dish, divide all the cooked onions and bacon evenly among four large, warmed bowls. Place one portion of sweetbreads in each bowl, drizzle with quince vinegar, top with two fennel fronds, and serve immediately.

GLASS PRIMING

Glass priming, the practice of swirling a small amount of wine in a glass and discarding it before pouring the wine, is a dining-room ritual in which form meets function to create orchestrated service art and one we observe conscientiously at Babbo. It is performed primarily to eliminate from the stemware any potential impurities that might mar the diner's wine-tasting experience. Glasses are always washed separately, then hand polished with a lint-free towel; the imperfections that may occur have nothing to do with the cleaning process. However, in the restaurant environment, glasses can capture a slight musty odor from the shelves they are stored on; cooking and food smells may be captured in the stem; and even chlorine residue from New York City tap water can adversely affect wine in a glass. But we readily admit that there is a bit of drama in the ritual as well.

I first saw glass priming while working in wine cellars in Italy. Wine makers, savvy tasters, and opinion leaders always primed a glass before using it, and swish, swirl, and pour was a prelude to any serious tasting. I began to take notice of the highly stylized technique with which some primers performed their task. The *avvinamento* was the preshow to the tasting. A dexterous glass handler could finish priming four glasses before the red stain that coated the interior of the stem dissolved. When the rinse of a particularly viscous high-alcohol wine is performed, the wine rinse coats the interior of the glass, creating a stained-glass effect. Now our servers use the technique of priming to announce to our customers both that we're serious about their enjoyment of the wine they've selected and that the pleasures of wine are not only in the glass.

—J.B.

grilled PORK TENDERLOIN
with JERUSALEM ARTICHOKES,
CIPOLLINE, AND CINZANO VINAIGRETTE

SERVES 4

½ cup dry **PORCINI** mushrooms, ground to a fine powder in a spice grinder

½ cup **BROWN SUGAR**

¼ cup hot **RED PEPPER FLAKES**

2 **PORK TENDERLOINS**, about 1½ pounds

1 pound **JERUSALEM ARTICHOKES**, scrubbed

2 cups **KOSHER SALT**, plus more to taste

½ pound **HARICOTS VERTS**, trimmed

¼ cup extra-virgin **OLIVE OIL**

1 pound cipolline or baby **ONIONS**, peeled

¼ pound **PANCETTA**, cut into ¼-inch cubes

½ cup **CINZANO VINAIGRETTE** (page 240)

Freshly ground **BLACK PEPPER**, to taste

We give these puppies a dry rub and then cook them 'til medium rare. The meat is virtually fat-free but has a succulence that is hard to match. Tie the beans into bundles with a blanched scallion green for a slightly fancy touch if you like.

1. In a small bowl, combine the porcini powder, brown sugar, and red pepper flakes and stir well. Apply the mixture as a rub to the pork tenderloins, using as much as possible to coat the meat evenly. Wrap the meat in plastic wrap and refrigerate for 12 to 24 hours.

2. Preheat the oven to 375°F.

3. Place the Jerusalem artichokes in a small roasting pan. Pour the 2 cups of salt over to cover and roast, uncovered, for 45 minutes, or until they are tender. Remove from the oven and, when cool enough to handle, slice ¼ inch thick. Set aside.

4. Bring 3 quarts of water to a boil and add 1 tablespoon of salt. Set up an ice bath nearby. Cook the haricots verts in the boiling water for 2 minutes, until somewhat tender but not cooked through. Remove and immediately refresh in the ice bath. Once cooled, drain and set aside.

5. Preheat the grill or broiler. Remove the pork from the refrigerator, brush off the excess rub, and place the tenderloins on the hottest part of the grill. Cook, turning every few minutes, for 13 to 15 minutes, or to an internal temperature of 130°F. on an instant-read thermometer. Allow the meat to rest for at least 5 minutes.

6. In a 12- to 14-inch sauté pan, heat the olive oil over medium-high heat. Add the onions and pancetta and cook slowly over medium heat until both are golden brown, or caramelized, about 10 minutes. Add the Jerusalem artichoke slices, the blanched haricots verts, and the Cinzano vinaigrette to the pan and toss over high heat for 3 minutes, so that the vinaigrette reduces and coats all the vegetables. Season with salt and pepper. Place some Jerusalem artichokes and onions on each plate and arrange the sliced pork on top. Pile the haricots verts over, drizzle with sauce, and serve.

PORK CHOP
milanese
with ARUGULA *and* TEARDROP TOMATOES

A spicy arugula and tomato salad accompaniment makes this a perfect light summer entrée that could easily serve as a one-dish meal, or a *piatto unico* as they are known in Italy. The trick is to cook the chops slowly over even, medium heat, so that they cook through without burning the bread-crumb crust.

1. Remove the bones from the pork chops. Using a meat mallet, carefully pound the pork chops until they are uniformly ¼ inch thick. Season the pork chops with salt and pepper. Dip each chop into the beaten eggs, allowing the excess to drip off. Dredge each chop in the bread crumbs and set on a plate.

2. In a 14- to 16-inch sauté pan, heat ¼ cup of the olive oil over medium heat until just smoking. Add the butter and allow it to foam for 10 to 15 seconds. Place the chops in the pan and cook until light golden brown on one side, about 5 minutes. Using tongs, carefully turn the chops and cook on the other side until light golden brown, about 5 more minutes. Add more oil if necessary, ½ tablespoon at a time, to avoid scorching the breading.

3. In a large bowl, combine the arugula and tomatoes. Add the remaining 3 tablespoons of olive oil, the lemon juice, and salt and pepper and toss to coat the greens.

4. Place one pork chop on each of four warmed dinner plates. Divide the arugula salad evenly among the plates, place a lemon wedge on each plate, and serve immediately.

SERVES 4

4 center-cut **PORK CHOPS**,
   1 inch thick

KOSHER SALT and freshly ground
   BLACK PEPPER

2 extra-large **EGGS**, lightly beaten

1 cup fresh **BREAD CRUMBS**,
   lightly toasted

¼ cup plus 3 tablespoons
   extra-virgin **OLIVE OIL**

1 tablespoon unsalted **BUTTER**

1 bunch of **ARUGULA**, stems
   removed

½ pound **TEARDROP TOMATOES**,
   halved lengthwise

1 tablespoon fresh **LEMON JUICE**

1 **LEMON**, cut into 4 wedges,
   seeds removed

grilled PORK CHOPS
with PEACHES *and* BALSAMIC VINEGAR

SERVES 4

4 8-ounce, double-cut PORK
    CHOPS

½ cup KOSHER SALT, plus more
    to taste

¼ cup SUGAR, plus more to taste

4 fresh PEACHES, halved and
    pitted

¼ cup extra-virgin OLIVE OIL

Freshly ground BLACK PEPPER

BROCCOLI RABE WITH GARLIC
    (page 204)

Best-quality BALSAMIC VINEGAR,
    for drizzling

Italians are not especially down with the notion of fruit on their meat, but they love the pairing of peaches with balsamic vinegar, so this dish is a convergence of two different ideas. The brining trick will change the way you think about pork chops by making them much more juicy and tender. Manodori is a brand of *aceto balsamico* that I like and use often. It's made by my friend Massimo Bottura of Ristorante La Francescana, one of Modena's best.

1. Place the chops in a nonreactive casserole. In a deep bowl, combine the salt, sugar, and about 2 quarts of water and mix well. Pour the mixture over the chops and let them brine in the refrigerator for 12 hours or overnight.

2. Prepare a grill or broiler.

3. Brush each pork chop and peach section with some of the olive oil, season both meat and fruit well with salt and pepper, and set the peaches aside. Place the pork chops on the hottest part of the grill and cook for 5 minutes on one side, then turn carefully with tongs and grill for 5 minutes on the other side.

4. While the second side cooks, place the peach halves on the grill and cook until lightly charred and juicy.

5. Place a mound of broccoli rabe on each plate and top with one pork chop. Garnish with the peach halves, drizzle both pork and peaches with the balsamic vinegar, and serve immediately.

PORK CHEEKS

in the FRIULIAN STYLE

SERVES 4

½ pound **PANCETTA** or slab bacon

½ cup extra-virgin **OLIVE OIL**

1 pound **PORK CHEEKS** or pork shoulder

KOSHER SALT and freshly ground **BLACK PEPPER**

2 **ONIONS**, one roughly chopped, the other finely chopped

1 **CARROT**, peeled and roughly chopped

4 **GARLIC** cloves, peeled

2 cups **DARK BEER**

1 cup **APPLE CIDER**

1 cup canned **TOMATOES**, crushed by hand

1 head of **SAVOY CABBAGE**, or green cabbage, cored and cut into 1-inch ribbons

2 tablespoons **SUGAR**

2 ounces **SPECK** or prosciutto, cut into ¼-inch cubes

½ cup **RED WINE VINEGAR**

PRUNE VINEGAR (page 221)

Although a true Friulian might not agree with the use of cider in the braise, this is my take on the flavors of Italy's northeast corner, birthplace of my partner Joe Bastianich's family. They may live here in the United States, but they do it in the style of the Friulians—at least on Sunday.

1. Preheat the oven to 375°F.

2. Cut half the pancetta into 2-inch batons and the rest in ¼-inch dice. Reserve separately.

3. In a Dutch oven, heat ¼ cup of the olive oil over high heat until smoking. Season the pork cheeks with salt and pepper and add them to the hot oil to sear on all sides, working in batches if necessary to avoid overcrowding the pan. Turn the cheeks until they are deep golden brown on all sides and remove to a plate lined with paper towels. Add the roughly chopped onion and carrot, the garlic cloves, and the pancetta batons and sauté until golden brown, about 7 minutes. Stir in the beer, cider, and tomatoes, scraping the bottom of the pan with a wooden spoon to dislodge any browned bits, and season with salt and pepper. Bring the mixture to a boil and return the pork cheeks to the pan. Cover and cook in the oven for 1 hour, or until the meat is fork-tender.

4. Meanwhile, in a 12- to 14-inch sauté pan, heat the diced pancetta over medium heat, to render out the fat and slightly brown the meat. Remove any excess fat (there should be no more than 2 tablespoons left in the pan) and add the finely chopped onion and the cabbage. Cook until the onion is softened and just light brown, about 7 minutes. Add the sugar, speck, and vinegar and bring to a boil. Cook for 5 to 6 minutes at a boil, then remove from the heat and keep warm.

5. Once the pork cheeks are cooked, remove from the oven and divide evenly, with some of their braising liquid, among four warmed dinner plates. Divide the cabbage evenly among the four plates, drizzle with some of the prune vinegar, and serve immediately.

Pork Cheeks

Your butcher should probably be able to find either pork cheeks or pork jowls for you. The cheek is the small muscular portion of the whole jowl, and is quite simple to remove. Do not discard the remainder; make it into *guanciale* (page 75). The cheek itself is very similar in texture to osso buco, as both are much-used muscles with fibrous, gelatinous textures that respond well to slow, moist cooking. My dad loves to use this sweet meat as the main ingredient for many of his *salumi*. If you really can't find the cheeks, an excellent substitute is pork shank meat or boneless pork shoulder.

GRILLED LAMB CHOPS
scottaditi
WITH BROCCOLI RABE PESTO

Rubbing the chops with mint and lemon and letting them sit overnight makes the flavor of the meat twice as intense. I love the bitter edge of the broccoli rabe pesto and the way it dances with the cumin-scented yogurt.

1. In the bowl of a food processor, combine the zest of 2 of the lemons (reserving the rest for garnish), the chopped mint, sugar, and 1 teaspoon each of salt and pepper. Process until the mixture has the texture of coarse sand. Rub each chop well with a small amount of the mixture, cover the chops, and set aside.

2. Bring about 3 quarts of water to a boil. Set up a large ice bath nearby. Blanch the broccoli rabe in the boiling water until tender, about 2 minutes. Drain, then immediately immerse in the ice bath. When completely cooled, drain the broccoli rabe again and pat dry. In the bowl of a food processor, combine the broccoli rabe, sliced garlic, capers, mustard, anchovy fillets, and chicken stock and pulse for 30 seconds. Slowly drizzle in the olive oil and pulse until emulsified to make a pesto. Do not overprocess.

3. Preheat the grill or broiler.

4. Grill the chops until medium rare, about 5 minutes on each side (internal temperature of about 130°F. on an instant-read thermometer).

5. Combine the yogurt and ground cumin and blend well. Add salt and pepper.

6. If necessary, reheat the broccoli rabe pesto gently over medium-high heat until warmed through, about 2 minutes.

7. To assemble the dish, place a mound of broccoli rabe pesto in the center of each of four warmed dinner plates. Drizzle the cumin yogurt, roasted red pepper jus, and parsley oil around the pesto. Tent 6 chops over the pesto on each plate, garnish with mint sprigs and the remaining lemon zest, and serve immediately.

SERVES 4

Zest of 3 LEMONS

¼ cup finely chopped MINT, plus 4 whole sprigs

1 tablespoon SUGAR

KOSHER SALT and freshly ground BLACK PEPPER

24 LAMB RIB CHOPS, about 4 pounds

1 bunch BROCCOLI RABE

4 GARLIC cloves, sliced

2 tablespoons CAPERS, rinsed and drained

1 tablespoon DIJON MUSTARD

2 ANCHOVY fillets, soaked in milk for 20 minutes and rinsed

1 cup BROWN CHICKEN STOCK (page 141)

¾ cup extra-virgin OLIVE OIL

1 cup GOAT MILK YOGURT, preferably Coach Farm brand

1 tablespoon CUMIN SEEDS, toasted in a 400°F. oven for 5 minutes and finely ground

¼ cup ROASTED RED PEPPER JUS (page 73)

1 cup PARSLEY OIL (page 50)

grilled venison

with SQUASH CAPONATA *and* TURRIGA

SERVES 4

1 VENISON LEG, cut into
    4 8-ounce portions

1 teaspoon JUNIPER BERRIES

2 sprigs of fresh ROSEMARY

4 GARLIC cloves, thinly sliced

2 cups plus 2 tablespoons
    extra-virgin OLIVE OIL

KOSHER SALT and freshly ground
    BLACK PEPPER

Caponata

4 tablespoons extra-virgin
    OLIVE OIL

1 RED ONION, diced

1 WHITE ONION, diced

1 FENNEL bulb, cut into
    ¼-inch cubes

1 large BUTTERNUT SQUASH,
    peeled and cut into ¼-inch
    cubes

1 large CELERY ROOT, peeled
    and cut into ¼-inch cubes

2 CELERY stalks, cut into
    ¼-inch cubes

½ cup CAPERS, rinsed and
    drained

Even though it has practically no fat whatsoever, venison has a full, sweet flavor. Because of its lack of fat, cooking this kind of meat beyond medium rare will dry it out, so be careful and use a meat thermometer; you do not want to go over an internal temperature of 120 to 125°F. The caponata would make an excellent appetizer, either all by itself or with a couple of buttons of fresh goat cheese and a small salad.

1. Place the venison in a nonreactive, shallow casserole. In a small bowl, combine the juniper berries, rosemary sprigs, sliced garlic, and 2 cups of the olive oil and pour over the venison. Cover the meat and refrigerate for at least 2 hours.

2. In the meantime, make the caponata. In a 12- to 14-inch sauté pan, heat 1 tablespoon of the olive oil until smoking. Add the red and white onions and the fennel and sauté until they are golden, about 5 minutes. Remove from the pan and transfer to a large mixing bowl. Sauté the butternut squash, celery root, and celery individually, adding 1 tablespoon of oil to the pan each time, and combining the sautéed ingredients in the bowl as you go. Gently stir in the capers, drained raisins, sweet garlic cloves, olives, pine nuts, roasted tomatoes, and bell peppers. In a small bowl, combine the cocoa powder, red pepper flakes, orange juice, thyme, and sugar and add to the cooked ingredients, stirring gently to combine.

3. To make the Turriga sauce, combine the red wine and sugar in a small nonreactive saucepan and bring to a boil over high heat. Lower the heat so that the wine simmers and cook until reduced by half to a syrupy consistency. Remove from the heat and add the cloves and cinnamon to taste.

½ cup **RAISINS**, steeped in
    ½ cup **RED WINE VINEGAR**
    for 2 hours or overnight

½ cup **SWEET GARLIC CLOVES**
    (page 133)

¼ cup pitted **BLACK OLIVES**

¼ cup pitted **GREEN OLIVES**

¼ cup **PINE NUTS**, toasted in a
    400°F. oven for 5 minutes

½ cup **OVEN-ROASTED**
    TOMATOES (page 146),
    chopped

1 **YELLOW BELL PEPPER**, roasted,
    seeded, and cut into julienne
    strips

1 **RED BELL PEPPER**, roasted,
    seeded, and cut into julienne
    strips

1 tablespoon **COCOA POWDER**

1 tablespoon hot **RED PEPPER**
    FLAKES

Juice of 1 **ORANGE**

1 tablespoon fresh **THYME** leaves

1½ teaspoons **SUGAR**

Turriga Sauce

2 cups **TURRIGA WINE**, or any
    other full-bodied red wine

½ cup **SUGAR**

Pinch of ground **CLOVES**

Pinch of ground **CINNAMON**

4. Preheat the grill. Remove the venison from the refrigerator, pat off the excess oil, and season with salt and pepper. Grill the venison pieces to medium rare, about 4 minutes on each side, or approximately 120°F. on an instant-read thermometer.

5. To assemble the dish, mound the caponata in the center of four warmed dinner plates. Slice the venison and arrange over the caponata. Drizzle each serving with the Turriga sauce and ½ tablespoon of extra-virgin olive oil and serve immediately.

PRE-DESSERTS AND CHEESE

The idea behind a cheese course and many of what we call pre-desserts is a delicious pause. At this point in the meal, the diner is approaching, but has not reached, fullness and may have a bit of wine from the main course left either in the bottle or in his glass. At this delicate moment we love to add a little something, a small course that is both an extension of the savory world and a hint of the sweet heaven to come.

At Babbo, pastry chef Gina DePalma spends a lot of time thinking and even worrying about this moment. Together, we have devised some cheese courses that will for many serve as desserts, due to the sweet or sweet-and-sour condiment that accompanies them. This might be a piquant cranberry mostarda (see page 234) or a delicate sour cherry compote to accompany goat cheese, but a simple drizzle of traditional vinegar over Parmigiano or warm chestnut honey over Pecorino can do the trick as well. You might pair a small portion of fresh berries from the market with a dollop of ricotta that has been sweetened or even flavored with a teaspoon of perfume-y rosewater.

We also have some less intensely sweet courses on the menu that can mingle quite mellifluously with the remainder of that dinner wine, without challenging the palate so much as to interfere with the decadence to follow. You can find recipes for these on the next few pages.

Even if the wine is finished, this pre-dessert is too much fun to skip, so we have suggested several wines (some outside the Italian peninsula) that make absolute sense at this stage of the game. The whole idea is to extend the pleasurable moments at the table and thus, extend life, because as every Italian knows, *Al tavolo, non s'invecchia mai*: "At the table, you simply never age."

OPPOSITE AND ABOVE:
Parmigiano-Reggiano

25
ITALIAN CHEESES
WE LOVE

Parmigiano-Reggiano
Pecorino di Pienza
Tuma d'la Paja
Brinata
Carnia
Gorgonzola Piccante

Asiago di Montegrappa
Robiola di Mondovi
Puzzone di Moena
Raviggiolo
Marzolino
Cacciotta Toscana
Ragusano
Canestrato
Stracchino
Toma del Maccagno
Robiola di Roccaverano
Castelmagno
Ambra di Talamello
Taleggio
Bitto
Montasio
Malga
Pecorino di Fossa
Caciocavallo

OPPOSITE: *Capriolo;* TOP: *Pecorino di Noce;* LEFT: *Coach Farm's Goat Cheese Pyramid with Black Pepper and Cranberry* Mostarda

ESPRESSO

TORRONE

with DRUNKEN CHERRIES

The combo of coffee and cherries had me worried at first, but the texture of the *torrone*—a nougat candy—makes the two work perfectly from the very first bite.

WINE SUGGESTION: Malvasia Passito by la Stoppa; *this passito has a beautiful balance of sweetness and acidity, with a lingering finish and honey–citrus tones.*

1. In the bowl of an electric mixer, whip the heavy cream to stiff peaks. Transfer the whipped cream to a large bowl, cover, and refrigerate. Line a large loaf pan with plastic wrap and set aside.

2. In a small saucepan, place the sugar, corn syrup, and honey. Clip a candy thermometer to the side of the pan and place over medium heat. While the sugar is cooking, place the egg whites and salt in the bowl of an electric mixer, and beat on low speed with the whip attachment.

3. As the sugar approaches softball stage (234° to 240°F.), increase the mixer speed so that the egg whites begin to form soft peaks. Cook the sugar to the softball stage. Remove from the heat. With the mixer on low, carefully drizzle the hot sugar syrup into the egg whites. Keep the stream of sugar against the side of the bowl to prevent the sugar from hitting the whip.

4. Increase the mixer speed to medium and beat until the bowl is cool to the touch. Add the espresso, coffee extract, and amaretto. Gently fold the egg white mixture into the whipped cream.

5. Spoon the mixture into the prepared pan and freeze until firm, at least 2 hours.

6. Place the cherries, vermouth, sugar, and vanilla bean in a nonreactive saucepan and bring to a boil. Lower the heat and simmer until the cherries are plump and have absorbed almost all of the liquid. Remove from the heat, discard the vanilla bean, and cool completely.

7. To serve, place a small scoop of espresso *torrone* in the center of a small plate. Ladle a spoonful of cherries and their liquid over the top.

SERVES 12

2¾ cups **HEAVY CREAM**

⅓ cup **SUGAR**

3 tablespoons **DARK CORN SYRUP**

½ cup **HONEY**

6 **EGG WHITES**

Pinch of **KOSHER SALT**

2 tablespoons **BREWED ESPRESSO**

1 tablespoon **PURE COFFEE EXTRACT**

2 teaspoons **AMARETTO**

Drunken Cherries

1 cup dried Michigan **CHERRIES**

1 cup **SWEET VERMOUTH**

3 tablespoons **SUGAR**

1 **VANILLA BEAN**, split and scraped

bigne

with HONEY MOUSSE

AND RED CURRANTS

SERVES 12 TO 14

Bigne

4 tablespoons (½ stick) unsalted **BUTTER**

Pinch of **KOSHER SALT**

2 teaspoons granulated **SUGAR**, plus more for sprinkling

¾ cup all-purpose **FLOUR**

3 **EGGS**

½ teaspoon pure **VANILLA EXTRACT**

¼ teaspoon **BAKING POWDER**

CONFECTIONERS' SUGAR, for dusting

Honey Mousse

3 **EGG YOLKS**

1 tablespoon **SUGAR**

½ cup **HONEY**

½ envelope powdered **GELATIN**

1 cup **HEAVY CREAM**

1 cup **MASCARPONE** cheese

1 pint fresh **RED CURRANTS**, stems removed

2 teaspoons **SUGAR**

This little mouthful captures nearly everything I love about good food. The harmonic convergence of the texture of the fritter *(bigne)*, the sweet and creamy mousse, and the acidity of the currants give me a Proustian jolt whenever I taste it.

WINE SUGGESTION: Dindarello by Macallan; *an elegant, medium-bodied moscato from the Veneto.*

1. To make the *bigne:* Combine ½ cup water, the butter, salt, and 2 teaspoons granulated sugar in a saucepan and bring to a boil. Dump in the flour all at once and stir vigorously to form a paste. Smash the paste against the bottom of the pan and gather it up repeatedly for 1 minute to cook the flour. Immediately transfer the mixture to the bowl of an electric mixer and beat on low speed with the paddle attachment to release some of the heat. Beat in the eggs, one at a time, until you have a very thick, shiny batter. Beat in the vanilla extract and baking powder. Chill the batter until it is somewhat firm, about 30 minutes.

2. Preheat the oven to 350°F.

3. Spoon the batter into a pastry bag fitted with a medium round tip. Pipe ¾-inch mounds, 1 inch apart, onto a parchment-lined baking sheet. Sprinkle the tops with granulated sugar. Bake for 12 to 15 minutes, or until they are golden brown and sound hollow when tapped. Remove the *bigne* from the oven and allow to cool on the baking sheet.

4. To make the mousse: In the bowl of an electric mixer, place the egg yolks and sugar and beat with a whip attachment until very thick and pale in color.

5. In a small saucepan, bring the honey to a boil. Remove from the heat and sprinkle with the gelatin; stir to dissolve. With the mixer on low speed, slowly drizzle the honey into the egg yolks. When all of the honey has been added, increase the mixer speed to medium and continue beating until the bowl is cool to the touch.

6. In another bowl, beat the heavy cream and mascarpone together to form stiff peaks. Gently fold the cooled honey mixture into the cream. Cover the mousse with plastic wrap and chill until firm, at least 4 hours.

7. Place the currants in a fine strainer. Rinse carefully under cold water and drain well. Place the currants in a bowl, sprinkle with the sugar, and set aside, stirring occasionally, until the sugar has dissolved and the currants have released some of their juices.

8. Slice the tops off the *bigne* and fill each with a spoonful of the honey mousse. (You can also place the mousse in a pastry bag and pipe it onto the *bigne*.) Replace the tops and dust lightly with confectioners' sugar. Serve with a spoonful of the sweetened currants.

PLUM & BAY LEAF
soup
with VANILLA YOGURT SORBETTO

SERVES 6

Sugar Syrup

6 cups **SUGAR**

5 cups **WATER**

Sorbetto

4 cups **YOGURT**, preferably Coach
 Farm goat yogurt

1 **VANILLA BEAN**

3 cups **SUGAR SYRUP**

Soup

8 ripe, dark-skinned red or
 purple **PLUMS**

2 cups **SUGAR SYRUP**

1 cup cold **WATER**

4 fresh **BAY LEAVES**

1 **VANILLA BEAN**, split lengthwise

¾ cup **MARZEMINO DOLCE**, a
 slightly sweet, sparkling red
 dessert wine

Juice of 1 **LEMON**

This is the reason why all other fruit soups exist and the best I've ever had. One taste of the dazzling tango between the cool, creamy yet acidic sorbetto and the exotically scented plum broth and you will know infinity. This recipe is made in three steps, beginning with the sugar syrup, which needs to cool before proceeding. Allow enough time to freeze the gelato before making the plum soup.

WINE SUGGESTION: Moscato d'Asti from Sarraco; *a sparkling moscato with tones of citrus, apple, and honey.*

1. To make the syrup: Combine the sugar and water in a medium saucepan and bring to a boil. Cook until the sugar is completely dissolved, then remove from the heat. Cool completely. You should have 5 cups.

2. To make the sorbetto: Place the yogurt in a blender. Split the vanilla bean and scrape the seeds into the blender. Blend until smooth, then strain through a fine sieve into a bowl. Stir in the 3 cups of sugar syrup. Transfer to an ice-cream maker and freeze according to the manufacturer's instructions.

3. To make the soup: Slice 6 of the plums into eighths, discarding the pits, and place in a medium saucepan. Add the 2 cups of sugar syrup, the water, bay leaves, and vanilla bean. Bring to a boil over low heat, then simmer gently for 5 minutes. Cool to room temperature.

4. Strain the soup through a fine sieve, discarding the plums and bay leaves. (Reserve the vanilla bean for future use.) Refrigerate the soup until completely chilled. Just before serving, add the Marzemino Dolce and lemon juice.

5. When ready to serve, thinly slice the remaining two plums and distribute them among six chilled soup bowls. Ladle in the plum soup. Top each serving with three small scoops of sorbetto.

goat cheese TORTA

This is the Babbo version of the really fancy cheese tortas the mythic Peck company of Milan has been perfecting for the last thirty years. Ours, of course, uses spectacular fresh goat cheese produced by my wife Susi's family at Coach Farm.

WINE SUGGESTION: *Gambellara Recioto by La Biancara; a semi-sweet white wine made in the Recioto style; nutty and complex.*

1. Grease an 8-inch square pan with extra-virgin olive oil.

2. In the bowl of an electric mixer, beat the butter until very smooth. Add the goat cheese in batches, making sure that there are no lumps of butter. Beat in the pepper and 1 teaspoon of the salt.

3. Combine the mint and parsley leaves, pine nuts, sugar, and the remaining ¼ teaspoon of salt in a blender. Add the olive oil and blend until the nuts are pulverized and the pesto is smooth.

4. Divide the goat cheese mixture into three equal portions. Using an offset spatula, carefully spread one portion of the goat cheese evenly over the bottom of the pan. Spread the pesto in an even layer over the cheese. Carefully layer another portion of the cheese over the pesto, using your fingers to pat the cheese gently into place.

5. Spread the jam evenly over the second cheese layer. Pat the remaining cheese mixture over the jam in an even layer. Cover the torta with plastic wrap and chill until firm.

6. To serve, cut the torta in squares and drizzle with best-quality extra-virgin olive oil and sprinkle with freshly ground black pepper.

SERVES 10 TO 12

¾ cup (1½ sticks) unsalted **BUTTER**, softened

2 pounds fresh **GOAT CHEESE**, preferably Coach Farm brand

¾ teaspoon freshly ground **BLACK PEPPER**, plus more for sprinkling

1¼ teaspoons **KOSHER SALT**

¾ cup packed fresh **MINT** leaves

½ cup packed fresh **PARSLEY** leaves

⅓ cup toasted **PINE NUTS**

1 teaspoon **SUGAR**

¾ cup extra-virgin **OLIVE OIL**

1½ cups **FIG JAM** or preserves

Best-quality extra-virgin **OLIVE OIL**, for drizzling

GORGONZOLA
with MINT, WALNUTS,
AND SOUR CHERRY JAM

This is a perfect example of a graceful segue between savory and sweet courses. The symbiosis among the four main ingredients is nearly magical.

WINE SUGGESTION: Recioto della Valpolicella by Allegrini; *a full-bodied, sweet red wine that resembles a port.*

1. Place the sour cherries and sugar in a medium nonreactive saucepan over medium heat and cook until the cherries have softened completely and released their juices, 8 to 10 minutes. Continue cooking until the juices have reduced and thickened. Cool completely, then refrigerate.

2. Using a sharp knife, chop the mint leaves, fine. Place the gorgonzola in a bowl. Using a fork, mash the gorgonzola until it is creamy and smooth. Add ½ cup of the chopped walnuts and all of the chopped mint and mix until completely incorporated. Refrigerate for 30 minutes, or until somewhat firm.

3. Roll the gorgonzola mixture into eight 1-inch balls, and roll the balls in the remaining chopped walnuts to coat completely. Refrigerate until ready to serve.

4. Serve each gorgonzola ball with a spoonful of sour cherry jam.

SERVES 8

1 pound **SOUR CHERRIES**, pitted

1¼ cups **SUGAR**

1 tightly packed cup of fresh **MINT** leaves

1 cup **GORGONZOLA**, cut into small pieces

1½ cups toasted **WALNUT** pieces, finely chopped

CHAPTER FIVE

Dolci

Having spent my formative years in Washington State, the fruit basket of the west, my favorite desserts growing up were not likely to be anything along the lines of *gâteau opéra* or Viennese linzertorte. My early memories of sweetness almost always derived from the bounty of the soil, with little interference from the cook. To a large extent, I feel the same way today. What I love about good desserts in Italy is how they are always appropriate to their surroundings. In a fancy ristorante I may be served an exquisite panna cotta scented with a hint of seasonal citrus; a casual trattoria may offer the traditional *sbrisolona*, or crumbly cake, with a glass of local dessert wine. Both are on the menu at Babbo.

When I first sat down with pastry chef Gina DePalma, one of the first things she stressed about her approach to dessert-making was her hope that we could bypass the ooey-gooey school of desserts. This said a lot about her confidence and was exactly what I wanted to hear; she has been an integral member of the Babbo team ever since.

Since then she has developed an incredible series of thoughtful and well-executed desserts that are entirely reflective of her style and ideology. The following are her recipes, which, like everything else we serve at Babbo, are inspired by the Italian way of thinking, eating, and dreaming, yet are unlike anything you have ever eaten there.

chocolate HAZELNUT CAKES

This is what Nutella would taste like in cake form; it was the first recipe Gina created for our original dessert menu.

SERVES 12

8 ounces **BITTERSWEET CHOCOLATE**

2 ounces unsweetened **CHOCOLATE**

4 ounces toasted **HAZELNUTS**

3 tablespoons **CONFECTIONERS' SUGAR**

¼ cup premium-quality Dutch-process **COCOA POWDER**

¾ cup (1½ sticks) unsalted **BUTTER**, softened

¾ cup plus 5 tablespoons granulated **SUGAR**

⅓ cup unsweetened **HAZELNUT PASTE** (available at specialty stores)

6 **EGGS**, separated

2 teaspoons strong **BREWED ESPRESSO**, cooled completely

2 teaspoons **FRANGELICO** (hazelnut liqueur)

2 teaspoons pure **VANILLA EXTRACT**

1. Preheat the oven to 325°F. Spray twelve 3-inch cake molds or one 9-inch springform pan lightly with nonstick cooking spray and set aside.

2. Fill the bottom of a double boiler one-third full with water and bring to a simmer over medium-low heat. Place a medium stainless-steel bowl over the water and melt the chocolates together, stirring constantly. Once melted, set aside to cool.

3. In the bowl of a food processor, pulse the hazelnuts with the confectioners' sugar and cocoa to form a fine, sand-like mixture.

4. In an electric mixer, beat the butter and ¾ cup of the granulated sugar until very light and fluffy. Beat in the hazelnut paste, scraping down the sides of the bowl with a spatula, then beat in the egg yolks, one at a time. Beat in the espresso, Frangelico, and vanilla extract, followed by the melted chocolate. Fold in the nut mixture.

5. In a separate mixing bowl, use the whip attachment to beat the egg whites until foamy. Gradually add the remaining 5 tablespoons of sugar and continue beating until soft peaks form. Using a rubber spatula, gently fold the egg whites into the cake batter. Place the prepared molds on a greased baking sheet and divide the batter evenly among them.

6. Bake the cakes just until they puff and crack slightly, about 14 minutes for the cake molds (45 to 50 minutes if using the springform pan). Remove from the oven and cool in the molds on a wire rack. When the cakes are almost completely cool, gently remove the molds, then chill in the refrigerator until firm. The cakes will last for up to 1 week, refrigerated in an airtight container.

MAPLE AND MASCARPONE
CHEESECAKE

SERVES 8

2 cups dark amber **MAPLE SYRUP**

½ cup **HEAVY CREAM**

1 tablespoon unsalted **BUTTER**

½ cup **RAW** or **TURBINADO**
   SUGAR

1½ cups **CREAM CHEESE**

⅓ cup granulated **SUGAR**

3 **EGGS**

1½ teaspoons pure **VANILLA**
   EXTRACT

1½ pounds **MASCARPONE** cheese

WALNUT SHORTBREAD
   (page 319)

This is without a doubt one of our all-time best-selling desserts. I must admit that at first I was very skeptical about the flavor combination, but it blows me out of the water to this day.

1. Place the maple syrup in a large saucepan and bring to a boil. (It is important to use a large saucepan because the syrup will bubble up a great deal.) Lower the heat so that the syrup simmers gently, and cook until reduced by two thirds, 30 to 35 minutes. Remove from the heat and stir in the heavy cream. Cool to room temperature.

2. Preheat the oven to 325°F.

3. Use the butter to grease eight 4-ounce ramekins. Sprinkle the raw sugar into the ramekins, completely coating the bottom and sides; tap out the excess. Place the ramekins in a baking dish large enough to fit them with at least an inch of space between each.

4. In the bowl of an electric mixer, beat the cream cheese and granulated sugar together until very soft and creamy. Scrape down the sides, then beat in the eggs one at a time, scraping down the sides after each addition. Beat in the vanilla extract. Add the mascarpone and beat only until the lumps disappear; do not overbeat, or the batter will break. Measure out ½ cup of the maple–cream mixture and beat it into the cheese mixture. Reserve the remaining maple–cream mixture.

5. Pour the batter into the prepared ramekins, filling them almost to the top, and arrange in the baking dish. Add enough hot water to the baking dish to come one third of the way up the sides of the ramekins. Cover the entire baking dish with aluminum foil and bake for 25 to 30 minutes, or until the cheesecakes begin to look set in the middle. Lower the oven temperature to 300°F. and continue baking for another 10 minutes, then remove the foil and bake for an additional 10 minutes uncovered. The cheesecakes will be

done when they puff slightly and are no longer liquid in the center. Carefully remove the baking dish from the oven and allow the cheesecakes to cool in the water bath for 30 minutes, then carefully remove and continue to cool to room temperature. Chill for at least 8 hours (preferably overnight).

6. To serve, run the tip of a knife along the top of each ramekin and shake gently to unmold onto a plate. Drizzle with some of the reserved maple reduction and serve with walnut shortbread.

lemon GOAT CHEESE CAKE

SERVES 8

1¼ cups plus 2 tablespoons
SUGAR, plus more for the pan

6 EGGS, separated

1½ pounds fresh GOAT CHEESE,
preferably from Coach Farm

2 tablespoons LIGHT RUM

3 tablespoons unbleached,
all-purpose FLOUR

Grated zest of 2 LEMONS

1 tablespoon plus ¼ cup fresh
LEMON JUICE

2 teaspoons pure VANILLA
EXTRACT

¼ teaspoon KOSHER SALT

2 pints fresh RASPBERRIES

Goat cheese in a dessert may scare off some timid diners but it's great. The lemon syrup would make gym shoes taste delicious.

1. Preheat the oven to 325°F. Spray an 8-inch springform pan with nonstick cooking spray and sprinkle the bottom and sides with sugar, shaking out the excess.

2. In the bowl of an electric mixer, beat the egg yolks and 1 cup of the sugar until the yolks are very pale. Slowly beat in the goat cheese, 1 cup at a time. Add the rum, flour, lemon zest, 1 tablespoon of the lemon juice, the vanilla, and salt and beat until creamy.

3. In another bowl, whisk the egg whites with a pinch of salt until foamy. Slowly add 2 tablespoons of the sugar and continue whisking until you have a soft-peaked meringue. Working in two batches, gently fold the whites into the cheese mixture.

4. Pour the batter into the prepared pan. Place the pan in a baking dish large enough to contain it comfortably. Pour enough hot water into the baking dish to reach approximately 1 inch up the sides of the pan. Cover the entire baking dish with aluminum foil and carefully place it on the middle rack of the oven.

5. Bake for 35 to 40 minutes, or until the cake begins to rise slightly and is somewhat set in the middle. Remove the foil and bake for an additional 10 minutes, or until the cake is completely set. Remove the cake from the oven and allow it to cool in the baking dish for several minutes.

6. Meanwhile, combine the remaining ¼ cup of lemon juice and ¼ cup of sugar in a small saucepan and bring to a boil. Boil rapidly for 1 minute, or until the mixture has thickened slightly. Remove from the heat and set aside to cool.

7. When the cake has cooled slightly, remove the pan from the baking dish. Refrigerate the cake until completely chilled. Remove the sides of the springform pan, then spoon the lemon syrup over the cake to glaze. Cut into wedges and serve with the berries.

OLIVE OIL AND
fresh rosemary cake

This is a classic example of what Italians really eat in the late afternoon, perhaps with a glass of vin santo. Gina serves it with braised fresh figs and a rosemary sorbet, but it would also be delicious with something simpler, like some bitter orange marmalade.

1. Preheat the oven to 325°F. Spray a 10-inch loaf pan with nonstick cooking spray and set aside.

2. In the bowl of an electric mixer, use the whip attachment to beat the eggs for 30 seconds. Add the sugar and continue to beat until the mixture is very foamy and pale in color. With the mixer running, slowly drizzle in the olive oil. Using a spatula, gently fold the rosemary into the batter.

3. In a separate bowl, whisk together the flour, baking powder, and salt. With the mixer on low speed, gradually add the dry ingredients to the egg mixture. Pour the batter into the prepared pan.

4. Bake for 45 to 50 minutes, rotating the pan halfway through for even color. The cake is done when it is golden brown, springs back when touched, and a skewer inserted in the center comes out clean. Allow the cake to cool briefly in the pan, then tip out onto a cake rack to continue cooling.

SERVES 8 TO 10

4 **EGGS**

¾ cup **SUGAR**

⅔ cup extra-virgin **OLIVE OIL**

2 tablespoons finely chopped fresh **ROSEMARY** leaves

1½ cups unbleached, all-purpose **FLOUR**

1 tablespoon **BAKING POWDER**

½ teaspoon **KOSHER SALT**

SEMOLINA
budino
with RHUBARB *and* MINT *marmellata*

SERVES 8

1 tablespoon unsalted **BUTTER**, softened

½ cup plus ¾ cup plus 4 tablespoons **SUGAR**, plus more for sprinkling

3 **RHUBARB** stalks, cut into ¼-inch slices

2 **VANILLA BEANS**, split lengthwise

4 **EGGS**, separated

½ teaspoon pure **VANILLA EXTRACT**

½ cup (1 stick) sweet unsalted **BUTTER**, melted and cooled

¾ cup whole **MILK**

¼ cup semolina **FLOUR**

⅓ cup bleached cake **FLOUR**

Pinch of **KOSHER SALT**

RHUBARB AND MINT *MARMELLATA* (see sidebar)

1 cup **HEAVY CREAM**

These succulent little puppies are delicious and can be made and eaten plain. Rhubarb is on my list of nostalgic childhood memories, so I always go wild when this is on the menu in late spring.

1. Use the butter to grease eight 4-ounce ramekins. Sprinkle them with granulated sugar to evenly coat the interior and tap out the excess. Place the ramekins in a baking dish large enough to fit them with at least an inch of space between each ramekin.

2. In a small saucepan, stir together the sliced rhubarb and ½ cup of the sugar. With the tip of a paring knife, scrape the insides of 1 vanilla bean into the saucepan. Cook over medium heat, stirring often, until the rhubarb is soft, about 15 minutes. Cool completely.

3. In the bowl of an electric mixer, combine the egg yolks and ¾ cup of the sugar. Beat until very light yellow. Add the vanilla extract and the melted butter, then beat in the milk. In a small bowl, combine the semolina and cake flours, then add them gradually to the egg mixture, beating lightly. Fold in the rhubarb with a rubber spatula. Beat or whip the egg whites with a pinch of salt until foamy. Gradually beat in 2 tablespoons of the sugar and whip until soft peaks form. Gently fold the egg whites into the batter.

4. Divide the batter among the ramekins. Add enough hot water to the baking dish to come one third of the way up the sides of the ramekins. Cover the entire baking dish with aluminum foil. Bake for 25 to 30 minutes, or until the *budini* begin to puff slightly. Remove the foil and continue to bake for another 10 to 15 minutes, or until slightly pale golden and set. Remove from the oven and transfer to a rack to cool.

5. While the *budini* bake, make the *marmellata:* In a large saucepan, mix together the rhubarb and sugar. Cook over low heat, stirring the mixture to dissolve the sugar as the rhubarb begins to soften and release its juices. Scrape the insides of the vanilla bean into the pan, add the mint, and continue to stir. Cook the mixture until the rhubarb is tender but still holds its shape, about 10 minutes. Remove from the heat and immediately transfer the *marmel-*

Rhubarb and Mint Marmellata

8 **RHUBARB** stalks, finely
   chopped

1½ cups **SUGAR**

1 **VANILLA BEAN**, split lengthwise

3 or 4 large **MINT** sprigs

lata to a shallow dish to facilitate cooling. When completely cool, discard the mint.

6. Combine the cream and the scraped insides of the remaining vanilla bean in a chilled mixing bowl. Whip on medium speed until soft peaks form. Gradually add the remaining 2 tablespoons of sugar and continue to whip until the cream holds its shape.

7. Unmold each *budino* from its ramekin and top with some of the *marmellata*. Serve with a dollop of the vanilla whipped cream.

HAZELNUT CAKE

Sometimes a recipe is so simple that I wonder what everyone is doing with the pages and pages of recipes they have copied from magazines and books. This is one of the simplest cakes I have ever seen made, and the flavor is pure Italy.

1. Preheat the oven to 325°F. Spray an 8-inch round cake pan with nonstick cooking spray and dust with flour, shaking off the excess.

2. In the bowl of a food processor, pulse the hazelnuts and ¼ cup of the flour until the nuts are finely ground.

3. In the bowl of an electric mixer, cream together the butter and sugar until very light. Beat in the hazelnut paste, then add the eggs one at a time. Scrape down the sides with a rubber spatula and beat in the vanilla extract. In a small bowl, mix together the nut-and-flour mixture, the remaining cup of flour, the salt, and baking powder. Beat the dry ingredients into the batter.

4. Spread the batter evenly in the cake pan. Bake for 25 to 30 minutes, or until the cake springs back lightly when touched and a cake tester inserted in the center comes out clean. Allow the cake to cool in the pan for 10 minutes, then gently remove from the pan. When cool, sift cocoa powder over the top.

SERVES 8

1 cup skinned HAZELNUTS, toasted in a 350°F. oven for 5 minutes

1¼ cups unbleached, all-purpose FLOUR, plus more for the pan

10 tablespoons (1¼ sticks) unsalted BUTTER, softened

¾ cup SUGAR

¼ cup HAZELNUT PASTE (available at specialty stores)

3 EGGS

1 teaspoon pure VANILLA EXTRACT

½ teaspoon KOSHER SALT

1 teaspoon BAKING POWDER

COCOA POWDER, for dusting

CRUMBLY CAKE

MODENESE

WITH FIGS

and SWEET BLACK PEPPER RICOTTA

SERVES 8 TO 12

Streusel

½ cup **PINE NUTS**

2 tablespoons **LIGHT BROWN SUGAR**, packed

¼ cup granulated **SUGAR**

¾ cup unbleached, all-purpose **FLOUR**

¼ cup (½ stick) unsalted **BUTTER**, melted and cooled

¾ cup **PINE NUTS**

1 cup plus 2 tablespoons all-purpose **FLOUR**

1 teaspoon **KOSHER SALT**

1 cup semolina **FLOUR**

½ teaspoon **BAKING POWDER**

¼ cup **LIGHT BROWN SUGAR**, packed

½ cup plus 2 tablespoons granulated **SUGAR**

¾ cup (1½ sticks) unsalted **BUTTER**, chilled and cut into cubes

3 **EGGS**

3 tablespoons extra-virgin **OLIVE OIL**

Finely grated zest of 1 **LEMON**

1½ teaspoons pure **VANILLA EXTRACT**

Here is the Babbo version of an Italian *sbrisolona,* another great example of the kind of cake Italians like to snack on all afternoon. The presence of salt and pepper in desserts is very stylish now, but this sweetened ricotta topping is no gimmick.

1. To make the streusel: Combine the pine nuts, sugars, and flour and pulse to combine. Add the melted butter and pulse until the mixture is combined and forms pea-size crumbs. Set aside.

2. Preheat the oven to 325°F. Spray a 9-inch springform pan with nonstick cooking spray.

3. Spread the ¾ cup of pine nuts evenly onto a baking sheet and toast in the oven until light golden brown, approximately 10 minutes. When the pine nuts have cooled, place them in the bowl of a food processor along with the flour, salt, semolina, baking powder, light brown sugar, and ½ cup of the granulated sugar and pulse to combine. Add the cold butter cubes and pulse until the butter has dispersed and the mixture is finely textured.

4. In a small bowl, combine the eggs, olive oil, lemon zest, and vanilla. Add this mixture to the pine nut mixture and pulse to combine, then process for about 30 seconds to completely emulsify the batter. Spread the batter evenly in the prepared pan and sprinkle evenly with the streusel.

5. Bake the cake for 30 to 35 minutes, or until it is golden brown and a cake tester inserted in the center comes out clean. Cool for 10 minutes, then remove the sides of the pan and allow the cake to cool completely.

6. Trim the figs and halve lengthwise. In a medium saucepan, combine the vin santo, honey, and the remaining 2 tablespoons of sugar. Bring to a boil over high heat and cook until reduced slightly, about 5 minutes, then add the figs. Toss with the hot syrup, and cook for about 1 minute, or until they are lightly coated. Remove from the heat and cool.

8 small **BLACK MISSION FIGS**

¼ cup **VIN SANTO**

¼ cup **HONEY**

Sweet Black Pepper Ricotta

1 cup **HEAVY CREAM**

2 tablespoons **SUGAR**

1¼ cups fresh **RICOTTA**

1 teaspoon freshly ground **BLACK PEPPER**

7. To make the pepper ricotta: In a chilled mixing bowl, whip the heavy cream and sugar until soft peaks form. Add the ricotta and black pepper and whip until stiff. Chill until ready to serve.

8. Cut the cake into wedges and serve each with a dollop of ricotta and one or two fig halves.

pumpkin cake

with TOASTED PINE NUTS
and OLIVE OIL GELATO

SERVES 12

Cake

¼ cup **PINE NUTS**

½ cup golden **RAISINS**

¼ cup boiling **WATER**

2 tablespoons **BRANDY** or **GRAPPA**

1 cup cake **FLOUR**

¼ teaspoon **KOSHER SALT**

1 teaspoon **BAKING SODA**

2 **EGGS**

¾ cup **LIGHT BROWN SUGAR**, packed

1 tablespoon finely chopped fresh **ROSEMARY** leaves

¾ cup extra-virgin **OLIVE OIL**

1 cup canned **PUMPKIN PUREE**

Gelato

6 **EGG YOLKS**

1 cup **SUGAR**

¾ cup extra-virgin **OLIVE OIL**

3 cups **MILK**

1 cup **HEAVY CREAM**

The olive oil gelato perplexed many of our wait staff—and guests—at first, but one bite and you will be slayed.

1. To make the cake: Preheat the oven to 325°F. Lightly spray twelve 3-inch individual cake molds or a 9-inch square cake pan with nonstick cooking spray.

2. Spread the pine nuts on a baking sheet and toast in the oven until light golden brown, about 10 minutes. Allow to cool. Place the raisins in a bowl and pour the boiling water and brandy or grappa over them. Set the raisins aside to plump.

3. In a medium bowl, stir together the flour, salt, and baking soda. In the bowl of an electric mixer, beat the eggs and brown sugar until very light. Add the rosemary leaves and then, with the mixer running, slowly beat in the olive oil. Beat in the dry ingredients, scraping down the sides of the bowl. Add the pumpkin and beat until smooth. Stir in the drained raisins and pine nuts.

4. Pour the batter into the prepared pan or pans and bake until golden brown, 35 to 40 minutes for the single pan or 25 to 30 minutes for the individual pans. Allow the cakes to cool slightly, then run a knife around the outside of each cake and gently remove the molds.

5. To make the gelato: Combine the egg yolks and sugar in the bowl of an electric mixer. Use the whip attachment to beat them for 5 minutes on medium speed, or until the mixture is thick and very pale in color and forms a ribbon when the whip is lifted. Continue beating and drizzle in the olive oil; beat for 2 more minutes. Add the milk and cream and continue to beat until all ingredients are combined.

6. Freeze the mixture in a gelato machine according to the manufacturer's instructions.

7. When ready to serve, cut the cake into wedges if baked in a single pan; otherwise, place an individual cake on each dessert plate and serve with a scoop of gelato alongside.

CASTAGNACCIO

Gina developed this recipe after a couple of conversations about the rich tradition of chestnut cookery in the hills between Bologna and Florence. Generally *castagnaccio* is a very acquired taste, but this one is very accessible.

1. Preheat the oven to 350°F. Brush the inside of a 9-inch springform pan with olive oil.

2. Spread the walnuts and pine nuts on a baking sheet and toast for 5 minutes, or until fragrant. Set aside to cool and reduce the oven temperature to 300°F.

3. Using a fine-mesh sieve, sift the chestnut flour into a large mixing bowl to remove any lumps. Stir in the all-purpose flour, salt, baking powder, cocoa, and sugars. Make a well in the center of the dry ingredients.

4. In a small bowl, whisk together the eggs, chestnut honey, and olive oil. Pour the wet ingredients into the well. Using your hands, gradually incorporate the dry ingredients into the wet ingredients. You will have a very sticky batter. Add the cherries, raisins, orange zest, walnuts, and pine nuts and mix well.

5. Using damp hands, evenly pat the mixture into the prepared pan. Bake for 20 minutes, rotating the cake pan 180 degrees after 10 minutes. The cake will puff slightly when done.

6. Meanwhile, combine the ingredients for the honey syrup in a small saucepan and bring to a boil. Simmer for 2 minutes and remove from heat.

7. Remove the cake from the oven and immediately brush with some of the honey syrup. Allow the cake to cool and remove the sides of the springform pan. Brush the cake with the remaining syrup. Just before serving, lightly dust the top of the cake with confectioners' sugar. Cut the cake into wedges and serve.

SERVES 8 TO 12

1 cup chopped WALNUTS

1/3 cup PINE NUTS

2 1/3 cups CHESTNUT FLOUR

2 tablespoons unbleached, all-purpose FLOUR

1 teaspoon KOSHER SALT

1 tablespoon BAKING POWDER

1 tablespoon Dutch-process COCOA POWDER

1/4 cup plus 2 tablespoons granulated SUGAR

1/4 cup LIGHT BROWN SUGAR, packed

3 EGGS

1/4 cup CHESTNUT HONEY

1/4 cup extra-virgin OLIVE OIL

3/4 cup DRIED CHERRIES

1/2 cup golden RAISINS

1/2 cup chopped candied ORANGE ZEST

Honey Syrup

1/2 cup CHESTNUT HONEY

1/4 cup VIN SANTO

2-inch strip of fresh ORANGE ZEST

CONFECTIONERS' SUGAR, for dusting

saffron
PANNA COTTA

The faintly metallic tang of saffron works beautifully in this ethereal flavor poem. Gina keeps this on the menu year round, changing its dance partner seasonally. Some of my faves are peaches and grapefruit.

1. In a medium saucepan, combine the cream, sugar, lemon or orange zest, and saffron threads. Bring the mixture to a boil, stirring gently, then remove from the heat. Let the mixture rest for 10 minutes to develop the flavor and color.

2. Stir the powdered gelatin into the cream mixture until it dissolves. Strain the mixture through a fine-meshed sieve, then stir in the milk.

3. Pour the mixture into chilled dessert cups or wine glasses. If desired, the panna cotta may be unmolded by running the tip of a knife around the edge of the cup, dipping the cup quickly into hot water, and gently shaking the custard onto a plate. Serve with fresh fruit.

SERVES 8 TO 12

3⅓ cups **HEAVY CREAM**

¾ cup **SUGAR**

Zest of 1 **LEMON** or 1 **ORANGE**

¾ teaspoon **SAFFRON THREADS**

½ tablespoon powdered **GELATIN**

1 cup whole **MILK**

DATE AND WALNUT
delizie
WITH
ORANGE *FIORE DI LATTE*

SERVES 12

1 heaping cup **WALNUTS**

¾ pound fresh **DATES**, pitted and
cut into 1-inch pieces

½ cup **MILK**

1½ cups **FLOUR**

1 teaspoon **BAKING POWDER**

1 teaspoon **BAKING SODA**

½ teaspoon **KOSHER SALT**

3 **EGGS**

½ cup granulated **SUGAR**

½ cup **DARK BROWN SUGAR**,
packed

2 teaspoons pure **VANILLA
EXTRACT**

½ cup (1 stick) unsalted **BUTTER**,
melted and cooled

1½ cups plus 2 tablespoons
HEAVY CREAM

Orange *Fiore di Latte*

1½ cups **CRÈME FRAÎCHE**

3 tablespoons **SUGAR**

Grated zest of 1 large **ORANGE**

1 cup plus 2 tablespoons fresh
RICOTTA

I love date season; fresh dates give a rich, sweet, and almost smoky flavor to anything they are in. *Fiore di latte* means the flower of the milk, and Gina's version is exceptional.

1. Preheat the oven to 350°F.

2. On a baking sheet lined with parchment paper, arrange twelve 3-inch by 2-inch cake molds. Lightly spray the cake molds with nonstick cooking spray.

3. Spread the walnuts on another ungreased baking sheet and toast them in the oven for 15 minutes, or until golden and aromatic. Remove and allow to cool, then chop the walnuts medium-fine. Place the dates in the bowl of a food processor with the milk. Process to make a chunky puree.

4. In a small bowl, sift together the flour, baking powder, baking soda, and salt.

5. In the bowl of an electric mixer, beat the eggs, granulated sugar, and brown sugar until light and airy, about 5 minutes. Add the vanilla extract and butter and beat well. Beat in the dry ingredients in two batches, scraping down the sides of the bowl between each addition. Beat in the date puree until thoroughly combined, then add the chopped walnuts. With the mixer on low speed, gradually add the heavy cream and beat until thoroughly mixed.

6. Spoon the batter into the molds, filling them by two thirds. Bake the *delizie* until they puff, turn golden brown, and appear set in the center, 20 to 25 minutes.

7. In a chilled bowl, combine the crème fraîche, sugar, orange zest, and ricotta and whip to form soft peaks. Refrigerate until ready to serve, or up to 3 hours.

8. Allow the cakes to cool until slightly warm, then gently remove the molds. Serve the *delizie* warm with a dollop of the *fiore di latte*.

chocolate and VALPOLICELLA *CREMA*

This is the most adult pudding you will ever encounter. The intensity of the wine's fruit-and-acid combo makes each bite a serious experience.

1. Combine the red wine and ½ cup of the sugar in a small saucepan. Bring to a boil, then reduce the heat and simmer until reduced by two thirds, about 15 minutes. Remove from the heat and allow to cool.

2. Heat both chocolates in a large bowl over a double boiler until melted. Whisk in the red wine syrup, followed by the egg yolks.

3. In a medium saucepan, combine the milk, 1 cup of the cream, and ¼ cup of the sugar. Heat until scalded, then whisk quickly into the chocolate mixture. Whisk in the butter. Divide the custard among individual custard cups or wine glasses. Chill until completely set.

4. Just before serving, whip the remaining 1 cup of cream to soft peaks. Add the remaining 2 tablespoons of sugar and whip to stiff peaks. Top each serving of custard with a small dollop of whipped cream.

SERVES 8 TO 12

1 cup **RED WINE**, preferably Valpolicella or another medium-bodied, fruity red wine

½ cup plus ¼ cup plus 2 tablespoons **SUGAR**

12 ounces **BITTERSWEET CHOCOLATE**, finely chopped

8 ounces **UNSWEETENED CHOCOLATE**, finely chopped

8 **EGG YOLKS**

1¼ cups **MILK**

2 cups **HEAVY CREAM**

1 tablespoon unsalted **BUTTER**

MEYER LEMON
SEMIFREDDO

SERVES 10

2½ cups **HEAVY CREAM**

1½ cups **SUGAR**

9 **EGG YOLKS**

¾ cup fresh Meyer **LEMON JUICE**

2 tablespoons freshly grated
   Meyer **LEMON ZEST**

½ teaspoon pure **VANILLA**
   EXTRACT

Huckleberry Sauce

1 pint fresh **HUCKLEBERRIES** or
   wild blueberries

⅓ cup **SUGAR**

Lemon *Brodo*

½ cup fresh Meyer **LEMON JUICE**

¾ cup **SUGAR**

1 **EGG YOLK**

½ cup **HEAVY CREAM**

Pinch of **KOSHER SALT**

This recipe is a knockout, both because it's not difficult to make, and because the lemon flavor is like a bullwhip crack of intensity.

If you prefer not to eat raw egg yolk you may delete it from the *brodo,* but it will be less rich.

1. In the bowl of an electric mixer, whip the cream to stiff peaks. Transfer the whipped cream to a large bowl and refrigerate. Line a large loaf pan with plastic wrap and set aside.

2. In a small saucepan, combine the sugar and ¼ cup water. Clip a candy thermometer to the side of the pan and cook over medium heat until the mixture reaches hardball stage (247° to 250°F.). While the sugar is cooking, place the egg yolks in the bowl of an electric mixer, and beat with the whip attachment at medium speed. The egg yolks should become thick and very pale in color.

3. When the sugar reaches hardball stage, remove it from the heat. With the mixer running on low speed, carefully drizzle the hot sugar into the egg yolks. Keep the stream of sugar against the side of the bowl to prevent the sugar from hitting the whip.

4. After all the sugar has been added, increase the mixer speed to medium and beat until the bowl is cool to the touch. Add the lemon juice, lemon zest, and vanilla. Gently fold the yolk mixture into the whipped cream. Spoon the mixture into the prepared pan and freeze until firm.

5. Place the berries and sugar in a small saucepan and cook until the juices have thickened slightly, about 5 minutes. Remove from the heat and place in the refrigerator to chill completely.

6. Meanwhile, combine the lemon *brodo* ingredients in a blender and blend until smooth and creamy. Chill thoroughly.

7. Place a scoop of semifreddo in a small bowl and pour several spoonfuls of the lemon *brodo* over each. Swirl 2 tablespoons of huckleberry sauce through the *brodo* of each serving and serve immediately.

sweet corn *CREMA*

with CORNMEAL *ZEPPOLE*

AND BLACKBERRIES

This is another of my all-time favorite Babbo desserts. I love the intellectual play of the corn used two ways, and the texture of the custard is a joyous surprise every time. Serve with the blackberry compote to hit the home run even further out of the park.

1. To make the *crema:* Preheat the oven to 300°F. Place eight 4-ounce ramekins or custard cups in a baking dish large enough to fit them with at least an inch of space between each ramekin.

2. With a sharp knife, slice the corn kernels off the cobs. Cut the cobs in half and place in a medium saucepan with the kernels, milk, cream, and 1/3 cup of the sugar. With the tip of a knife, scrape the vanilla bean into the pan. Bring to a boil over medium heat, stirring occasionally, then remove from the heat and steep until cool.

3. Discard the corncobs, then use an immersion blender to puree the mixture until somewhat smooth. This step may also be done in a regular blender in small batches. Bring the mixture back to a boil, stirring constantly, then set aside. In a medium bowl, whisk the egg yolks with the remaining 1/3 cup of sugar until completely blended. Gradually whisk half of the hot corn custard into the yolks, then pour the tempered yolk mixture back into the remaining custard and whisk well. Strain through a fine sieve, pressing the corn kernels to extract as much liquid as possible. Stir in the salt.

4. Divide the custard evenly among the ramekins. Add enough hot water to the baking dish to come one third of the way up the sides of the ramekins. Cover the entire baking dish with aluminum foil. Bake the custards on the middle oven rack for about 40 minutes. The custards will be done when they are no longer liquid in the center and are completely set.

5. Carefully remove the baking dish from the oven and discard the foil. Allow the custards to cool in the water bath for 20 minutes and then refrigerate until completely chilled.

(continued on next page)

SERVES 8

Crema

2 ears of fresh sweet CORN

1 cup MILK

2 cups HEAVY CREAM

2/3 cup SUGAR

1/2 VANILLA BEAN, split lengthwise

8 EGG YOLKS

Pinch of KOSHER SALT

Zeppole

5 tablespoons unsalted BUTTER, softened

1/3 cup plus 2 cups SUGAR

4 EGGS

1 tablespoon VANILLA EXTRACT

2 tablespoons whole MILK

1 2/3 cups unbleached, all-purpose FLOUR, plus more for sprinkling

1/2 cup plus 2 tablespoons instant POLENTA

2 tablespoons BAKING POWDER

3/4 teaspoon KOSHER SALT

6 cups VEGETABLE OIL, for frying

BLACKBERRY COMPOTE (page 308)

Blackberry Compote

Makes 2 cups

2 pints **BLACKBERRIES**
2 tablespoons **CRÈME DE CASSIS**
¼ cup **SUGAR**

Place the berries in a medium saucepan and toss with the crème de cassis and sugar. Place the pan over low heat and cook slowly, shaking the pan occasionally to cook the berries evenly. When the berries have softened somewhat and released their juices, remove from the heat and allow to cool.

6. To make the *zeppole:* Cream together the butter and ⅓ cup of sugar until very light. Add the eggs and continue to beat; the mixture will appear broken. Scrape down the sides of the bowl, then add the vanilla extract and milk.

7. In a small bowl, stir together the flour, polenta, baking powder, and salt. Add the dry ingredients to the creamed mixture and beat until completely incorporated. You will have a very soft, sticky dough. Sprinkle the dough liberally with flour and wrap tightly in plastic. Chill until somewhat firm, at least 8 hours.

8. When the dough is completely chilled and firm, flour a board liberally and unwrap the dough. Roll to ¾-inch thickness, using as much flour as needed to prevent the dough from sticking.

9. Using a small doughnut cutter, cut out as many *zeppole* as possible, re-rolling the scraps as necessary until you have used all the dough. As you cut the *zeppole*, place them on a baking sheet sprinkled lightly with flour to prevent them from sticking. Return the *zeppole* to the refrigerator and chill for 30 minutes.

10. In a large, heavy-bottomed pot, heat the vegetable oil to 340°F. Place the remaining 2 cups of sugar in a shallow bowl. Line several baking sheets with two layers of paper towels.

11. Fry the *zeppole* a few at a time in the hot oil, until golden brown on both sides and cooked through. Drain on the paper towels, and while they are still hot, roll them in the bowl of sugar to coat each one completely. The *zeppole* may be fried up to 4 hours before serving, but they are especially good served hot.

12. Spoon some of the compote over each serving of *crema* and serve with a warm *zeppole*.

SPOON CRUMBING

A shiny silver tablespoon races across the padded linen table as your bread crumbs voluntarily jump, just as shipwrecked passengers bobbing in the cold North Atlantic Sea scramble into lifeboats. The spoon is a precise, elegant, amusing, and deftly functional tool, certainly more adept than the traditional aluminum crumber that lives among a forest of lint in a waiter's pockets with matches, change, and other necessities. A spoon belongs to the table, whereas anything one keeps in one's pocket does not.

—J.B.

strawberries *and* PEACHES

with BALSAMIC ZABAGLIONE

This quick little pan roast really captures the spirit of Italian food culture although I've never seen anything quite like it in Italy. The balsamic-flavored zabaglione is a nod to the classic Modenese osteria dessert of raw strawberries with balsamic vinegar and black pepper.

1. To make the zabaglione: In a medium bowl, whip the heavy cream to stiff peaks. Cover and refrigerate.

2. In a stainless-steel bowl, whisk the egg yolks with the sugar, vin santo, and balsamic vinegar. Place the bowl over a saucepan of simmering water or transfer to the top of a double boiler and whisk vigorously, using a balloon whisk. Continue whisking over the simmering water until the mixture is thick and foamy. Remove the bowl from the heat and continue whisking until the zabaglione is completely cool. Gently fold the zabaglione into the whipped cream and chill for 30 minutes.

3. While the zabaglione is chilling, place the strawberries and peaches in a large bowl. In a small saucepan, combine the vin santo, honey, and sugar and bring to a boil. Stir to completely dissolve the sugar, then cook the mixture until reduced slightly. Pour the hot syrup over the fruit and toss to coat. Spoon the fruit into dessert dishes or wine glasses and top with a dollop of the zabaglione.

SERVES 6 TO 8

Zabaglione

1 cup HEAVY CREAM

4 EGG YOLKS

¼ cup SUGAR

¼ cup VIN SANTO

1 tablespoon aged BALSAMIC VINEGAR

1 pint ripe STRAWBERRIES, cleaned and cut into ¼-inch slices

2 ripe PEACHES, pitted and cut into ¼-inch slices

½ cup VIN SANTO

½ cup HONEY

2 tablespoons SUGAR

peach crostata
with HONEY BUTTER
and HONEY VANILLA GELATO

SERVES 8 TO 10

1 recipe **TART DOUGH**
(page 315), chilled

1½ cups blanched, sliced **ALMONDS**

½ cup (1 stick) unsalted **BUTTER**

1 cup sifted **CONFECTIONERS'**
SUGAR

1 **EGG**

½ teaspoon **VANILLA EXTRACT**

Pinch of **KOSHER SALT**

Streusel

6 tablespoons unsalted **BUTTER**

1¼ cups all-purpose **FLOUR**

½ cup blanched, sliced **ALMONDS**

¾ cup **SUGAR**

¼ teaspoon **KOSHER SALT**

6 medium ripe **PEACHES**

1 tablespoon fresh **LEMON JUICE**

1 teaspoon **VANILLA EXTRACT**

2 tablespoons all-purpose **FLOUR**

½ cup **SUGAR**

2 pints **HONEY VANILLA GELATO**
(page 314)

When the perfect summer pie happened to take a little ride uptown this beautiful confection was the result. Gina's *frolla* pastry has just the right texture to hold the juiciness of perfect peaches without becoming too firm or heavy.

1. Preheat the oven to 350°F.

2. Roll the chilled Tart Dough into a 12-inch circle, large enough to line the bottom and sides of a 10-inch tart pan with removable bottom. Press the dough into the sides and trim the top so that the dough is flush with the tart pan. Place the pastry shell in the refrigerator and chill until completely firm, about 30 minutes.

3. To make the filling: Spread the almonds evenly on a baking sheet and toast in the oven until light golden brown, 5 to 6 minutes. Allow to cool completely, then place the nuts in a food processor and pulse until finely chopped but not powdery.

4. In the bowl of an electric mixer, cream the butter and the confectioners' sugar until very smooth and creamy. Beat in the egg, followed by the vanilla and salt. Scrape down the sides of the bowl. Thoroughly beat in the ground almonds. Set aside.

5. To make the streusel: Melt the butter and set aside to cool. Place the flour, almonds, sugar, and salt in the bowl of a food processor and pulse to combine. Add the melted butter and pulse to form pea-size crumbs. Spread the streusel out onto a cookie sheet and chill briefly.

6. Peel the peaches and cut into ¼-inch wedges. In a large bowl, toss the peach wedges with the lemon juice, vanilla, flour, and sugar. Spread enough of the almond filling on the bottom of the tart to completely cover it, and arrange the peach slices densely on top. Sprinkle the streusel crumbs over the tart. Place the tart on a baking sheet to catch any juices and bake for 45 to 50 minutes, or until the crust and streusel are nicely browned and the juices are bubbling. Allow to cool completely before removing the tart from the pan.

Honey Butter

1 cup **HONEY**

½ **VANILLA BEAN**, split
  lengthwise

¼ cup (½ stick) unsalted
  BUTTER, softened

7. To make the honey butter: In a small saucepan, combine the honey and the insides of the split vanilla bean. Bring to a boil, lower the heat, and simmer for 10 minutes, or until the honey is reduced by two thirds. Whisk in the butter until it is completely incorporated.

8. Serve with a scoop of Honey Vanilla Gelato and drizzle with the honey butter.

HONEY VANILLA gelato

MAKES 2 PINTS

9 EGG YOLKS

½ cup HONEY

Pinch of KOSHER SALT

2¼ cups MILK

¾ cup HEAVY CREAM

1 plump VANILLA BEAN, split
   lengthwise

2 tablespoons SUGAR

Honey not only contributes an intriguing sweetness to this gelato, but it also lends a very unusual mouth feel.

1. Place the egg yolks in a small bowl and whisk together with the honey and salt.

2. Combine the milk and cream in a medium saucepan. Add the vanilla bean and sugar and bring to a boil over medium heat. When the milk and cream come to a rolling boil, quickly whisk some of the boiling milk into the egg yolk mixture, then return the egg yolk mixture back to the pot. Whisk well to combine the rest of the milk with the egg yolk mixture. Strain through a chinois or fine-mesh strainer and save the vanilla bean for future use.

3. Chill the custard completely, then freeze in a gelato maker according to the manufacturer's instructions.

Tart Dough

Makes one 12-inch tart crust

2⅓ cups unbleached all-purpose **FLOUR**

⅓ cup granulated **SUGAR**

½ teaspoon **KOSHER SALT**

½ teaspoon **BAKING POWDER**

Grated zest of 1 **ORANGE**

¾ cup (1½ sticks) unsalted **BUTTER**, very cold, cut into small cubes

1 **EGG** plus 1 **EGG YOLK**

1 teaspoon pure **VANILLA EXTRACT**

2 teaspoons **HEAVY CREAM**

In the bowl of a food processor, combine the flour, sugar, salt, baking powder, and orange zest. Add the cold butter cubes and toss lightly to coat. Pulse until the butter is the size of small peas.

In a separate bowl, combine the egg, egg yolk, vanilla, and heavy cream, and add it to the flour–butter mixture. Pulse to moisten the dough, then pulse until it begins to come together. Turn the dough out onto a lightly floured board and knead by hand. If the dough is too dry, add a few drops of heavy cream. Shape into a small disc, wrap, and chill thoroughly for at least 3 hours or overnight.

THE COOKIE PLATE

***Even guests who won't commit to a full-fledged
dessert seem willing to nibble on a little cookie or
two from the selection*** Gina sends out on the cookie plate
each night. The assortment might include my son Benno's favorite
polenta shortbreads (which make a killer ice-cream sandwich) or
her intriguingly textured fig and hazelnut biscotti. Each of these
cookies is perfect on its own, but when they are presented in full
regalia with a little *affogato*—a glass of chilled espresso with a scoop
of gelato and a touch of softly whipped cream—they're even more
dramatic.

AMARETTI

MAKES ABOUT 30 COOKIES

1¼ cups whole blanched
    ALMONDS

1½ teaspoons **CORNSTARCH**

½ cup **CONFECTIONERS' SUGAR**

2 **EGG WHITES**

Pinch of **KOSHER SALT**

⅓ cup plus 2 tablespoons
    granulated **SUGAR**

½ teaspoon **ALMOND EXTRACT**

1 tablespoon **AMARETTO**

½ cup **TURBINADO SUGAR**, for
    sprinkling

Gina made this recipe very simple because it goes on the *piccola pasticceria* plate we serve to every table after coffee.

1. Preheat the oven to 300°F.

2. Place the almonds, cornstarch, and confectioners' sugar in the bowl of a food processor and pulse until the almonds are very finely chopped. Place the egg whites in the bowl of an electric mixer and add the salt. Using the whip attachment on medium speed, beat the whites until foamy and light. Gradually add the granulated sugar in a steady stream, continuing to beat until the egg whites are somewhat stiff and glossy. Beat in the almond extract and amaretto.

3. Using a rubber spatula, fold in the ground almonds, taking care not to deflate the meringue. Spoon the batter into a pastry bag with a medium round tip and pipe into 1-inch mounds on ungreased baking sheets. Alternatively, drop the meringue onto the baking sheets by heaping teaspoonfuls. Sprinkle each cookie generously with the turbinado sugar.

4. Bake for 15 minutes, or until the cookies have begun to turn pale golden and are just beginning to crack slightly. Lower the oven temperature to 200°F., and leave the oven door ajar to release some of the heat. Leave the cookies in the oven for at least 25 to 30 minutes, or until they are completely dry and crisp in the center. Allow the cookies to cool briefly on the baking sheets, then transfer them to a rack to cool completely. Store in an airtight container.

walnut SHORTBREAD

These are my son Leo's number ones; he calls them nutty bars.

1. Preheat the oven to 325°F. Spread the walnut pieces on a baking sheet and toast for 5 to 7 minutes, or until golden brown and fragrant. Cool completely, then transfer to the bowl of a food processor and pulse until just finely ground. Set aside. Reduce the oven temperature to 300°F.

2. In the bowl of an electric mixer, cream the butter, brown sugar, and confectioners' sugar together until very smooth and creamy, then beat in the vanilla extract.

3. In a separate bowl, stir together the ground nuts, flour, and salt. Add the dry ingredients to the butter mixture and beat to form a soft dough. Wrap the dough tightly in plastic wrap and chill until firm enough to roll, at least 30 minutes.

4. Lightly grease two baking sheets or line them with parchment.

5. Divide the dough into two pieces, and roll one piece out to ½-inch thickness on a lightly floured board. Using a cookie cutter, cut out as many cookies as you can and place them on the baking sheet. Repeat with the remaining dough. (You may re-roll the scraps, but the cookies will not be as tender.) Sprinkle each cookie with granulated sugar.

6. Bake the cookies for 12 to 15 minutes, or until they turn light golden brown. Remove to a wire rack to cool completely and store in an airtight container.

MAKES ABOUT 36 COOKIES

4 cups **WALNUT** pieces, toasted and finely ground

1 cup (2 sticks) unsalted **BUTTER**, softened

¾ cup **DARK BROWN SUGAR**, packed

¾ cup **CONFECTIONERS' SUGAR**

2 teaspoons pure **VANILLA EXTRACT**

2 cups sifted unbleached, all-purpose **FLOUR**

½ teaspoon **KOSHER SALT**

Granulated **SUGAR**, for sprinkling

fig and walnut
BISCOTTI

MAKES ABOUT 55 COOKIES

2 cups **WALNUT** pieces

2 cups dried Turkish or
 Calimyrna **FIGS**, quartered

¾ cup (1½ sticks) unsalted
 BUTTER, softened

½ cup granulated **SUGAR**, plus
 more for sprinkling

¾ cup **DARK BROWN SUGAR**,
 packed

4 **EGGS**

2 teaspoons **VANILLA EXTRACT**

Grated zest of 1 large **ORANGE**

3¾ cups unbleached, all-purpose
 FLOUR

2 teaspoons **BAKING POWDER**

½ teaspoon **BAKING SODA**

½ teaspoon **KOSHER SALT**

2 teaspoons ground **CINNAMON**

½ teaspoon ground **NUTMEG**

¼ teaspoon ground **CLOVES**

1 **EGG WHITE**, lightly beaten

Figs give these biscotti an unusual texture.

1. Preheat the oven to 325°F.

2. Spread the walnuts on a baking sheet and toast for 5 to 7 minutes, or until golden brown and fragrant. Allow the walnuts to cool completely.

3. Place the walnuts and dried figs in a food processor and process until they are finely chopped.

4. In the bowl of an electric mixer, cream together the butter and sugars until light and fluffy. Add the eggs, one at a time, and beat until incorporated, scraping down the sides of the bowl with a spatula occasionally. Beat in the vanilla and orange zest.

5. In a medium bowl, stir together the flour, baking powder, baking soda, salt, and spices. Beat the dry ingredients into the butter mixture to form a somewhat firm dough. Add the walnuts and figs and beat until thoroughly combined. Wrap the dough tightly in plastic and chill 30 to 45 minutes, or until completely firm.

6. When the dough has chilled, divide it into equal portions. Lightly grease two baking sheets. On a floured board, use your palms to roll each piece of dough into a log the length of the baking sheet. Place the logs on the baking sheets 1½ inches apart. Brush each log with the egg white to glaze, then sprinkle with granulated sugar.

7. Bake the logs for 17 to 20 minutes, or until they have become light brown and firm in the center. Remove from the oven and reduce the temperature to 200°F. Allow the logs to cool until they are firm enough to slice, 10 to 15 minutes. Using a sharp, serrated knife, cut each log on a slight bias into ¼-inch slices. Arrange the slices on a baking sheet in a single layer. Toast the biscotti until they are dry and crisp, approximately 30 to 40 minutes. Allow the biscotti to cool, then store in an airtight container.

MASCARPONE
JELLY
thumbprints

You can substitute any jam or thick fruit puree for the raspberry jelly here.

1. In the bowl of an electric mixer, beat the butter until creamy and smooth. Add 1 cup of the sugar and cream together until light and fluffy. Beat in the egg and vanilla extract, scraping down the sides of the bowl with a spatula occasionally. Add the mascarpone and beat just until smooth.

2. In a medium bowl, stir together the flour, baking powder, baking soda, and salt. Beat the dry ingredients into the butter mixture to form a soft dough. Wrap the dough tightly in plastic wrap and chill for 30 minutes, or until firm.

3. Preheat the oven to 325°F. Divide the dough into 4 equal portions. Working with one portion of dough at a time, break off small pieces and roll each into a half-inch ball. Roll each ball in the remaining ½ cup of sugar, then place on a lightly greased baking sheet, about 1 inch apart. Using the blunt end of a wooden skewer, poke a deep hole in each ball, using a circular motion to widen the opening at the top.

4. Bake the cookies for 12 to 15 minutes, or until they just begin to turn pale golden at the edges. Remove from the oven and if necessary, gently poke the centers to redefine the indentation. While the cookies are cooling, heat the raspberry jam slightly in a small saucepan until melted. Using a very small spoon, carefully fill the centers of the cookies with the jam. Allow the cookies to cool until the jam is set. Store in an airtight container with sheets of wax paper or parchment between the layers.

MAKES ABOUT 36 COOKIES

½ cup (1 stick) unsalted **BUTTER**, softened

1½ cups **SUGAR**

1 **EGG**

½ teaspoon pure **VANILLA EXTRACT**

½ cup **MASCARPONE** cheese

2¾ cups unbleached, all-purpose **FLOUR**

1 teaspoon **BAKING POWDER**

½ teaspoon **BAKING SODA**

½ teaspoon **KOSHER SALT**

1 cup seedless **RASPBERRY JAM**

polenta shortbread

MAKES ABOUT 36 COOKIES

1¼ cups unbleached, all-purpose **FLOUR**

1 cup quick-cooking **POLENTA**

⅔ cup **SUGAR**, plus more for sprinkling

1½ teaspoons **BAKING POWDER**

½ teaspoon **KOSHER SALT**

1 **EGG**

1 **EGG YOLK**

6 tablespoons unsalted **BUTTER**, melted and cooled

Grated zest of 1 **ORANGE**

This is my son Benno's favorite cookie and for good reason—it is delicious. These also make excellent mini ice-cream sandwiches.

1. In the bowl of an electric mixer, stir together the flour, polenta, sugar, baking powder, and salt. Add the egg, egg yolk, butter, and orange zest, and beat with the paddle attachment for about 3 minutes to form a sticky dough. Scrape the dough onto a sheet of plastic wrap, flatten into a disc, and wrap tightly. Chill the dough until it is firm enough to roll.

2. Preheat the oven to 325°F.

3. Lightly flour your work surface and, using a rolling pin, roll the dough to ¼-inch thickness. With a round or square cookie cutter, cut out as many cookies as you can, transferring them to a parchment-lined or greased baking sheet. Re-roll the scraps and continue cutting cookies until you have used all the dough. Sprinkle the cookies evenly with sugar.

4. Bake the cookies until they just begin to turn golden brown around the edges. Cool on the sheets for a few minutes, then remove to a rack to cool completely. Store in an airtight container.

BITTERSWEET
CHOCOLATE
cookies

When you need a chocolate fix, this will do the trick.

1. In the bowl of an electric mixer, cream the butter until very soft and creamy. Add the granulated sugar and beat until light and fluffy. Beat in the egg, followed by the vanilla extract, scraping down the sides of the bowl with a spatula occasionally. In a medium bowl, stir together the flour, cocoa powder, baking powder, and salt. Beat the dry ingredients into the butter mixture, followed by the chopped chocolate and nuts. Wrap the dough tightly in plastic wrap and chill for 30 minutes, or until firm.

2. Preheat the oven to 325°F.

3. Divide the dough into 4 equal portions. Working with one piece at a time, break off 1-inch pieces of the dough and roll each piece into a ball. With your thumb, flatten each ball into a small disc and roll in the confectioners' sugar to coat completely. Arrange the cookies on greased baking sheets.

4. Bake the cookies for 8 to 10 minutes, or until they are just beginning to puff and crack. Allow the cookies to cool, then re-roll them in the confectioners' sugar. Store in an airtight container.

MAKES ABOUT 32 COOKIES

1 cup (2 sticks) unsalted **BUTTER**, softened

½ cup granulated **SUGAR**

1 **EGG**

1 teaspoon pure **VANILLA EXTRACT**

2 cups unbleached, all-purpose **FLOUR**

⅓ cup Dutch-process **COCOA POWDER**

½ teaspoon **BAKING POWDER**

½ teaspoon **KOSHER SALT**

5 ounces **SEMISWEET** or **BITTERSWEET CHOCOLATE**, finely chopped

½ cup whole **HAZELNUTS** or sliced almonds, finely chopped

1½ cups **CONFECTIONERS' SUGAR**

DIGESTIVI

One of the most memorable parts of a great meal in Italy is the *digestivo,* or after-dinner drink. Italians have a way of associating a special taste or drink with nearly every moment of the day, and the art of digestivi is particularly well developed throughout all of Italy, with each region producing a special type and/or flavor. Of these, no doubt the best known is grappa, that clear yet lethal liquid sold in intriguingly stylish bottles for stratospheric prices.

Grappa culture truly started in Friuli and the Veneto, and it is there that we find both the best and the most humble examples of the genre. Grappa was originally a by-product of winemaking, using a second pressing of the grapes, which produced a rough, raspy beverage traditionally associated with old guys in hats. In the 1970s the Nonino family began making distillates from the first pressing of grapes and other fruits and bottled the more refined, softer grappa in modern glass bottles that resembled elegant laboratory beakers. The grappas you'll encounter at a neighborhood trattoria in Italy are divided among the two styles, the old being rough and fiery, the new being soft and more feminine. Today grappa is made in almost every province in Italy, and while many are delightful, not all of them are great. At Babbo we take an inexpensive traditional bottling and mellow its fire by adding cooked or raw fruit that we allow to macerate for as long as six months. In this way we are able to entice the unaccustomed diner to try one, or two, or . . .

But grappa is just the beginning. *Amari* refers to the bitter or bittersweet family of digestivi generally made with herbs, spices, and fragrant nuts and made either from wine or neutral spirits. At Babbo my friend Cesare Casella and I make a *nocino,* a liqueur made out of green walnuts, based on his family recipe from Lucca. In the middle of June my friends Ridgley and Colleen Evers, from Healdsburg, California, send us a box of green walnuts, which we soak and marinate for five months before bottling the liqueur. In addition to the homemade *nocino,* we serve Averna, Fernet Branca, and Montenegro, each from its own town and with its own memorable flavor. One of the things I like best about traveling the Amalfi coast is enjoying their version of the digestivo, *limoncello.* Our pastry chef, Gina DePalma, makes her own with Meyer lemons and blood oranges and people just love it. The trick to these infused liqueurs is to serve them stinging cold— almost frozen, in fact—and to partake in moderation; these will kill you the next day.

We're not entirely Italo-centric when it comes to after-dinner quaffs, though. We have been known to suggest a glass of port or Madeira, both fortified wines with their own fascinating histories. For an especially momentous meal we might even pour one of the great vintages dating back to the nineteenth century. But don't wait for a big, fancy deal to serve a digestivo. Most of what they drink in Italy is inexpensive yet considered as integral a part of a proper meal as the pasta course. Offering a selection after a meal is a great way to continue the flow of hospitality that started with the aperitivo.

TOOLS OF THE TRADE

CHEESE RASP (also called a microplane grater) We use this elegant tool to shave *bottarga* over *Maccheroni alla Chitarra* (page 147) just before it leaves the kitchen. More delicate than a box grater and decidedly sexier, the cheese rasp also allows a cook more control in garnishing a dish with cheese or other "gratables."

EGG MOLDS While we strive to keep ingredients close to their natural shapes, there are times when a thing is made better with a little help, such as this egg mold, which I like to think of as a girdle for the lovely curvaceous duck eggs we serve as appetizers (see pages 69 and 74).

FOIL CUPS Surely one of the most efficient kitchen accessories since the advent of electricity. Ramekins are expensive and take up a lot of space, and their beveled interiors are a busy dishwasher's worst nightmare. Foil cups, on the other hand, cost pennies apiece, compress down to nothing, and are painless to part with. We use them for our various *sformatti* (vegetable flans), as well as for pastries. Next time you're in your favorite restaurant, enjoying the inevitable molten chocolate cake, take a closer look—you'll probably recognize the shape as having come from one of these little foil life-savers.

HEAVY-DUTY MIXER More sturdy than a hand-held and infinitely more stylish, it's an investment worth making for the home or professional kitchen. The dough hook attachment is perfect for kneading pasta, and the sausage stuffing attachment will rock your world.

KNIVES With the exception of slicing bread, any kitchen task can be accomplished with one of two knives: a chef's knife and a paring knife. Knives are as personal to a cook as his tongs, with the added dimension of being infinitely variable. The cooks' knife-sharpening rituals can take on the competitive nature of brightly colored birds preening and displaying their plumage.

MANDOLINO Without succumbing to the Italian-American cliché, a lot of thinly sliced garlic gets used at Babbo. More than one line cook owes his fingertips to the garlic *mandolino,* used in place of a simple knife (too slow) or inexpensive plastic mandoline (too dangerous for something as small as a clove of garlic).

NONSTICK PAN Even a seasoned line cook, master of flipping a twelve-egg frittata with perfect grace, needs a little help when it comes to the delicate matter of crespelle or flaky white fish.

PARCHMENT Used most often in the pastry department to keep delicate petits-four from adhering to the baking pan (or each other), parchment paper also forms the steaming packet for *in Cartoccio* dishes (see pages 161 and 172), a method that has been delighting diners in French and Italian restaurants for years.

PASTA CUTTER At Babbo, making fresh pasta is a full-time job for two people. With the volume they're required to produce every day, these guys don't have time to idle over the perfect 2-inch rectangle. Hence, the adjustable rolling pasta cutter, a tool that horrifies some of my Italian friends, yet keeps daily pasta production a manageable two-man affair.

QUART CONTAINERS Most recognizable from any take-out deli, these plastic lidded containers are the building blocks of every cook's *mise en place,* and are often horded jealously.

RAVIOLI STAMPS For each town and to each cook, *ravioli* means something different, whether it's the fold or the size; the easiest way to distinguish your personal stuffed pastas is to buy a ravioli stamp. They come in hundreds of shapes and sizes. Be sure to buy one with brass or teflon, as they are much easier to use and keep clean.

SAUTÉ PANS To optimize temperature control and sanitation, each piece of fish or meat and each order of pasta is cooked in its own sauté pan. With over 200 customers served per night, that's a staggering number of sauté pans, enough to keep cooks and dishwashers doing the "more pans, please!" and "here they are!" call-and-response all night, every night. For the home cook I recommend two 6-inch, two 10-inch, and two 14-inch pans.

SLICER There is simply no other method for cutting silky layers of prosciutto and other *salumi.* For service we use an electric model; for special occasions and cooking demos we bring out a gorgeous hand-cranked model.

SQUIRT BOTTLE When used with the proper restraint, a squirt bottle affords the user perfect control in dispensing oils and sauces. Enough has been made of the "Pollock-izing" of otherwise beautiful plates that to weigh in at this point would be redundant; suffice it to say that plates at Babbo know nothing of squiggles or, God forbid, heart-shaped borders. We use squirt bottles to quickly put the right amount of sauce in exactly the right place.

TONGS At Babbo, tongs are used for everything from plating pasta to turning grilled meats to tossing salads to carrying a hot pan to the sink. To a line cook, tongs are an extension of his hand, not unlike a set of metallic opposable thumbs. A newcomer to the kitchen will not make the mistake of "borrowing" another cook's tongs in the heat of service more than once. You'll want a set of your own.

TRUFFLE SHAVER Its shape is more suggestive of a medieval hand puppet with killer teeth than the perfect instrument for doling out just the right amount of precious truffles. At the height of the season we shave them over pastas, salads, and meats.

VEGETABLE PEELER I am constantly amazed that, in a world of perfect tools, some people insist on using the cumbersome, prehistoric tools of yesterday. So it is with the vegetable peeler. We use the plastic-handled, Y-shaped ones as opposed to the old metal wand-type. They are far stronger and produce straighter lines, and they achieve an unsurpassed length on curls of semi-hard cheeses.

TASTING MENUS

At Babbo we create new tasting menus weekly to showcase the best seasonal offerings and pair them with great wines. The following are examples of a traditional tasting and a pasta tasting, each with complementary desserts and our suggestions for wine matches. Use them as a template for your own tastings, varying them to reflect the season and your preferences.

TRADITIONAL TASTING MENU

Duck *Bresaola* with Borlotti and Red Onion Jam
Cavalleri "Collezione Rosé" NV

Goat Cheese Tortelloni
with Dried Orange and Fennel Pollen
Malvasia Istriana, Edi Kante 1999

Gnocchi with Oxtail Ragù
Valpolicella Superiore, Marion 1997

Grilled Quail with *Scorzanera alla Romana,*
Braised Dandelions, and Blood Oranges
Flaccianello della Pieve, Fontodi 1997

Coach Farm Goat Cheese
Gattinara, Nervi 1982

Bigne with Honey Mousse and Red Currants
Moscato Rosa, Zeni 1998

Maple and Mascarpone Cheesecake
with Walnut Shortbread
Loazzolo, Forteto della Luja 1997

PASTA TASTING MENU

Black Pepper Tagliatelle with Parsnips
and Pancetta
"Valentino Brut Zero," Rocche dei Manzoni 1995

Bitter Greens and Sorrel Ravioli
Gewürztraminer "Sanct Valentin,"
San Michele-Appiano 1999

Perciatelli with Cardoons, Garlic, and Pecorino
"Vespa Bianco," Bastianich 1999

Gnocchi with Venison and Rosemary
Aglianico "Naima," Bruno DeConciliis 1998

Pappardelle Bolognese
Tignanello, Antinori 1990

Espresso *Torrone* with Drunken Cherries
Brachetto "Birbet," Cascina Ca'Rossa 1999

Sweet Corn *Crema* with Cornmeal *Zeppole*
and Blackberries
"Le Passule" Librandi 1998

SOURCES

ARMANDINO'S SALUMI
Cured meats made by my dad
RETAIL STORE:
309 Third Avenue South
Seattle, WA 98104
(206) 621-8772

ARTHUR AVENUE CATERERS
Cured meats, specialty items, and cheeses
2344 Arthur Avenue
Bronx, NY 10458
(718) 295-5033
(866)-2-SALAMI
WWW.ARTHURAVENUE.COM

BALDUCCI'S
Cheese, cured meats, fish, produce, olive oil, and vinegars
MAIL ORDER CATALOG:
(800) 225-3822
RETAIL STORE:
424 Sixth Avenue (at West 9th Street)
New York, NY 10011
(212) 673-2600
WWW.BALDUCCI.COM

D'ARTAGNAN
Fresh game and poultry
RETAIL STORE:
280 Wilson Avenue
Newark, NJ 07105
(800) 327-8246
WWW.DARTAGNAN.COM

DEAN AND DELUCA
Cured meats, cheeses, olive oil, vinegar, blood orange juice, and specialty produce
MAIL-ORDER CATALOG:
(800) 221-7714
RETAIL STORES:
560 Broadway
New York, NY 10012
(212) 226-6800 or

697 South St. Helena Highway
St. Helena, CA 94574
(707) 967-9980
WWW.DEAN-DELUCA.COM

DIPALO
Italian cheeses (including eighty-five types of pecorino), cured meats, olives, oil, vinegar, and pasta
206 Grand Street
New York, NY 10002
(212) 226-1033

FAICCO
Cured meats, dry pasta, oils, and vinegar
RETAIL STORE:
260 Bleecker Street
New York, NY 10014
(212) 243-1974

FORMAGGIO KITCHEN
Cheese, olive oils, vinegars, pasta, and specialty foods
MAIL-ORDER CATALOG:
(888) 212-3224
RETAIL STORE:
244 Huron Avenue
Cambridge, MA 02138
(617) 354-4750

GRATEFUL PALATE
Olive oil, vinegar, wine, and Bacon-of-the-Month Club
MAIL-ORDER CATALOG:
(888) 472-5283
WWW.GRATEFULPALATE.COM

ISCHIA
Italian cheeses, cured meats, olives, oils, vinegars, pasta, and spices
MAIL-ORDER CATALOG:
5-12 37th Avenue
Woodside, NY 11377
(718) 446-0134

MANICARETTI
This company imports many of the specialty products used at Babbo, including bottarga (dried, pressed mullet roe), saba, estate-produced olive oils and vinegars, high-quality grains and rices, and superb pasta. Catalog and mail order available through The Pasta Shop.
MAIL-ORDER CATALOG:
(888) 952-4005
WWW.MANICARETTI.COM

MURRAY'S CHEESE SHOP
Extensive cheese selection, olives, oils, pasta, vinegar, and imported specialty items
MAIL-ORDER CATALOG:
(888) 692-4339
RETAIL STORE:
257 Bleecker Street
New York, NY 10014
(212) 243-3289
WWW.MURRAYSCHEESE.COM

VINO E OLIO
Beans, cheese, coffee, mushrooms, pasta, truffles, oil, vinegar, cookware, and specialty items
MAIL-ORDER CATALOG:
(877) 846-6365
WWW.VINOEOLIO.COM

ZINGERMANS
Cheese, specialty items, olive oils, vinegars, and produce
MAIL-ORDER CATALOG:
(888) 636-8162
RETAIL STORE:
422 Detroit Street
Ann Arbor, MI 48104
(734) 663-DELI
WWW.ZINGERMANS.COM

INDEX

CONVERSION CHART

EQUIVALENT IMPERIAL AND METRIC MEASUREMENTS

American cooks use standard containers, the 8-ounce cup and a tablespoon that takes exactly 16 level fillings to fill that cup level. Measuring by cup makes it very difficult to give weight equivalents, as a cup of densely packed butter will weigh considerably more than a cup of flour. The easiest way therefore to deal with cup measurements in recipes is to take the amount by volume rather than by weight. Thus the equation reads:

1 cup = 240 ml = 8 fl. oz.   1/2 cup = 120 ml = 4 fl. oz.

In the States, butter is often measured in sticks. One stick is the equivalent of 8 tablespoons. One tablespoon of butter is therefore the equivalent to ½ ounce/15 grams.

LIQUID MEASURES

Fluid Ounces	U.S.	Imperial	Milliliters
	1 teaspoon	1 teaspoon	5
¼	2 teaspoons	1 dessertspoon	10
½	1 tablespoon	1 tablespoon	14
1	2 tablespoons	2 tablespoons	28
2	¼ cup	4 tablespoons	56
4	½ cup		120
5		¼ pint or 1 gill	140
6	¾ cup		170
8	1 cup		240
9			250, ¼ liter
10	1¼ cups	½ pint	280
12	1½ cups		340
15		¾ pint	420
16	2 cups		450
18	2¼ cups		500, ½ liter
20	2½ cups	1 pint	560
24	3 cups		675
25		1¼ pints	700
27	3½ cups		750
30	3¾ cups	1½ pints	840
32	4 cups or 1 quart		900
35		1¾ pints	980
36	4½ cups		1000, 1 liter
40	5 cups	2 pints or 1 quart	1120

SOLID MEASURES

U.S. and Imperial Measures		Metric Measures	
Ounces	Pounds	Grams	Kilos
1		28	
2		56	
3½		100	
4	¼	112	
5		140	
6		168	
8	½	225	
9		250	¼
12	¾	340	
16	1	450	
18		500	½
20	1¼	560	
24	1½	675	
27		750	¾
28	1¾	780	
32	2	900	
36	2¼	1000	1
40	2½	1100	
48	3	1350	
54		1500	1½

OVEN TEMPERATURE EQUIVALENTS

Fahrenheit	Celsius	Gas Mark	Description
225	110	¼	Cool
250	130	½	
275	140	1	Very Slow
300	150	2	
325	170	3	Slow
350	180	4	Moderate
375	190	5	
400	200	6	Moderately Hot
425	220	7	Fairly Hot
450	230	8	Hot
475	240	9	Very Hot
500	250	10	Extremely Hot

Any broiling recipes can be used with the grill of the oven, but beware of high-temperature grills.

EQUIVALENTS FOR INGREDIENTS

all-purpose flour—plain flour
baking sheet—oven tray
buttermilk—ordinary milk
cheesecloth—muslin
coarse salt—kitchen salt
cornstarch—cornflour
eggplant—aubergine

granulated sugar—caster sugar
half and half—12% fat milk
heavy cream—double cream
light cream—single cream
lima beans—broad beans
parchment paper—greaseproof paper
plastic wrap—cling film

scallion—spring onion
shortening—white fat
unbleached flour—strong, white flour
vanilla bean—vanilla pod
zest—rind
zucchini—courgettes or marrow

Al tavolo non s'invecchia mai.

At the table one never gets old.